Library of
Davidson College

Family Life in Central Italy, 1880–1910

Family Life in Central Italy, 1880–1910

Sharecropping, Wage Labor, and Coresidence

David I. Kertzer

RUTGERS UNIVERSITY PRESS
New Brunswick, New Jersey

Library of Congress Cataloging in Publication Data

Kertzer, David I., 1948–
Family life in central Italy, 1880–1910.

Bibliography: p.
Includes index.
1. Family—Italy—Bertalia—History. 2. Italy—History—1870–1915. 3. Italy—Rural conditions. 4. Kinship—Italy—Bertalia. 5. Sharecropping—Italy—Bertalia. 6. Labor and laboring classes—Italy—Bertalia. I. Title.
HQ629.K47 1983 306.8′5′09456 82-22958
ISBN 0-8135-0978-5

Copyright © 1984 by Rutgers,
The State University

All rights reserved

Manufactured in the United States of America

For Molly Emilia and Seth Evan

Contents

List of Maps and Figures
ix

List of Tables
xi

Preface
xv

1. Introduction
1

2. Economy and Social Organization in Rural Bologna
17

3. Sharecropping and Coresidence
57

4. Urbanization and Coresidence
86

5. Migration
111

6. Coresidence in Life Course Perspective
131

7. Kinsmen beyond the Household
162

8. Conclusions
188

Appendix: Methods of Household Study
199

Contents

Notes
211

Bibliography
223

Index
241

Maps and Figures

Maps

1. Italy and the Central Sharecropping Regions
   19
2. The Provinces of Emilia–Romagna and Their Capitals, 1880
   21
3. The Province of Bologna and Its Topographical Zones
   22

Figures

6.1. Individuals' Coresidential Situation in 1890 as a Function of Their Coresidential Situation in 1880, by Ten-Year Birth Cohorts
   138

6.2. Individuals' Coresidential Situation in 1880 as a Function of Their Coresidential Situation in 1890, by Ten-Year Birth Cohorts
   140

6.3. Individuals' Coresidential Situation in 1910 as a Function of Their Coresidential Situation in 1900, by Ten-Year Birth Cohorts
   144

6.4. Individuals' Coresidential Situation in 1900 as a Function of Their Coresidential Situation in 1910, by Ten-Year Birth Cohorts
   146

7.1. Percentage of Households Having No Kin Links to Other Bertalia Households, by Age of Household Head—1880, 1890, 1900, 1910
   176

List of Maps and Figures

A.1. Complex Family Household Categorization
207

A.2. The Household as Longitudinal Unit
208

Tables

1.1. Occupations of Bertalia Males, 1867 and 1880
13

3.1. Crude Deathrate in Bertalia, 1880–1889
61

3.2. Age Distribution of Deaths in Bertalia, 1880–1889
62

3.3. Composition of Bertalia Households, 1880
63

3.4. Coresidence of All Bertalia Residents by Age and Sex, 1880
66

3.5. Household Composition by Age of Household Head, Bertalia, 1880
68

3.6. Household Composition of Wage Laborers and Sharecroppers, Bertalia, 1880
71

3.7. Number of Generations in Bertalia Households as an Attribute of All Residents, by Age, 1880
72

3.8. Mean Size of Households of Different Composition, Bertalia, 1880
74

3.9. Sharecropper and *Bracciante* Household Composition in the Suburbs of Bologna, 1847
76

List of Tables

3.10. Household Composition for All Individuals Living in Households Headed by Sharecroppers and *Braccianti*, in Two Communes of the Province of Bologna, 1881
77

3.11. Sharecropper Household Composition in Three Communes of Ravenna, Emilia-Romagna, 1811
78

3.12. Household Composition in Northern France
81

3.13. Household Composition in Central and Southern France
82

4.1. Composition of Households in Bertalia, 1880–1910
92

4.2. Coresidence of All Bertalia Residents, 1880–1910
93

4.3. Coresidence of All Bertalia Residents by Age and Sex, 1910
94

4.4. Household Composition of the Elderly, by Sex and Marital Status, Bertalia, 1880 and 1910
96

4.5. Household Composition by Occupation of Household Head, Bertalia, 1880 and 1910
98

4.6. Coresidential Situation of All Bertalia Residents by Occupation, 1880 and 1910
100

4.7. Household Size by Occupation of Household Head, Bertalia, 1880 and 1910
102

4.8. Household Composition by Occupation of Household Head, Bertalia, 1910
104

5.1. Birthplace of Persisters and Immigrants over Age Ten, Bertalia, 1890 and 1910
117

List of Tables

5.2. Birthplace of Persisters in Bertalia, by Age, 1910
118

5.3. Proportion of Bertalia Population Having Entered Parish within Previous Decade, by Age, 1890 and 1910
119

5.4. Migration Characteristics of Various Occupations in Bertalia, 1890 and 1910
120

5.5. Composition of Households Headed by Persisters and by Immigrants, Bertalia, 1890 and 1910
121

5.6. Coresidential Situation of Persisters and Immigrants in Bertalia, by Age, 1890
122

5.7. Coresidential Situation of Persisters and Immigrants in Bertalia, by Age, 1910
124

5.8. Migration Characteristics of Nonhousehold Heads Linked to Migration Characteristics of Their Household Heads, Bertalia, 1890 and 1910
127

5.9. Age, Marital Status, and Sex of Immigrants Living in Multiple Family Households Headed by Persisters, Bertalia, 1890 and 1910
128

6.1. Occupational Mobility of Nonmigrant Males, Ages 20–59 at Initial Year: Percentage Switching Occupation
134

6.2. Occupational Mobility by Age: Percentage of Nonmigrant Males Switching Occupation
135

6.3. Occupations of Male Youths Ages 0–9 at Initial Year, Ten Years Later
136

6.4. Stability and Change in Household Composition of Nonmigrants, 1880–1890 and 1900–1910
137

List of Tables

7.1. Nature and Frequency of Kin Links between Bertalia Households
166

7.2. Nature and Frequency of Indirect Affinal Kin Ties Linking together Bertalia Households
167

7.3. Proportion of Households Having Kin Links to Other Bertalia Households, by Household Composition
169

7.4. Frequency of Kin Links of Specified Kind, by Household Composition
170

7.5. Relationship between Age of Household Head and Frequency of Kinsmen Living in Other Households
174

7.6. Kin Ties with Other Bertalia Households, by Occupation of Household Head, 1880 and 1910
178

7.7. Occupational Characteristics of the Household Heads of Kin-Linked Households, 1880
180

7.8. Occupational Characteristics of the Household Heads of Kin-Linked Households, 1910
182

7.9. Relationship between Age of Household Head and Absence of Kin Ties with Other Bertalia Households: Persisters versus Immigrants
186

Preface

Closely tied to both kinship and economic organization, coresidential arrangements have an important impact on people's lives from birth to death. The infant living in a home with no adults other than his or her parents may receive a different kind and amount of attention than an infant sharing a home with a grandmother or aunt. Children living with cousins, uncles, and aunts face a different set of demands than children growing up with only their parents present. A woman's decision in the middle years to work outside the home may be influenced by the presence of other women in the household. And the life experiences of elderly widows and widowers are likely to vary widely depending on whether or not they live with their married children and grandchildren.

Yet, despite the social importance of such coresidential arrangements in Italy, they have until recently received little scholarly attention, an oversight linked to an overall dearth of empirical family studies. The long domination of elitist and politically oriented research traditions in Italian historiography help account for this ignorance in the historical realm, while the slowness with which an empirical research tradition has developed in sociology and anthropology has also been a factor. Fortunately, this situation has now begun to change, with demographers and sociologists joining anthropologists and historians in trying to shed light on the evolution and diversity of Italian family life.

The history of family life in Italy is not only of interest to those seeking a better understanding of Italian society but also to those who seek a broader understanding of changing family forms in Western Europe. The possibilities for historical family study in Italy are great, for Italy has an unusual wealth of historical documentation pertaining to the family. In the modern period, these range from annual parish censuses, going back a number of centuries, to the comprehensive population registers that were begun in the 1860s and continue today. Moreover, along with the social and cultural heterogeneity of the Italian peninsula we find a multi-

Preface

plicity of family forms. For scholars who seek to identify the determinants and social consequences of different family arrangements, such diversity provides a treasured resource.

This book focuses on family organization and, especially, coresidential arrangements in central Italy, with a particular emphasis on Bologna, which lies at the northern edge of this area. This part of Italy was for centuries dominated by sharecropping agriculture. During the latter part of the nineteenth century, however, the economic and social system in which sharecropping played such a major role began to come apart. A severe agrarian crisis, in addition to the gradual expansion of modern industrialization, brought about change in many sectors of life. It should be emphasized, however, that this is not a study of *the* Italian family or of *the* Italian household in this period, for Italy encompasses a number of different family and household patterns, linked in part to regional differences in economic organization. Rather, my intention is to shed light on household processes in a sizeable and theoretically interesting part of Italy; only through research in other parts of the nation can we obtain a full picture of Italian family and household patterns.

Work on this study was begun in 1972, but not until 1975, with a two-year grant from the National Institute of Child Health and Human Development (HD09557), did it get fully under way. Since 1979, together with Andrea Schiaffino of the University of Bologna, I have been the recipient of another NICHD grant (HD13415) for a related historical demographic study of the impact of industrialization on demographic processes and coresidence. Work supported by this grant has influenced my perspective in writing this book. I should note Andrea Schiaffino's influence in my thinking, particularly his insistence that individuals rather than households must be the basic unit of analysis in the longitudinal study of coresidence.

This study could not have been completed without the kind cooperation of the parish priests of Bertalia. I would like to acknowledge with gratitude the help provided by the late don Nino Diolaiti and by don Giuliano Gaddoni who acted as my guides to the parish archives and facilitated my work there. I would also like to thank Arturo Parisi, who acted as consultant in the early stages of the research. Carlo Poni has for years taken the time to share his unparalleled knowledge of Bolognese social history with me and has expertly guided me through the complexities of Italian archives and libraries. To him I am most grateful. Thanks are also due to Lorenzo del Panta and Carlo Corsini for their bibliograph-

Preface

ical aid in Florence. I would also like to acknowledge the generosity of Marzio Barbagli, who has given me permission to make use of unpublished data from his ongoing study of household composition in Emilia-Romagna.

For their assistance in various stages of this research I am happy to note the contributions made by Marco Melega, Donna Muncey, Frank Kelcz, Mark Porter, and Jeff Tracy. Jonathan Bye, who also worked as a research assistant, helped in drafting chapter 5. I am grateful to Mark Nelsen, who provided expert aid in computer programming.

Work for this book was supported in part by various grants from Bowdoin College, including a faculty research award and a research travel grant. This book was written while I was supported by a sabbatical leave provided by Bowdoin in 1981–1982. For this research support, as well as for various other amenities, I am most appreciative. Final revisions were completed in 1982–1983 while I was at the Center for Advanced Study in the Behavioral Sciences, supported in part by a grant from the John and Catherine MacArthur Foundation.

Final archival and library work in Bologna was conducted in the fall of 1981. I would like to express my gratitude to Athos Belletini, director of the Istituto di Statistica of the University of Bologna, for hosting me during that period.

Finally, I would like to thank those who provided helpful comments on drafts of the various chapters of this book. Andrea Schiaffino provided valuable advice on a number of chapters; Lutz Berkner offered insightful comments on an earlier version of chapter 3; Carlo Poni critiqued chapter 2; and thanks are due to Anne Foner for her helpful remarks on earlier drafts of chapters 3 and 4.

Incorporated into chapter 3 is material that first appeared in a 1977 article in the *Journal of Family History*. Chapter 4 contains material that first appeared in a 1978 article in *Urban Anthropology*. An earlier and much shorter version of this book was published in Italy by Il Mulino in 1981. It is titled *Famiglia Contadina e Urbanizzazione*.

I dedicate this book to my children, Molly and Seth, who have provided me with so many delightful lessons in family life.

1

Introduction

How did the great mass of peasants in Western Europe live their lives? What changes took place in their lives as they passed from youth to old age? What was the social context of their everyday experience? And how were they affected by the traumatic upheavals of agricultural transformation, industrialization, and urban expansion that shook much of Europe in the nineteenth century?

One of the keys to an understanding of this social history is provided by family life and coresidential experience. People's lives—their plans, hopes, and fears for the future—were intimately bound up with family and coresidential arrangements. There are, of course, many significant spheres of experience outside the domestic context—relations at workplaces outside the home, relations with political authorities, relations with other men and women outside the orbit of family and household—but even these relationships were conditioned by and had an impact on family life and coresidential arrangements.

Our conceptions of European social history as well as our understanding of the continuities and discontinuities between the lives of contemporary Europeans and those of their forebears are conditioned by our conceptions of what family life was like in the past. Yet these conceptions themselves have been changing. Today's scholarly community is sharply divided on the nature of family life in the past; moreover, there is little similarity between what many scholars claim family life was like in the past and the conceptions of so-called traditional family life that most people have.

These popular conceptions are based on the premise that family life was more tightly knit and more important to the people in Europe's preindustrial past than it is today. In this view, families have been undermined by the massive changes that have taken place over the past two centuries, with disastrous social and psychological consequences. The web of mutual obligation provided by the family and reflected in a presumed predilection for extended family households began to disintegrate under the influence of such forces as industrialization and urbanization.

Yet, in recent years this portrait has come under sharp attack by scholars seeking to discredit the romantic notion of stable, nurturing family life in the preindustrial past. Edward Shorter (1975), in his history of family life in Europe, has gone so far as to claim that the so-called traditional European family was less a source of emotional nurturance than an unsentimental mechanism for productive and reproductive ends. The mother, in Shorter's view, had many higher priorities than caring for her offsprings' welfare; her primary concern was wresting a living from a cruel world. Nor were conjugal ties typically steeped in affection; couples were brought together for material rather than emotional reasons.

How can we decide which of these models is closer to historical reality and what were the important factors in differentiating among family patterns found in different places and at different times in the same places? Until the past fifteen years or so, as Anderson (1972a: 47) has noted, historians relied on three principal sources for their knowledge of family life: novels written in the past; nonfiction writings of various kinds dating to the period under study; and the oral history provided by elderly informants. Although useful for some problems, none of these sources can provide satisfactory evidence for the nature of family life among the illiterate masses of the past. Those who wrote accounts of the world around them—whether fictional or nonfictional—were themselves drawn from the small, highly literate, middle- or upper-class elite. Insofar as they described family life other than that which they or their social peers experienced, their information was both fragmentary and biased by their own class perspective. Information provided via oral history (cf. Bernardi, Poni, and Triulzi 1977), though avoiding the problem of class bias and simultaneously minimizing the problem of social representivity, is itself both imperfect and limited. It is imperfect in that people's memories are selective and certain biases creep into oral recollections of events that occurred decades before. More to the point here, they are limited in time to the life-span of living individuals and hence do us little good in inquiring into life in past centuries.

The dramatic upsurge in historical study of European family life is linked to the increasing use of a fourth data source: demographic records.[1] By utilizing a variety of such sources—birth, marriage, and death records, as well as periodic enumerations of local populations—scholars from a variety of disciplines have been able to examine the experiences of the great mass of people in the past, minimizing the problem of class bias and eliminating problems stemming from the oral historical approach.[2] With the development of these methods, the question of whom people lived their lives with, and how their coresidential situation changed over their life course and through historical time, could finally be addressed more systematically.

Issues in the History of Coresidence in Western Europe

The use of demographic records allowed historians to ask a broad range of questions that had previously been dealt with only in imprecise terms, if at all. One of these questions provides our focus in this book: what were the characteristics of coresidence in preindustrial Europe and what impact did the great economic, social, and political changes of the past two centuries have on people's coresidential experience? More precisely, we would like to plot and to explain variations in time and space in coresidential patterns.

The complexities of European social history have become better recognized of late, making the answers to these questions more difficult than many had previously thought (C. Tilly 1979: 29). The notion that there had been a simple transformation of the rural peasantry to an urban proletariat, upon which many of our ideas of family history are based, can no longer be supported. It has become increasingly clear that even before the first factories were constructed large segments of the population were engaged in wage labor of one kind or another, and this includes rural areas as well as urban. Large portions of the eighteenth- and early nineteenth-century population of rural Europe were involved in protoindustrial production, taking in materials and orders from merchants and, typically employing all available household members, turning out the finished product to be put on the market by the merchant. Moreover, in many areas it was unusual for the agriculturalists to own their own land, and they worked not for their subsistence but for wages or for their share of the proceeds from a cash crop. When the first factories were erected, then, the social order being affected was not that of the simple self-sufficient peasant society but a much more variegated and stratified society already long tied into an international market system.

One of the major issues in European social history, directly linked to the new demographic methods of study, concerns the transition from high to low fertility. Most commonly this question has been studied without regard to coresidence, but there has been increasing recognition that fertility decisions are made within the household context and that no adequate understanding of changes in childbearing patterns can be achieved without investigating the possible influence of people's co-residential situation on their decision to have children (Van de Walle 1976: 92–93; C. Tilly 1978: 46). Depending on the economic pressures on households, there may be advantages or disadvantages in having large numbers of children. Of relevance, too, are alternatives to raising one's own children to maturity, such as those that existed in preindustrial Europe in the form of domestic service, apprenticeship, and putting babies out to wet nurses or abandoning them as foundlings.

Another major aspect of European life experiences was the departure of the individual from the parental home. Whether the individual viewed this departure with jubilation or dread, there is little question that the move represented a significant life transition. This transition is all the more interesting because patterns of departure from the parental home showed much greater variation in preindustrial European societies than in contemporary Europe. Yet strikingly little is known about the departure of individuals from the parental home (Wall 1978: 181). We do know that large numbers of individuals were cast off from the parental home days after birth in eighteenth- and nineteenth-century France and Italy (Buffini 1845; Shorter 1975; Corsini 1976, 1977). We know, too, that millions of prepubescent children were sent into domestic service, while some still to be determined proportion never left the parental home, taking it over as their parents retired or died. Just what these patterns are and what factors account for them remains one of the major challenges for contemporary historians.

Introduction

Preindustrial Europe is notable for another demographic trait linked to coresidence as well: its marriage system. Indeed, there may be no other marriage system quite like it in the world, with its dual distinctions of a high age of marriage for both males and females, and a high proportion of people who never marry (Hajnal 1965). For many years in much of Western Europe, women typically married only in their mid-twenties, while men married closer to thirty years of age. This meant that there were large numbers of adult men and women living in households headed neither by themselves nor their spouses. Not only does this represent a substantial part of the life course, but, insofar as a sizeable segment of the population never married (sometimes up to 20 percent, though generally closer to 10 percent), it has important implications for any simple family-cycle model of the coresidential life course. Indeed, the millions of people who never married represent the phantom population of European history, which has been systematically ignored in the family history literature.

Just as the likelihood that an individual would be cast off from his or her natal home at a tender age is linked to the characteristics of the coresidential unit, so are the life chances of any individual largely determined by the domestic group with which he or she is associated. Not only are people's life chances linked to the economic characteristics of their parents, but they are related as well to birth order, and to the number and sex both of their siblings and, later, of their own children. Seen from a somewhat different perspective, people make decisions about their coresidential situation based on their desire to improve their life chances, to improve the quality of their lives in the present, and to insure a secure future. These decisions may involve having more children, getting rid of an excess of unproductive dependents, or acquiring children or adults through domestic service or apprenticeship to "make up" for a lack of domestic labor power (Santini 1977: 371–80; Netting 1979: 57).

The key factors to which individuals react, in the minds of most historians and social scientists, are economic. At the individual level, a coresidential situation is sought that confers the greatest benefits at the least cost. From the household perspective, the number and types of members are a function of whether the household is the unit of production and, if so, what the labor demands of the productive process are (C. Tilly 1978: 48; Lee 1981: 162–163). Insofar as the household is the unit of production, it can be analyzed as a firm that requires a certain kind of labor force and can afford a certain level of operating expenses. Where the household is not the unit of production, as in the typical proletarian case, household composition is based on the advantages to be conferred by pooling wages, by having people available for child care (and hence freeing the mother to enter the wage labor force), by sharing available housing, and by arranging for support in old age.

This last point raises an important issue in European social history that has yet to get the attention it deserves, namely, what was life like for the elderly? A fair amount of attention has been devoted to the lives of elderly peasant farmers who had property to pass down to an heir and thus were in a good bargaining position to provide for their old age. However, only a minority of the aged in preindustrial Europe fell into this category. What happened to the people who owned no property? Did their adult children feel responsible for maintaining them? And what of those who had no living children, a sizeable proportion in a population having high child mortality rates and large numbers of children who never married?

Having quickly sketched some of the principal components or coresidential processes—fertility, departure from the parental home, marriage, and the care of the elderly—it is time we looked more comprehensively at the characteristics of households in the European past. Here we would like to focus on the issue of the structure of households in the *preindustrial* period, leaving our discussion of the impact of urbanization and industrialization to chapter 4. Of course, before we can address the question of how household characteristics have changed over the past century or two, we must determine what households looked like before these recent forces were at work.

Peter Laslett deserves the credit for reopening the issue of household composition in preindustrial Europe, long assumed to be uninteresting because the answer was thought to be well known. The traditional view, that the preindustrial population lived in complex family households, was challenged by Laslett, who propounded the contrary thesis. Joined by a number of his colleagues from the Cambridge Group for the History of Population and Social Structure, Laslett argued that the conjugal family household had been the "standard form for the co-residential domestic group" in England since at least the late sixteenth century. Extended family households were "quite rare," and parents seldom lived with their married children (Laslett 1973: 21). The implications of this position for

Introduction

understanding the impact of industrialization and urbanization are clear: if the extended family had never been a common coresidential unit in preindustrial times, the view that these massive social changes led to the nuclearization of coresidence was untenable (Laslett 1972b: 126).

If Laslett's thesis were limited to England, the historical and theoretical interest in his work would be limited. But Laslett was more ambitious, seeking to characterize family life for all of Western Europe, despite the geographical limitations of his data. As he saw it, the extended family household was a product of European mythology rather than of empirically grounded history. To overcome that ideological heritage, he issued a call for a "properly historical sociology" (1972a: 73). This book represents one response to that call, though its results may not be altogether in keeping with Laslett's attempted myth slaying.

Although Laslett's generalizations are inductive in nature, based largely on his analysis of English population listings of past centuries, similar conclusions have been drawn deductively by Marion Levy, Jr., on the basis of demographic considerations. Levy has maintained that "the general outlines and nature of the actual family structures have been virtually identical in certain strategic respects in all known societies in world history for well over 50 percent of the members of those societies" (1965: 41–42). Given mortality rates prevailing in preindustrial societies, he argues, three-generation households would be rare even should cultural norms favor such households.[3] In this view, where life expectancy is relatively short, most parents die before their children marry and have offspring, and thus the demographic potential for three-generation households is limited. Of course, this argument says nothing about the potential for lateral extension, it being assumed that complex households are generally the result of vertical linkage.

In short, the most notable historical and theoretical literature over the past decade and a half has sought to minimize the significance of complex family households in preindustrial Western Europe and, in a related vein, sought to dispel the notion that economic changes over the past century or two have led to a nuclearization of coresidential arrangements. My aim in this book is to cast these propositions in a somewhat different light than usual by examining an Italian case and considering the implications for these broad generalizations of a society organized in a quite different way from the one with which Laslett and his associates are most familiar.

The Significance of Italy

In the many debates that have raged within and about the new demographic approaches to European family history, the Italian case has been often mentioned but rarely studied. Moreover, most of the few studies in Italian family history that have been conducted focus on an earlier period than that of the great transformation to an urban, industrial society.[4]

But of what significance is the Italian case beyond that of Italian history? The answer is that no generalizations regarding family life and coresidence in Western Europe can be made until the Italian case is well understood. for Italy's coresidential patterns show great contrast with the pattern found in the paradigmatic case of Britain. Nor can it be argued that Italy's peculiarities may be dismissed as an example of her Mediterranean, as opposed to European, orientation, for the greatest contrast with northern Europe occurs not in southern Italy, but in the center and north, those regions culturally and socially closest to the rest of Western Europe.

In recent years, Italy has become a common caveat in generalizations about the European family of the past. Even some of the most vociferous proponents of the thesis that the peasantry lived in nuclear family households have pointed to central Italy as a possible exception to their generalizations (Laslett 1977a: 98; Wrigley 1977: 78).[5] Yet, though these champions of the revisionist cause have begun to voice increased caution in generalizing about Western Europe, the large number of social historians who have been influenced by their work have not shown comparable restraint. Typical is the interpretation provided by the British sociologist C. C. Harris:

> Laslett and the Cambridge Group for the History of Population and Social Structure have concentrated on the "family" as a domestic group, and have had little difficulty in demonstrating that in Western Europe domestic groups composed of an elementary family and its extensions, vertically and horizontally, were a rarity long before industrialization took place. This does not come as a surprise to anyone who has even the most rudimentary knowledge of the demographic characteristics of pre-industrial populations, or an understanding of the nature of a bilateral system of kinship (1977: 76–77).

Introduction

In effect, the demographic logic of Levy is here combined with the historical results reported by Laslett to conclude not only that all Western Europe was characterized by nuclear family households but that it could not have been any other way. Similarly, two of the most prominent American social historians, Hareven and Vinovskis (1978: 14), write that "one of the important contributions of demographic studies of preindustrial family and household patterns was to dispel prevailing myths about household complexity and extensions in the past." They then go on to quote approvingly Goode's comments about such beliefs as being the product of "Western Nostalgia," and they conclude that "contrary to prevailing theories of social change, the emergence of nuclear households was not a consequence of industrialization; it has been, in fact, the dominant household structure in Western society for the past three hundred years."

Of greater importance than its role as an impediment to generalization about coresidential norms in European history, the Italian case provides us with the opportunity to understand better under just what conditions more complex household forms may emerge and what factors may be responsible for the demise of such complex household forms where they do come to predominate. If, for example, there existed in Italy areas where complex family households were common, the logic that explains the absence of northern European household complexity on demographic grounds (e.g., mortality) must itself be questioned. To pursue this point a moment, we consider Lawrence Stone's recent comments on this subject. Stone recognizes that the nuclear family coresidential pattern characteristic of northwest Europe and New England in preindustrial times may well not have been characteristic of southern Europe. But he later argues that the northwest European pattern may be explained by high mortality rates, which make three-generation households uncommon (1981: 62). Yet Stone is certainly not suggesting that mortality rates were higher in northern Europe than in the south. If this is the case, there is nothing obvious about why northern Europe should have been characterized by nuclear family households, while parts of southern Europe should have had high frequencies of household complexity.

Another reason for the theoretical importance of the Italian case lies in the prevalence of sharecropping throughout large parts of Italy, particularly in the center and north. Most explanations of coresidential behavior have been based on economic parameters, and in the case of agriculturalists these have primarily concerned land ownership and rules of

9

inheritance. The "peasant," the Western ideal type of preindustrial agriculturalist, owns his own plot of land and must coordinate his household to make best use of this land, to expand it where possible, and to provide for his heirs. Much of the literature on past rural populations of Europe focuses on just these matters. Accordingly, complex family households have been most often identified with conditions of peasant land ownership. Where farmers did not own their own land, on the other hand, complex family households were not to be expected (Verdon 1979: 97, 102–103).[6]

Yet, as the Italian case demonstrates, there existed in preindustrial Europe a large number of agriculturalists who neither owned their own land nor worked for wages. Insofar as these sharecroppers commonly formed complex family households, we must reframe our generalizations about the link between land tenure and coresidence.

In recent years there have been increasing calls for going beyond the mass of information that has been collected for Britain and France and turning to other parts of Western Europe to trace more fully the history of Western family life. As Plakans concluded, after making just such a point, "the larger picture still remains elusive; the parts do not yet fit into a neat whole" (1979: 88). This is true not only for our understanding of preindustrial family life in Europe but also for our knowledge of the impact of industrialization and the related processes of social transformation that have affected Western Europe over the past two centuries. Illustrative is the recent apologetic comment by Merriman in an edited volume on European social history, a book whose chapters focus only on England and France. He writes that "despite some excellent work, we know relatively little about the experience of German urbanization and industrialization, particularly as they affected ordinary people. The Italian experience is even more obscure" (1979: 3). It is our hope that this book will, in a modest way, encourage historians to incorporate the Italian case into their analyses of the course of European family history, while enabling students of society to identify factors underlying household complexity by expanding the range of variation available in the Western European literature.

It is especially unfortunate that so little attention has been given to Italy in the European family history discussions because the historical data on coresidence in Italy are of unsurpassed quality (Sonnino 1975: 95). European historians have recognized this wealth of data for Renaissance times and the late Middle Ages. Indeed, Herlihy has maintained

Introduction

that the Tuscany data of that period are "probably the richest documentation, illuminating demographic patterns and movements, extant anywhere in western Europe" (1977: 135). But Italy's wealth of coresidential and related demographic data for the past two centuries is no less extraordinary. Indeed, the French demographic historians, Aymard and Delille (1977: 452), have claimed that *"leur richesse, leur densité [sont] sans equivalent dans les autres pays européens."*

Two sources are of particular importance enabling researchers to study coresidential processes in greater depth than is afforded by the sources available in the much more heavily studied areas of Britain and France. These are the *status animarum* (the annual parish census) and, since 1865, the *anagrafe* (population register). The *status animarum*, or *stato d'anime*, was recorded each year, generally during pre-Easter home visitations, by the priest of each parish. The church first called on the parish priests to undertake these regular enumerations in 1614, though the practice had begun in a number of parishes before that date. However, the oldest surviving high quality *stati d'anime* in substantial numbers date to the early eighteenth century (Bellettini 1974: 4–5). These record information on each resident of the parish and are divided by household. Data include first and last name of mother and father, age, sex, marital status, and, occasionally (particularly beginning in the latter part of the nineteenth century), occupation.[7] Where these documents have survived and where they had been diligently completed each year for long stretches of time, they provide us with a rich source for the historical analysis of coresidence.

The major source of Italy's historical demographic wealth is the population register, kept by every commune (the lowest level of city administration, corresponding to a village, town, or city) as a continuous record of each of its residents and each of its households through time. The population register, when used in conjunction with other demographic records, is an almost ideal source for the study of demographic and coresidential history, for rather than providing a series of snapshots, it provides a fully continuous picture of demographic and coresidential processes (see Van de Walle 1976; Schiaffino 1977; Bradley and Mendels 1978: 381n).

Hence, though the Italian case has heretofore been little considered in the British- and French-dominated debates on household composition and economic change, *il caso italiano* shows promise of being one of the decisive areas for the elucidation of coresidential processes through time and for the testing of theoretical propositions regarding household composition.

Bertalia

Our goal is to provide insight into coresidential processes in the sharecropping area of Italy and the effect on these processes of the initial stages of urban/industrial transformation. We do this through the detailed study of one particular parish that is well situated to reflect these forces. The parish is Bertalia, lying just a few kilometers outside the walls of the central city of Bologna, located in the midst of the rich agricultural region of Emilia-Romagna. The period under study, from 1880 to 1910, encompasses the initial transformation of a once agricultural community to one that is increasingly incorporated into the expanding city. After a twenty-seven-year period in which the population grew just 9 percent, between 1880 and 1910, the population grew 73 percent (from 1,780 to 3,085), as large numbers of immigrants entered the parish from the rural areas surrounding the city of Bologna (Bellettini 1961). Indeed, the population showed great flux, with large numbers of individuals leaving the parish as well, some bound for other agricultural areas and some bound for the more urban center of the city.

The parish extends roughly four kilometers north to south and a kilometer and a half east to west, with the great majority of the land in the late nineteenth century being devoted to agriculture. Large farmhouses, with adjacent barns, dotted the land; clusters of multifamily housing, accompanied by taverns and artisan shops, provided less than hygenic shelter for the rest of the population. Separated from the city by walls and a gate that was closed every evening, the parish was also cut off from its agricultural neighbor on the west, Borgo Panigale, by the Trebbo River. Bertalia adjoined a virtually identical parish, Beverara, on its east, and both were isolated from the more urban suburb of Arcoveggio by a major canal. To the north lay the agricultural communities of the Po Valley.

Bertalia in 1880 was dominated by agriculture, though the beginnings of Italian industrialization had already reached the parish in the form of railroad employment. Of the men in the labor force, 56 percent farmed the land, 10 percent were artisans, 8 percent worked in a variety of service and construction jobs (e.g., bricklayers, street sweepers, coach driv-

Introduction

Table 1.1. *Occupations of Bertalia Males, 1867 and 1880*

	1867		1880	
	N	Percentage	N	Percentage
Braccianti	143	25	204	33
Sharecropper	142	25	102	17
Salaried	7	1	22	4
Renters	17	3	7	1
Other agricultural	0	—	8	1
Cultivator total	309	55	343	56
Noncultivator total	253	45	267	44
Total (active male population)	562	100	610	100

SOURCE: 1867 data: Diolaiti (1973: 26); 1880 data: Bertalia parish *status animarum*.

ers), 7 percent held railroad jobs, and 6 percent were servants, largely working on the farms. The remainder of the population included small numbers of merchants and a tiny elite (of eighteen men). Indeed, the land was not owned by any of the residents of the parish but rather by wealthy landowners who lived in the city of Bologna and had scattered landholdings throughout the province. A few of these had summer villas in Bertalia, but none owned more than a few of the parish farms, and most owned only one or two.

The agricultural population of Bertalia, as through the province of Bologna in general, was primarily divided between sharecroppers (30 percent) and *braccianti*, or agricultural wage laborers (60 percent). Of lesser importance were the *boari*, salaried farmers, who composed 6 percent of the agricultural work force, and the farm renters, just 2 percent. The proportion of the population directly engaged in agriculture remained constant from 1867, when we have the first detailed occupational figures for the parish, to 1880 (see table 1.1). A significant shift had taken place, however, in the relative proportion of the sharecroppers and *braccianti*. In 1867 there had been equal numbers of each, whereas by 1880 the *braccianti* outnumbered the sharecroppers by a two to one margin. This reflects a long-term decline in sharecropping and a growth in agricultural wage labor linked to the rise of capitalism in the agricultural sector (Sereni 1968). The nature of this decline and its impact on the family lives of the people of this area are examined in chapters 2 and 3.

As already discussed, this part of Italy provides us with a sharp contrast in coresidential behavior to that found in northern Europe. In the mid-nineteenth century, rural communities exhibited substantial proportions of complex family households, and the frequency of such complex households was especially high in areas where sharecropping was predominant. In Bertalia in 1880, 43 percent of all individuals lived in complex family households. Moreover, given life cycle factors, it is likely that a majority of the rest of the population spent (or would spend) part of their lives living in such households. In certain age groups, notably young children and the elderly, more people lived in complex family households than in simple family households.

Overview

Our intention in this book is to move the Italian case more to center stage in the current debates over changing patterns of coresidence in Western European history. We do this largely through the analysis of a particular community over a thirty-year period of socioeconomic change, but we use what other coresidential data on Italy exist in order to judge the representativeness of this single case. We also make use of the now substantial literature on coresidence in other parts of Europe to determine where the Italian case fits into the larger picture. Through all this our concern is not with description but rather with the factors responsible for producing certain forms of coresidence and why these forms change through time.

Chapters 2 and 3 are devoted to the agricultural system that typified the province of Bologna through much of the nineteenth century and to the relationship between that system and coresidence. The importance of distinguishing between the two main kinds of agricultural labor—sharecropping and wage labor—is stressed, and the differences in coresidential behavior between the two groups are described and explained. In brief, the sharecropper's household is a unit of production, and household composition is in good part determined by the labor demands imposed by this economic arrangement. By contrast, the households of agricultural laborers are not units of production, and they are much less likely than sharecroppers to live in complex family units. Italian sharecroppers represent a major type of the preindustrial Western Euro-

Introduction

pean population that *did* live according to the "myth" of the large, extended family.

We examine the impact of urbanization on coresidence in chapter 4, having previously detailed the social and economic context in which late nineteenth-century Italian urbanization took place. The impact of urbanization depends both on the preexisting processes of coresidence and on the specific elements of urbanization and related social changes affecting the locality. In the case of the Bologna area, rural proletarianization had already undermined the household as a unit of production, and thus in some respects early urbanization had relatively little impact on household forms. Moreover, in certain respects urbanization encouraged the development of large and complex family households.

In societies experiencing rapid urbanization, high rates of rural-urban migration are often cited as one of the major social forces operating to change people's lives. In terms of our subject here, it is often claimed that such migration undermines complex family households and brings about household nuclearization. Yet, though this issue has often been addressed in contemporary third world studies, it has rarely been the subject of empirical historical investigation elsewhere. In chapter 5, we thus compare the more migratory population of Bertalia with the less transient population to determine what relationship exists between migration and household complexity.

Historical studies of coresidence have often been criticized for failing to follow households through time and for relying on cross-sectional data that lead to a static picture of what is a dynamic process. In chapter 6 we attempt to remedy this problem by following the coresidential experiences of individuals through these years. In this way, we look at how various, over time, are the coresidential arrangements in which individuals find themselves. We discover that only a minority of the nonmigratory Bertalia population lived in simple family households at both ends of any decade, though this proportion increased through our period. We also see how strong the patrilocal bias of the population is, with sons bringing their brides into their parental home. And we see the variability in coresidence introduced by the facts of mortality (as, for example, death rates result in higher or lower rates of orphanage) and marriage (as, for example, may be produced by a higher or lower proportion of individuals never marrying).

It has become a commonplace of the coresidential literature that it is not enough to examine kin ties within households but that kinship must also be placed in the larger context of ties that link different households. This seems sensible enough, yet empirical studies of kin ties among households in Western European history are almost nonexistent. In chapter 7 we attempt to take a step in the right direction by examining just how common it was for people to have kinsmen living in other households in the community of Bertalia, and what differentiated those who had such kin ties from those who did not. In addition, we ask just what sort of kin ties linked households, and what factors lay behind these patterns.

In our concluding chapter we assess the significance of the Bertalia case and, more broadly, the case of sharecropping central Italy for the understanding of Western European family history and for theories of coresidence. In doing so, we relate the Bertalia findings to what is already known about Italian social history and ask why the Italian coresidential pattern differs from much of Western Europe.

Finally, in the Appendix we discuss some of the controversies surrounding various methods of historical household study and suggest what the best options are. The importance of methodological issues is discussed, and deficiencies in a number of the methods commonly in use are identified and examined.

2

Economy and Social Organization in Rural Bologna

The distinguishing features of family life and coresidential behavior in central Italy—those that set them apart from life in northern Europe—are intimately connected to the sharecropping economy that dominated this area. To explain the system of family relations we must first examine this economy and the social relationships associated with it. In this chapter, we provide a general historical economic background. We begin by looking in some detail at the economic and social relations associated with the kind of sharecropping economy that was found in the province of Bologna in the early post-Unification period (1860–1880). We then look at the effects of the spread of rural capitalism and the demographic changes that took place in the last decades of the nineteenth century.

Sharecropping in Italy

A sharecropping system is based on an agreement between a person who controls land and people who offer their labor to farm the land. Those providing the labor are compensated by the proprietor of the land by receiving a previously agreed upon proportion of the crop. In this sense, sharecropping has an ancient history in Italy, going back to the Romans.

From the late Middle Ages until the Second World War it was the principal form of agriculture in a sizeable portion of the Italian peninsula. Its stronghold was in central Italy—Tuscany, Umbria, and the Marches—and the adjoining northern region of Emilia-Romagna, extending along the Po Valley (see map 1).[1] It was here that the classic *mezzadria* system, already well entrenched throughout Emilia-Romagna by the 1500s, flourished (Landi 1977: 143). However, sharecroppers of various kinds could be found in almost all of Italy's regions, and even by the time the decline of this system had been long under way, at the turn of this century, over 20 percent of Italians employed in agriculture worked as sharecroppers (Faina 1905: 263; Bruno 1923: 11). These ranged from the Sicilian form—described by one observer as the direct descendant of slavery (Garbaglia 1906: 688)—to that found in the northern regions of Lombardy and Piedmont.

The classic sharecropping system, which is the most fully developed form of sharecropping, has a number of distinguishing traits. It is this version of sharecropping with which we will be concerned in this book, and it is this system that is behind the form of family organization found in much of central Italy. Silverman (1975: 46) has conveniently identified three "essential elements" of this system:

> The unit of land worked is an integrated farm characterized by polyculture,
> The unit of labor is not the individual but rather an entire family,
> Both the land proprietor and the sharecropper take an active role in the operation of the farm.

Each of these elements has important implications for the lives of the sharecroppers, as we shall shortly see.

The sharecropping system has often been portrayed as an essentially subsistence economy, with sharecroppers growing the crops necessary to feed and clothe their families without resorting to the market. In this view, it was the intrusion of a large-scale market economy and, particularly, the encroachment of rural capitalism and the world economy that brought about the demise of the sharecropping system. But the sharecropping system can be more accurately viewed as a compromise between the former feudal relationship that tied the peasantry to the nobles, and the developing capitalistic relationship between a rural work force and an expanding urban-based bourgeoisie (Sereni 1957: 36, 1968: 177–278). The *mezzadria* had, in fact, been part of an interna-

Map 1. *Italy and the Central Sharecropping Regions*

tional market system for centuries. The ultimate demise of sharecropping was a result of changes in the relationship between Italy and the national and world economy, rather than a consequence of the entrance of the peasantry into a market economy.

The Economy of Bologna

The capital of the rich agricultural region of Emilia-Romagna, at the juncture between central and northern Italy, Bologna had long been part of the papal states, falling briefly under French control in the Napoleonic era and, after a brief restoration of papal authority, entering the new Italian state in 1860. Protected, like so many ancient Italian cities, by huge walls built around 1300, the city of Bologna was a hub of regional commercial activity and the home of a landowning elite that controlled the countryside. More than merely a regional center, it also had a long tradition of commercial manufacture and international trade.

From 1581 to the mid-nineteenth century, the population living within the walls of the city hovered around seventy thousand, with periodic plunges linked to a variety of epidemics (Bellettini 1978). The city lies in the center of what is now the province of Bologna, previously organized under papal rule as a diocese (with different borders). Bologna, in turn, lies in the center of the region of Emilia-Romagna, which is composed of provinces arranged side by side, running from the northwest to the southeast along the Po Valley: Piacenza, Parma, Reggio, Modena, Bologna, Ferrara, and Ravenna (see map 2). Running along the south side of the region are the Appenines, which divide most of the provinces into areas of mountains, hills, and plains. The city of Bologna lies at the crossroads of the foothills and the plain (see map 3.).

The mountains of the province of Bologna, with their short growing season and poor soil, have long been marked by poverty, as peasants tried to make a living from farming scattered parcels of land, from livestock, and from what use they could make of the forests. Although sharecropping was common here, the mountains are notable as the only part of the province where many peasants owned some land. Northeastward down the mountains are the hills. The land becomes increasingly fertile as the elevations decline. This is the heartland of the sharecropping system, with medium-sized farms, and agriculture based on grains, grapes, and livestock. In the plains lie the most fertile lands, some of

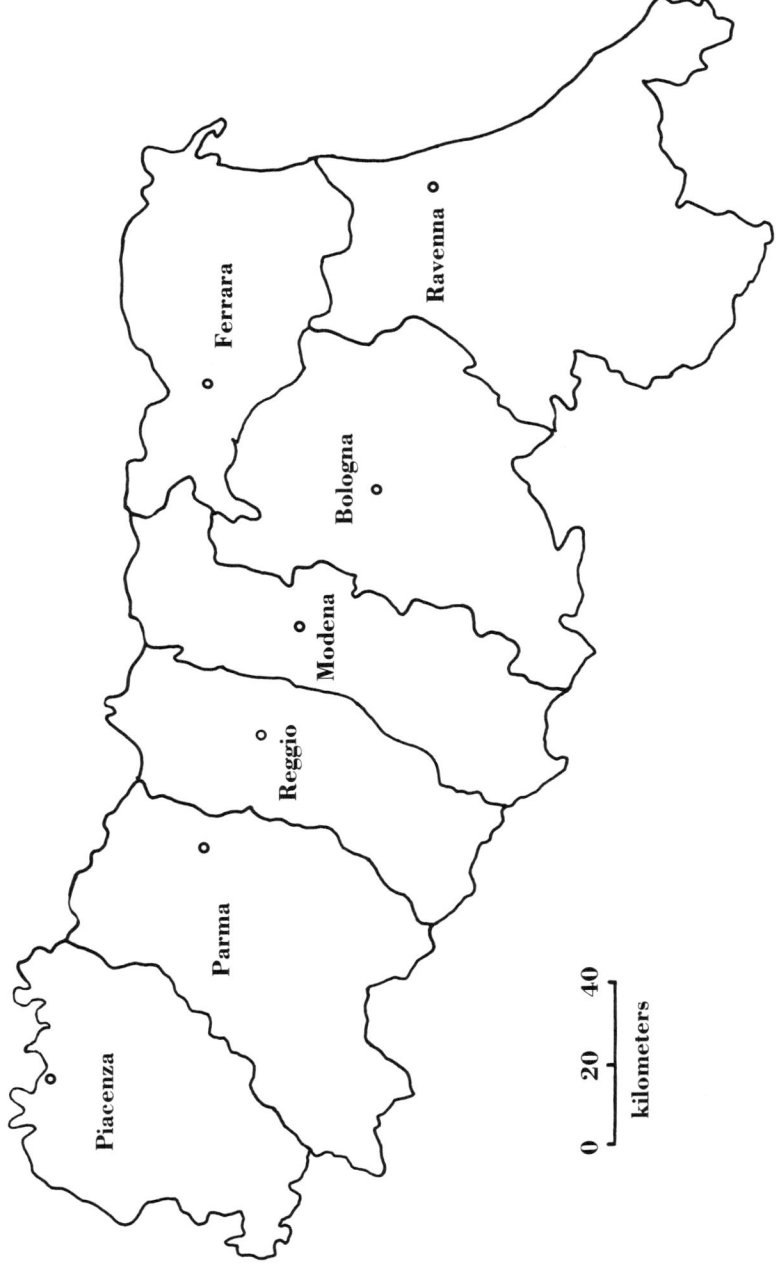

Map 2. *The Provinces of Emilia-Romagna and Their Capitals, 1880*

Map 3. *The Province of Bologna and Its Topographical Zones*

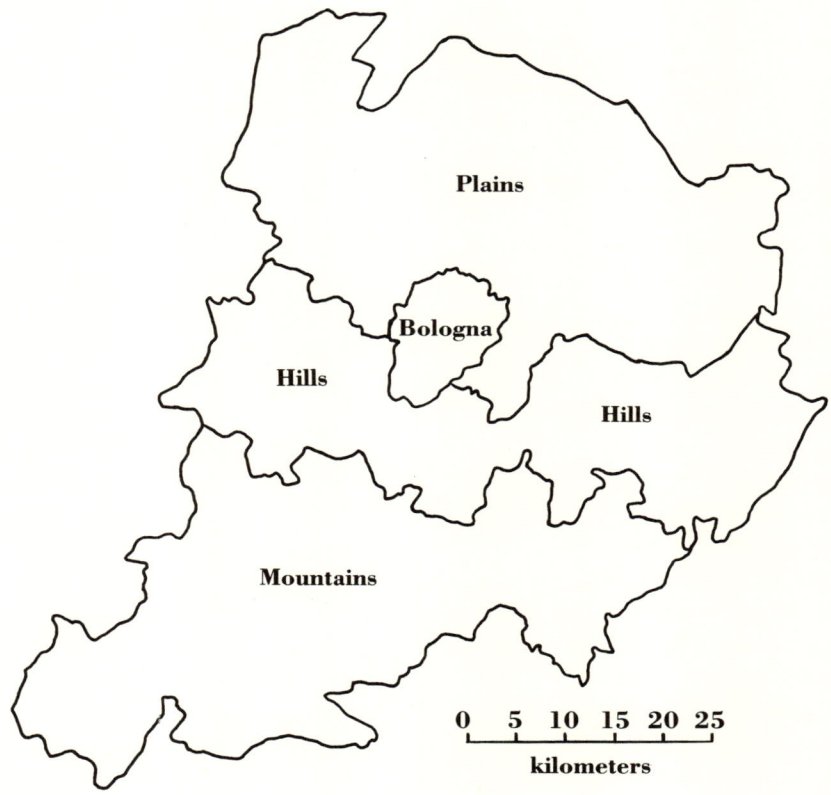

SOURCE: **Consiglio Provinciale (1932:393, 480).**

which are irrigated. Here, alongside areas in which sharecropping prevailed, the nineteenth century saw the expansion of the agricultural wage laborer populations (*braccianti*). Many of these laborers worked on large landholdings that had heavy capital investments in machinery and fertilizer. In addition to grain production, the plains had long concentrated on the cash crops of hemp and, later, sugar beets (Consiglio Provinciale 1932: 392). Through the nineteenth century large-scale land reclamation projects continued to bring new land into cultivation; consequently rice became an important crop in these low-lying areas.

Weather in Bologna shows considerable seasonal variation: summers are very hot and winters are cold; heavy fog is common from November through February. Frost is generally limited to December through early March, with some snow falling during the same period, but heavy snowfalls are rare in the plain. Average monthly temperatures range from 1.5° C in January to 25.2° C in August (Comizio Agrario 1881).

By the nineteenth century agriculture in this region was characterized by large-scale production of wheat and hemp. Grain production, always important as the primary means of feeding the population, became increasingly productive in the latter years of the century. The total grain produced in 1909 was three and a half times greater than that produced in the region a half century before. However, rather than being a sign of agricultural modernization, the continuing emphasis on cereal production indicates the conservatism of Emilian agriculture, a conservatism linked to the *mezzadria* system of production. Sharecroppers had struggled with the landholders for centuries in an attempt to maximize subsistence crops and to thwart the landlords' interest in producing cash crops (Jacini 1860: 77; Finzi 1980: 96). Hemp, chief among the cash crops, had been a Bolognese specialty since the 1500s and was exported to other European nations as well as to other parts of Italy. The story of the increasing commercialization of Emilian agriculture in the nineteenth century is largely the story of the increased production of hemp. In this process, too, must be noted the effect of Italian Unification, which brought the disparate political units of the peninsula under a common government. This served to unify the economic system by creating a national market system and integrating the national economy into the international market (Evangelisti 1980: 77). The principal economic beneficiaries of this development were the northern regions of Lombardy and Piedmont, not only centers of the new industrial production but also the first areas of agricultural capitalist development. However, albeit at a slower pace, Emilia-Romagna and Tuscany were also affected by this burst of capitalism.

Bologna had not experienced a unilinear development in its role in the world economic system. Indeed, at the time of Unification it had sunk to a low point in its centuries-old role as industrial producer. The high point of Bologna's industrial importance in Europe is probably to be found in the seventeenth century, when it was famous for its silks, as well as for its hemp products. As recently as 1806, Bologna counted 7,286 workers employed in silk factories, a number that was halved within the subsequent five years as a result of changing tastes and changing import tax structures on the continent (Dal Pane 1969: 247–287).

Second in importance to silk was the hemp industry, which enjoyed the benefit of sufficiently large hemp cultivation to provide it with locally produced raw materials. The city of Bologna considered hemp cultivation and production its rightful monopoly as early as 1500. An official notice, posted in 1519, announced the death penalty for anyone from Bologna who introduced hemp cultivation and methods of production to any other locality. For many years hemp was in great demand for the production of bedding materials and rope for rigging ships. In the sixteenth century it is estimated that between 12,000 and 20,000 inhabitants of Bologna were involved in the production of hemp from the raw crop. Yet, in the eighteenth century, new import policies in such places as Venice, Lombardy, and Tuscany forbidding the importation of finished hemp products from Bologna contributed to the decline of the Bologna hemp industry (Dal Pane 1969: 287–308).

Through the eighteenth century sharecropping families formed the backbone of the rural population; each family lived on the land being farmed. But as the population began to grow at a rapid rate, and as large landowners sought to run their holdings on a more capital-intensive basis, the proportion of the rural population who lived by wage labor, the *braccianti*, became more and more important.

According to an 1847 pontifical census of the diocese of Bologna, 58.6 percent of the agricultural population lived in households headed by sharecroppers, whereas 36.4 percent lived in households headed by *braccianti*. *Braccianti* were twice as common in the plain than they were in the hills (39.3 percent to 20.2 percent). In the agricultural lands lying outside the walls of the city of Bologna but within municipal jurisdiction, 57.3 percent of those in the agricultural labor force were sharecroppers, and 38.5 percent were *braccianti* (Bellettini 1971: 150, 174).

Throughout the nineteenth century, Bolognese landowners and leaseholders hailed the sharecroppers as the moral foundation of the rural population at the same time as they castigated the sharecroppers as conservative and an impediment to increased productivity (Commissione per lo Studio 1883).[2] As long as the farm's produce would be split equally between sharecropper and proprietor, there was little incentive for either one to invest heavily in capital. Landowners, in contact with their counterparts in northern Italy and elsewhere in Europe and aware of the great profits being made from large-scale, capitalist agriculture, made increasing attempts to substitute sharecroppers with wage laborers and salaried workers, organized in larger-scale units (Goretti 1883; Preti 1955; Sereni 1957, 1968).

Who were the landowners of Bologna? Few were the farmers who owned their own land, except in the poor mountainous area. Fortunately, the *Inchiesta Agraria* of 1881 provides data on sizes of landholdings for Emilia-Romagna (Tanari 1881: 160). It divides the province of Bologna into three zones, the major one containing the city. In this zone there was a total of 12,518 landholding units, of which 70 percent were under 10 hectares and another 27 percent were between 10 and 99 hectares. Yet the 3 percent of the landholding units greater than 100 hectares included 43 percent of all the land, with a mean size of 216 hectares. As these figures refer to contiguous units rather than total landholdings for any one owner, the high degree of concentration of land ownership in the hands of a small elite can be appreciated.

A typical sharecropping farm unit is roughly ten hectares. Thus, though sharecroppers lived on their land, a large proportion of them lived in farms adjacent to other farms owned by the same proprietor. This had important implications for the administration of the farm, for in the case of large landholdings the individual sharecropping family's affairs were directly linked to those of the other operations of the larger holding. Capital, both mechanical and animal, could be shared, and a level of specialization of production could be demanded by the proprietor that would not be appropriate for a small, individual holding (Bissoli 1979: 389). Larger holdings in the latter part of the nineteenth century tended to prosper, benefitting from economies of scale, while the small and middle-sized holdings (under 100 hectares) faced difficulties (Tanari 1881: 244).

Large landholders in nineteenth-century Bologna had the option of running their holdings themselves, through the intermediaries of *fattori* or *aggenti*, whom they hired to oversee their lands, or to lease their lands to *affituari* who then administered the farms themselves. Many of the large landholders opted for the latter arrangement, securing themselves a comfortable income while freeing their time for more dignified pursuits in the city. These were long-term arrangements, generally for nine years, and in them the *affittuario* was contractually obligated to make certain capital improvements on the land (Comizio Agrario 1881; Ministero di Agricoltura 1891: 357–358).

To understand why so few farmers owned their own land, something should be said about land prices. The price of each hectare of farmland in the Bologna area ranged from 1,750 to 2,500 lire, with particularly fertile pieces going for over 5,000 lire (Tanari 1881: 439). To give some idea of the difficulty of saving this amount of money, the wage paid to the agricultural workers of the time was generally one to two lire per day. Although the sharecroppers enjoyed a more favorable economic position than the wage laborers, this advantage was not easily converted into cash savings. The case of the sharecropper who became a landowner was rare indeed.

The Sharecropping Contract

The sharecropping system that dominated central Italy for many centuries was based on a contract between landowner (or leaseholder) and the family of sharecroppers. Already by the thirteenth century contracts were drawn up that resemble those used in the first part of the twentieth century. The crop is divided equally between the farmer and the landholder, with a feudal legacy evident in the contractual obligation of the sharecropper to provide the *padrone* with chickens, eggs, and hams for his table (Landi 1977: 140).

Although signed only by the male household head of the sharecropper family, the contract bound the entire labor force of the family, with the exact number of men and women registered in the agreement. The household head, the *reggitore*, in the language of the standard contract of the eighteenth century, "Promises and guarantees that this [number] will thus be maintained for the entire course of the sharecropping contract." Should any members leave the family, the *reggitore*, unless specifically exempted by the proprietor, "must immediately substitute another individual who is qualified to replace him" (Commissione Mista 1874: 23).

Linked to this provision was the prohibition, affecting all household members, against doing any work off the farm. They were forbidden to transport material for others in their carts; they could not help others with their farming; and they could not engage in artisanal work beyond that needed to maintain the household. This was of considerable significance, for it meant that there could be no coresidence without full-time participation in the household unit of production (Commissione Mista 1874: 31; Comizio Agrario 1905: 9; Poni 1969: 237–239).

Control of the farm remained in the hands of the proprietor, though in practice the proprietor or his agent might consult with the *reggitore* before making a decision affecting the way the farm operated. It was the prerogative of the proprietor to determine what crops should be grown, what rotation should be used, how much fertilizer should be purchased, what animals should be raised, what capital improvement projects should be undertaken, and where and at what price the produce of the farm should be sold (Ministero di Agricoltura 1891: 352–353). It was also the prerogative of the proprietor to determine each year whether to renew the sharecroppers' contract, to replace the family with another, or to place the farm on a wage labor basis and do away with the sharecropping arrangement altogether.

The feudal aspects of the sharecropping contract are evident in a number of ways. The proprietor, who provided the house that the sharecroppers lived in, enjoyed the right to inspect the premises, unannounced, at any time of the day or night. This intrusion on the personal lives of the sharecroppers may be seen in an 1860 sharecropping contract in Romagna, in which the members of the family are forbidden to wear store-bought clothes without the express permission of the proprietor (Giorgetti 1974: 302). The fact that the proprietor had contractual control over the residents of the sharecropper household also meant that his permission had to be obtained before any of the children of the household could marry. In some cases, where the proprietor believed the labor power of the family to be insufficient for the size of the farm, he could exert pressure on the young men in the family to marry, thus enlarging the work force (Sereni 1968: 180).

Written into all sharecropping contracts of the nineteenth century was the feudal practice of payment of *onoranze,* or tribute, to the proprietor. In a common contract, these payments consisted of a specified number of live hens, containers of milk, eggs, pullets, and hams. In addition, the sharecropper agreed to spend a specified amount of time in such work as carting and manual labor for the proprietor, even where these activities had nothing to do with the farm (Poni 1969: 248). Of course the other side of this often humiliating relationship was the expectation that the proprietor would act as a patron of the members of the sharecropping family, particularly in their dealings with state authorities and in other situations where literacy was required (Poni 1977: 117).

With the establishment of the new Italian state, the terms of the sharecropping contract became a part of the civil code. However, the code left room for locally agreed upon arrangements to substitute the terms specified in the code. Sharecropping contracts had a term of just one year, which in Bologna ran from November 1 to October 31. This meant that sharecroppers always had to be concerned about pleasing the proprietor so that their contract would be renewed. There was, however, a date by which, if the proprietor did not formally terminate the contract, the sharecropping agreement would be automatically renewed for another year. This date, which was May 31 in the mid-nineteenth century, had been moved back to the end of February by the beginning of the twentieth (Commissione Mista 1874: 22; Comizio Agrario 1905: 3–4).

The formally approved grounds for nonrenewal of the sharecropping contract provide insight into the proprietor's power over the sharecroppers' lives. The list published for Emilia-Romagna in 1891 included the following:

- if the sharecropper uses the farm's animals to cart material for others;
- if he does not attend to the work in the fields, following good agricultural practices and the instructions he has been given;
- if he is found to have concealed even the smallest portion of the produce to avoid proper division of the goods;
- if he does not pay proper homage to the proprietor;
- if he needlessly frequents taverns or takes part in any illegal organization;
- if he indulges in luxury beyond his economic means;
- if he does not obey all the orders given to him by the proprietor.

(Ministero di Agricoltura 1891: 356–357)

Economy and Social Organization

In looking for a new sharecropping family, the proprietor sought one that was large enough to farm the land but that did not have too many small children or infirm members (*bocche inutili*, useless mouths). Families were judged most desirable if they had no debts and they owned the necessary capital, including a carriage, implements for farming, and household furnishings. Ideally, they also had sufficient reserves of food to get them to the first harvest and, more generally, they were to be of good character, with family members obedient to the household head and the household head obedient to the *padrone*. The result of this continual evaluation of sharecropping families, both those already under contract and those who might be employed to replace them, was that there was a continuous process of selection and elimination (Poni 1977: 116–117). The proprietors controlled who had access to the best farms and who was extruded from sharecropping and forced into a less secure, less comfortable existence. This process of selection was both affected by, and in turn affected, processes of household formation.

Although the sharecropper was subservient to the proprietor, sharecropping families themselves had to have a certain amount of capital goods in order to get a sharecropping contract in the first place. It was this initial capital that made it difficult for other agricultural workers to move up to sharecropper status. These capital requirements were also of importance in regulating the marriages of children of sharecroppers and, especially, the decision of whether to leave the parental household. Whether and when a married sharecropper couple left a multiple family household was very much related to their ability to bring sufficient capital goods with them to acquire a sharecropping household of their own. The materials they needed included agricultural tools, plows, machinery, a stock of hay and foodstuffs, livestock, and a considerable supply of household furnishings (Ministero di Agricoltura 1891: 353; Comizio Agrario 1905: 5; Marangoni 1948: 18). In the Bologna area, unlike some sharecropping regions where the livestock was entirely owned by the proprietor, livestock was shared equally between sharecropper and proprietor. Part of the sharecropping contract specified the number of steer, cows, calves, pigs, and sheep to be maintained on the farm (Comizio Agrario 1905: 15–16). Of special importance were the cattle, who furnished the power to till the soil and to transport materials.[3]

The produce of the farm was split evenly between the sharecropper and the proprietor, regardless of the fertility of the land. This fact naturally led to considerable competition among sharecropping families for the most fertile farms, where they could expect considerably greater return for their investment of labor (Martelli 1854: 133–134). The sharecropper's half of the subsistence crops could be kept for domestic consumption, but all cash crops had to be consigned to the proprietor, who sold the harvest and credited half the price to the sharecropper. It was generally from these funds that the sharecropper's debts were annually deducted. Just as the harvest was shared equally, most expenses of farm operation were divided equally: fertilizer, fodder, seeds, stakes, and insecticides (Pasolini 1891: 17; Comizio Agrario 1905: 7, 9–10). Although the proprietor was entirely responsible for property taxes on the land, taxes on livestock were equally divided, while the annual household tax, based on an estimate of personal income, was paid entirely by the sharecropper (Commissione Mista 1874: 31).

The general expectation was that all labor needed for the farm was the responsibility of the sharecropping family and, where such labor power was lacking, day laborers had to be employed by the sharecropper. Should the sharecropper not carry out certain agricultural tasks that the proprietor judged essential, the proprietor could employ wage laborers to do the work, deducting their wages from the sharecropper's account. One partial exception to this policy concerned the plowing of the fields, for in some Bolognese contracts the proprietor provided one-third of the wages, the sharecropper providing the other two-thirds. In such cases the sharecropper was also responsible for providing the *braccianti* with food and drink while they worked (Commissione Mista 1874: 25; Comizio Agrario 1905: 6).

One concession made to the sharecroppers was the right to keep a certain number of chickens on their own. This provided highly prized eggs and the occasional chicken dinner for special holidays (Commissione Mista 1874: 25).

Of great importance to the sharecropper-proprietor relationship was the sharecropper's frequent need to turn to the proprietor for loans, which placed the sharecropper in an even more unfavorable and subservient position. The need for such loans was especially common in years following a bad harvest, and the sharecropping contract specified that the proprietor was obligated to loan the family both sufficient grain to feed themselves until the next harvest and sufficient seeds and other materials to permit the full operation of the farm. These loans were most often made in the spring, when the sharecroppers had exhausted the previous year's harvest, and the cost of the loan was computed on the basis of current prices, the highest of the year. The sharecropper made repayment on the loan at the time of the harvest, when prices were at their annual low, much to the benefit of the proprietors and the chagrin of the sharecroppers (Commissione Mista 1874: 25; Carrara 1896: 126; Comizio Agrario 1905: 6–7).

A large proportion of all sharecroppers found themselves in debt, and this debt both diminished their annual income and threatened to drive them out of sharecropping and into the wage labor force (Tanari 1881: 228; Sereni 1968: 182). Although this debt relationship strengthened the hold that the *padroni* had over the sharecroppers, the proprietors often complained about the abuses the debt relationship led to. Since regular payment on the accumulated debt was generally subtracted from the cash crop portion of the produce, many sharecroppers did as little as possible to benefit the harvest of such crops (especially hemp), putting as much effort as they could into the subsistence crops that would provide them with their food for the year to come (Ramponi 1892: 116–118).

The sharecroppers not only felt victimized by the landowners, who could rob them of their livelihood, but also by the state, which they saw as an outside power that robbed them of their income and of their sons. Distrust of the ruling powers had a long history in the area, with church officials being viewed with suspicion if not hostility. For the sharecroppers, the state was largely felt through the taxes imposed on their crops, and especially the *imposta sul macinato*, the flour tax. This tax had been one of the central sources of revenue for the pontifical state but was suppressed in the 1500s in response to peasant protest. When the French tried to reinstate the flour tax in 1809, it provoked a bitter anti-French insurrection in the countryside. Six decades later when the new Italian state, desperate for revenues, reimposed the flour tax, the rural population of Bologna again rose up in violent protest. The tax fell most heavily on those whose diet consisted largely of grain, and the sharecroppers were among its greatest victims (Tanari, 1881: 444–445; Zangheri 1957).

Taxes levied by the state, provincial, and municipal authorities also affected the sharecroppers in a more direct way. Land taxes became a more prominent revenue source in the latter part of the nineteenth century, impelling the landowners to demand greater production per hectare in order to protect their profit margin. A contemporary observer has argued that these taxes were a principal cause of the push for more intensive agriculture, a push that was closely tied to the increasing capitalization of Bolognese agriculture (Ramponi 1892: 103).

The Sharecropper Family

Among the sharecroppers, the household was the unit of production and it had a distinctive division of labor. The head of the household, the *reggitore*, was the family director of the agricultural enterprise and the legal representative of the entire family in its relations with the proprietor. Family members were expected to show considerable deference to the *reggitore*, particularly if he was of a senior generation. It was his responsibility to assign each family member particular duties on the farm and to insure that they were performed satisfactorily. He determined, on the basis of age, sex, and personal abilities, what jobs each individual should perform. One of the men of the family (the *bifolco*) was put in charge of the large animals, including all the farm operations involving animal-powered transportation. A child generally assisted him in this work. Another of the men of the family was designated as the director of cultivation (*campagnuolo*), and all other family members working on the land had to obey his instructions.

As the only family member in direct contact with the landowner or the landowner's agent, the *reggitore* mediated between the wishes of the landowner and the exigencies of the sharecropping family. When the *padrone* or his agent visited the farm, he was accompanied by the *reggitore*, but the *padrone* had the right to give orders and demand obedience from any household member. It was the responsibility of the household head not only to oversee the farm's operations but also to make decisions regarding family expenditures for food, clothing, and household goods. Within the limits set by the proprietor, it was also up to the *reggitore* to go to the regular fairs and markets to buy and sell livestock (Goretti 1883: 54–55; Ministero di Agricoltura 1891: 354).

Contemporary observers all characterized the traditional sharecropping family as patriarchal, stressing the fact that all family members took orders, directly or indirectly, from the household head, and that decisions of the head were *insindacabile*, not open to further appeal (Nardi 1957: 270). But there is reason to question this image of domestic tyranny. Toscanelli, writing in 1861, for example, describes the *reggitore* sitting in the evenings by the fire, discussing farm affairs with the other men of the family. True, it is the head who ultimately decides what is to be done, but he does this after consulting the other adults who have relevant expertise or who will be directly affected by the decision (1861: 258). The extent to which actual decison-making power was shared undoubtedly depended not so much on the personality of the *reggitore* as on the demographic and family composition of the household. Where the head was the only man of the senior generation, and there were no other married adult men, centralization of authority was likely to be great. On the other hand, when the *reggitore* had married brothers in the household, it is likely that their wishes were seriously weighed before any decisions were made.

In addition to the *reggitore*, the male head of household, each home also had its corresponding female head, the *reggitrice*, generally the wife of the *reggitore*. She was a woman of great domestic authority, especially in determining the tasks of the women of the household. She was in charge of most aspects of running the household, including preparing meals, spinning thread and making clothes, doing the laundry and the cleaning, taking care of the henhouse and the pigs, making cheeses, selling eggs, buying oil, salt, and other small household necessities. The women of the household did not do only domestic chores, however. They worked in the fields from March to October, aiding the men in all but the heaviest chores. Each married woman was responsible for her own children and for the care of the living space they occupied (Tanari 1881: 237; Goretti 1882: 144; Pasolini 1891: 20; Nardi 1957: 270; Anselmi 1978: 150; Broccoli 1979: 60).

Sharecropping families took advantage of all the labor power they had, including that provided by children and the elderly. Small children made themselves useful by watching the chickens to make sure they did not get into the crops. They also ran various errands, such as bringing drinks to the people working in the fields (Broccoli 1979: 20). Before the age of ten, however, the children were more liability than asset to the farm. There then followed a period in which the youths gradually contributed more and more to the farm labor, until by about the age of eighteen they were able to work as an adult (Jacini 1882: 459; Faina 1905: 269; Pagani 1930: 24).

As people gradually lost their strength and grew old, their work schedules were adjusted accordingly. There were hundreds of little tasks that could be done around the house, and the old folks spent their time doing what they could to be useful. They helped make brooms and baskets, greased the harnesses of the horses and oxen, and kept watch over the household and the adjacent fields (Broccoli 1979: 95).

According to cultural norm, the sharecropper household consisted of the patrilaterally extended family. The household was under the authority of the old father and mother, coresiding with their married sons, unmarried daughters, daughters-in-law, and grandchildren. At marriage sons brought their wives into the household, while daughters moved into the households of their husbands. The ideal sharecropper family, then, was ruled by a male head of the senior generation and contained two or more conjugal families, depending on the number of sons who had reached marital age.

The extent to which this cultural norm was realized in practice is the subject of chapter 3. It is worth noting here, though, that observers had been bemoaning the decline of this extended, patriarchal family form for many decades, even before Italian Unification. By the early 1880s this lamentation had grown into a clamorous chorus (Comizio Agrario 1881; Tanari 1881: 238). Many contemporary observers, themselves often landowners and leaseholders, blamed the decline of large, extended sharecropping families on the increased desire for independence on the part of the adult family members who were not themselves household heads or *reggitrici*. Goretti, for example, described the Bolognese situation as follows:

> Generally speaking the sharecropper families of today are breaking up and dividing due to the rising lack of respect, obedience and subordination toward the household heads, whose virtues provided the cement that bound together the old families and gave them their well-being. The sons of the family, just as soon as they are able to do all the farm work, begin to want to take part in the direction of the farm, and want money to pay for their habits and vices; they want clothes with better materials than those made at home, and they want much more spending money than was ever requested in the old families. (1883: 58)

Often blamed for the tensions that led to the dissolution of the extended families were the women who married into the family. Although compelled to obey the *reggitrice*, typically their mother-in-law, they often resented her authority and sought to enlist their husbands to fight on their sides. Indeed, the life of the young wife could be difficult, for she enjoyed little privacy and was expected to obey both her husband and

Economy and Social Organization

her husband's mother. In the tensions that resulted, it is not surprising that these women were often blamed for fomenting dissension in the household.

The *reggitore* and the *reggitrice* had to be ever conscious of the need to appear evenhanded in dealing with their various siblings, sons, sisters-in-law, daughters-in-law, nephews, nieces, and grandchildren. Broccoli tells the story, in this regard, of a *reggitore* who spurned the pleas of his daughter's teacher to have the girl continue school past the third grade. The teacher argued that the girl was the brightest in the class and should not abandon her studies, but the father refused, for he feared what his brothers would say if only *his* daughter were allowed to continue her schooling (1979: 247–248).

With or without encouragement from their wives, the sons were also quite capable of forming alliances to benefit themselves and to exclude other siblings. Although the late nineteenth-century observers lamented these tensions, intrigues, and divisions as new developments, it is unlikely that this is the case.[4] However, what was to change by the end of the century were the alternatives available to the men who were not household heads, making their departure from the sharecropping household more economically feasible (Faina 1905: 276; INEA 1931: 20; Nardi 1957: 272–273; Broccoli 1979: 326).

At the basis of the sharecroppers' extended family structure was the fact that the household was the basic unit of production, and that the primary capital good, the land, required a certain number of adults to optimize productivity. This number was greater than two, and often considerably greater, given the requirements of minimum farm size needed to make efficient use of basic capital goods and to allow a comprehensive agricultural operation. If the family was to be adequate to the task, it would have to be extended or contain unmarried nuclear family adult members.

Within certain limits, it was in the landowner's interests to maximize the labor power on his land and thus to contract with the largest family of adults as possible. The landowner was conscious, however, of the ill effects of having a larger family on the farm than could be supported, for this would only drive the sharecroppers into debt and also augment the possibility that they would expropriate produce during the year to feed themselves.[5] But within those limits, each adult laborer added to the farm meant increased total output and, hence, a greater share for the proprietor.

The sharecroppers' calculation of the most desirable situation was different; they generally sought the largest farm possible. The more land they had per laborer, the more they could produce per effort invested. Moreover, since there were various economies of scale, larger families, with larger farms, were more prosperous than smaller families on smaller farms. Sharecroppers especially sought to avoid having to employ wage laborers to help with their planting and harvest, thus minimizing their out-of-pocket expenditures. This could only be done by having sufficient family labor power to cope with even the busiest labor season (Livi 1915: 94–95; Perdisa 1935: 6; Anselmi 1978: 121–122; Cazzola 1980b: 83).

The number of adults in the household was thus a factor in accounting for differences in wealth among sharecroppers, and it was rare for a household with just two adults to be able to continue for long on a farm (Martelli 1854: 131). Accordingly, sharecropper families sought to maintain a fairly large adult labor size and to find relatively large farms. Families living on large farms whose adult size decreased through death or fission were in a vulnerable position, given the eagerness of families on smaller farms to acquire larger ones, and given the interest of the proprietor in contracting with a larger family.

Where a proprietor owned a large holding, with several sharecropper family farms on it, he was in a position to move families from one farm to another as the families changed in size. In this way loyal and productive families who had lost adult members would not have to be thrown out but, rather, could be placed on a smaller farm. Hence moving from one farm to another was not necessarily tantamount to being cast out by one landlord and having to search for a new one (Bissoli 1979: 397–402; Finzi 1980: 94).

Of crucial importance to understanding life in the sharecropping areas of Italy is this matter of how often people moved from farm to farm and what these movements meant to them. There is a romantic image of the sharecropper as living for generations on the same farm, with an entrenched patron-client relationship tying the sharecropping family to that of the *padrone*. Yet the economic logic that there be a fairly close correspondence between the size of the family work force and the size of the farm, along with the vagaries of the domestic family cycle and the unpredictability of fertility and mortality, undercut such permanence of sharecropper tenure.

Unfortunately there are few empirical studies of this matter. The most reliable relevant study to date, conducted by Conenna, examines sharecropper families in the Siena area of Tuscany during the eighteenth century. There is reason to believe that this was a time and an area in which sharecropper farm stability was relatively great. Conenna found that of 203 sharecropper families studied, half (102) had moved off their farms within ten years (1980: 132).

The question of property division among sharecroppers arose when a household head died and when members of the household having a share of the patrimony decided to leave the farm. There was a complex, codified system of inheritance that assigned certain property to each member of the household upon the death of the head and the dissolution of the remainder of the household. However, the general practice was to do everything possible to keep the patrimony intact, for unless the basic minimum capital was retained and centralized, all successors risked falling from the sharecropper ranks and becoming wage laborers (Dal Pane 1969: 400–401). In fact, the sharecropper contracts specified that where one segment of a family branched off and left the farm, it had no right to take with it its share of the livestock (Commissione Mista 1874: 37). Nor could a group of family members simply get up and leave the household, for they were bound by the terms of the contract and thus had to give several months' notice (Biagi 1935: 45).

Of course young women regularly left the household as they married, but though they had some claim to the family's patrimony, everything possible was done to limit their claims through payment of dowry. Women did not normally share in the basic capital goods of the farm. However, when a family did split and divide the patrimony, elaborate provision was made to ensure that each young unmarried woman of the family would have an adequate dowry (Rabbeno 1895: 83–84; Biagi 1935: 49). Moreover, when the mother died, her trousseau was equally divided among her daughters (Broccoli 1979: 100).

Large households typically split following the death of the parents when the married brothers could no longer tolerate living together, or when the family had become too numerous to be supported on the farm. In dividing the patrimony, distinction was made between number of family branches (*stirpe*) and number of mouths (*bocche*). Most of the capital goods of the family were divided equally among the *stirpe*, that is, each inheriting son received an equal share, regardless of the size of his nuclear family. Most of the foodstuffs and smaller livestock were divided by *bocche*, with each adult entitled to an equal share, and children entitled to a fraction of that share commensurate with their age (Comizio Agrario 1881; Biagi 1935: 45–49).

The Sharecroppers' Neighbors

Although the sharecroppers constituted the backbone of the rural population in much of central Italy for several centuries, they were never alone. They were surrounded by agricultural day laborers, artisans of various kinds, and an assortment of salaried farmers and small farmer-proprietors. Moreover, living in the sharecropper households were servants who came from families that could not easily provide for them. Although most of these servants were youths, many were adults, some of whom spent their entire lives in agricultural service.

By far the most important occupational group in the Bolognese countryside, aside from the sharecroppers, were the *braccianti*, the agricultural wage laborers. For centuries the *braccianti* had provided labor flexibility in the countryside, allowing a greater force to be assembled during the most hectic agricultural periods and permitting special work forces to be assembled when major projects (e.g., the building of irrigation canals) needed to be undertaken. Lacking the security of the sharecropper and generally suffering from a lower standard of living, the *braccianti* were composed of those who did not have sufficient resources to become sharecroppers and those who had come from sharecropping families that had lost their contracts and been unable to find new ones (Pagani 1932: 44–45).

There were two principal kinds of *braccianti*: those who had a direct arrangement with a single *padrone*, who provided them with housing, often a plot of land, and regular employment, and those *braccianti* who were on their own, seeking work each day from whomever was looking for daily labor. The mushrooming of the *braccianti* in the nineteenth century corresponded with a relative decline in the proportion of *braccianti* who were *obbligati*—having an ongoing relationship with a single proprietor—and an increase in those who were *disobbligati*, who had to fend for themselves to find work each day (Finzi 1980: 95–96).

Throughout the latter half of the nineteenth century the proprietors continuously lamented the decline of the sharecropper population and the increase in the *braccianti*, believing that the latter had low morals, could not be trusted, and were prone to revolt (Sereni 1968: 304–305). However, the rise of the *braccianti* was in good part a result of the increasing preference for wage labor on the part of the proprietors themselves, who were seeking to place their agricultural holdings on a more capitalistic basis. A major part of this effort involved a shift away from subsistence crops and toward cash crops, especially hemp. Additionally, the large-scale land reclamation projects in the lower plains of the province, which brought large tracts of fertile wetlands under cultivation, heavily favored *braccianti* in the new monocultural (often rice) enterprises that resulted (Goretti 1882: 142–143; Commissione per lo Studio 1883: 88–96; Ramponi 1892: 97; Nardi 1957: 268).

By the mid-nineteenth century there were approximately equal numbers of sharecroppers and *braccianti* in Emilia-Romagna, a proportion that stabilized for a period (Zangheri 1957: 112). However, in the later years of the nineteenth century increasing numbers of farms in the plains were taken out of sharecropping and given over to wage labor. In the hills and mountains change was to come much more slowly (Società Agraria 1883: 80).

Next in importance to the sharecroppers and *braccianti* among the agricultural population were the *boari*, salaried farm workers who lived on the farm and were responsible for the livestock. There was, in fact, a wide variety of *boaro* arrangements, including some that bordered on sharecropper contracts. Of particular importance in late nineteenth-century Bologna was the predilection of proprietors to remove large landholdings from sharecropping and place a more limited number of *boari* on them. These *boari*, who received a monthly salary and generally enjoyed yearlong contracts, took care of the farm animals and related equipment. The land itself was then farmed by *braccianti*, under the direction of an agent of the proprietor (Comizio Agrario 1881; Tanari 1881: 221–233, 434; Goretti 1882: 142; Commissione per lo Studio 1883: 90; Preti 1955: 27–28; Sereni 1968: 302).

As in much of Europe, servants were common in the sharecropping areas of Italy, and service provided a significant part of the early life course experience for a large proportion of the population. A study of the agricultural land surrounding the city of Bologna showed that in 1847 over one-third (35.6 percent) of all sharecropper households contained at least one servant and that 17.7 percent of all households had a servant. Yet, as we would expect, just 1 percent of *braccianti* households had servants (Angeli and Bellettini 1979: 162). Indeed, it was the children of *braccianti* who were going into service in the homes of the sharecroppers.

The agricultural servant was termed a *garzone*, and he or she lived with the family and was treated largely as a family member. Service might begin as early as ten years of age, though more commonly a bit later, with males often continuing in service until they could get work as *braccianti*, and females remaining in service until marriage. *Garzoni* received an annual salary, the size of which was related to their age, and they were also fed and clothed by the family. The sharecropper family's need for servants was obviously linked to its household composition. Where adult labor was lacking, adult or near-adult *garzoni* were taken in. However, as the cost of paying, feeding, and clothing such a person was considerable, the investment would only be made if necessary (Toscanelli 1861: 257; Tanari 1881: 237; Pasolini 1891: 21; Broccoli 1979: 116–117).

Not all the rural population was engaged in agriculture; there were merchants, artisans, priests, doctors, pharmacists, construction workers, and others. However, altogether these made up but a small proportion of the rural population through most of the nineteenth century. Merchants ran small stores, though increasing numbers of taverns opened up in the latter part of the nineteenth century that catered largely to the swelling ranks of the *braccianti*, most of whom had much time (though little money) on their hands. The artisans—primarily tailors and shoemakers—performed those tasks that the rural population could not do itself, going from home to home taking measurements and orders. Most clothes, though, as well as many other household goods, were made in the home by the women. Indeed, winter evenings were most often devoted to spinning, sewing, and working hemp (Poni and Fronzoni 1979).

Making a Living as a *Bracciante*

Given the great importance of the *braccianti* in this part of Italy it is worth looking at them more closely. We begin here by asking how they found their work and what kind of work they found.

We have already made the distinction between those *braccianti* who had relatively secure positions, living on farmland in housing provided by a proprietor who also gave them regular work, and those *braccianti* who lived in nonagricultural settlements and who had to find work each day wherever it was located. The former, the *braccianti obbligati*, were most often found on large landholdings. In such cases the *bracciante* family was sometimes provided with a small plot of land on which they could grow some vegetables for domestic consumption. In the larger holdings, the *braccianti* were organized under a foreman, who himself served under an agent of the proprietor. They were paid weekly, sometimes based on a straight daily rate and sometimes on a piecework basis (Goretti 1882: 139–147; Ministero di Agricoltura 1891: 362).

Although this form of *bracciante* arrangement had been common in previous years, by the latter part of the nineteenth century 80 percent of all *braccianti* in the region were *disobbligati*, or *avventizi* (literally, temporary). These people had no stable bonds with any *padrone* and were the most likely to participate in class-based movements. They were the major recruits of the first socialist leagues that blossomed in rural Emilia in this period, and they were feared and often vilified by the landowners. The *braccianti* were hired daily in the early morning labor markets, where agents sometimes worked in groups, sometimes alone (Schiavi 1904: xiv–xx; Preti 1955: 48).

Wages were low. The highest pay, about one and a half lire, was received in the summer months when demand for labor was greatest as was the number of hours worked per day. In the winter months, though, when any work was eagerly accepted, the *braccianti* men were paid just one lire per day, with women receiving sixty *centesimi* and youths forty. One lire of 1880 was equal to forty cents in American money of 1952 (Preti 1955: 37–38, 54).

The *braccianti* received low wages for their work in the fields; moreover, they were often unable to even earn these paltry wages, for it was only during the peak periods of agricultural activity that there was sufficient work to absorb the labor force. The *braccianti* survived by finding other kinds of work, some linked to farm operations and some not. Perhaps the greatest sources of such employment were the various public works projects, particularly in land reclamation and in construction of irrigation works and roads. In addition, work was found building railroads and in various seasonal industries, such as sugar refining, food preservation, and packaging. The *bracciante*, then, at least by the mid-nineteenth century, was no longer simply an agricultural figure but a wage laborer who found work in whatever sector—agricultural or nonagricultural—offered employment (Tanari 1881: 239, 248; Grabinski 1892: 171; Pasolini 1892a: 326; Schiavi 1904: xxiii; Pagani 1932: 12; Poni and Fronzoni 1979: 28; Cazzola 1980a: 24, 53).

Women constituted a large portion of the *bracciante* work force and were often in fact preferred by the proprietors because they were paid much less for nearly the same amount of work. Typically, if a man was a *bracciante*, his wife also worked as a *bracciante*, though the two would not generally work together. Women were involved in a wide variety of labor, including reaping, raking, threshing, husking, and hemp preparation (Sezioni di Agricoltura 1889: 61–62; Schiavi 1904: xxxiii). As Pagani (1932: 46) wrote for a somewhat later period:

> In the *bracciante* family it is hard to find a woman who devotes herself exclusively to housework. The reaping sickle, the hoe for breaking up the earth and the hoe for weeding, the pitchfork for haying, and the shears for harvesting the grapes are as common, and perhaps even more common, than are their kitchen utensils.

The income that the women provided to the household was essential. Households with just one income-earner and several mouths to feed were threatened by malnourishment, cold, and eviction.

Braccianti families had to move from place to place in search of employment. When large public works projects were under way, people swarmed into the area from distant parts of the province. When these projects ended, the workers moved elsewhere. But this continuous movement was geographically restricted. Few *braccianti* moved outside the province, and foreign migration, though becoming a mass phenomenon in southern Italy in this period, was rare in Emilia-Romagna. Despite the heavy burden of poverty, few *braccianti* ever considered leaving their native land (Pasolini 1891: 8–9).

Bracciante Family Life: Two Case Histories

At the end of the nineteenth century, Countess Maria Pasolini (1891, 1892a, 1892b) published a remarkable series of sketches of sharecroppers and *braccianti* who lived on land owned by her family in Ravenna, the province of Emilia-Romagna bordering Bologna on the east. Instead of providing an abstract discussion of *bracciante* family life here, we may get more insight by presenting two of her portraits. The first, focusing on Luigi Poletti, is the story of a relatively prosperous *bracciante*. The second, the story of Angiolo Tassinari, tells of a *bracciante* who has come upon hard times despite his continuous struggle to make ends meet.

Luigi Poletti's father was a sharecropper on a small farm belonging to the hospital of Ravenna. When he died, he left his widow with three children: Luigi, aged two, and two girls, one four years old and one just seven months. Lacking a sufficient labor force, the family was forced off the farm, but they remained in the same parish, where they rented a small room. Luigi's mother combined spinning at home with some wage work in the fields. This barely kept them from starvation.

The family could not be supported this way for long, and at the age of seven Luigi was sent to work as a servant in the home of a sharecropper. In the meantime one of his sisters had died, so his mother had just one child to support at home. As a small child, Luigi received no wages for his work, but he was given meals, housing, and clothing. Later, Luigi moved to the home of a sharecropper who needed more help and who was willing to take on an older child and to pay him modest wages. He spent a year and a half with this family but was then let go when it was decided that the family could no longer afford the expense of keeping him.

Luigi's mother's brother found him his next position as *garzone* to a sharecropper. But at the age of nineteen, he contracted pneumonia and was sent to the hospital. By the time he got out, his employers had already replaced him, but he was able to locate another sharecropper family who needed a *garzone*, and there he earned his highest salary, ninety lire per year (the year was 1857).

Luigi's mother, meanwhile, continued to live with his sister, aided by the money he regularly sent to them. But when his sister subsequently married, leaving his mother alone, Luigi felt obligated to return to her, leaving his position as *garzone* and becoming a *bracciante*. He worked hard to support his ailing mother, giving her bits of meat each day and paying for her doctor and her medicines. While working in the fields he met a young women who also worked as a *bracciante*, and after three years they got married and rented a room near his mother's so that he could continue to care for her. However, within a year of the marriage Luigi's mother died.

In 1876, when Luigi was thirty-nine years old, his first child was born, a son. In keeping with the prevailing view that it was just as easy to care for two infants as one, Luigi's wife took in a foundling from the orphanage in Ravenna and nursed both children together. For this service the orphanage paid the family 120 lire the first year, 96 for the second, 78 for the third through eighth, and 72 from the eighth through eleventh. Although the child had been taken in for economic reasons, ties of affection quickly developed, and the girl was treated as a daughter.

Finally one other daughter was born, leaving the family with five members. Luckily all remained in good health, and with the wages earned by the hardworking Luigi and his wife, they were spared hunger or debt.

The story of Angiolo Tassinari is less happy, though Pasolini describes him as a strong worker and a good man. Like Luigi Coletti, Tassinari married rather late, yet unlike Coletti he proceeded to have numerous children. By 1892 the family consisted of seven people, including three girls (the eldest of whom was fourteen) and two boys (the elder being nine). In 1890 Angiolo could find work for only seven months, which, along with a few miscellaneous sources of income, yielded a total of 479 lire to support the family for the year. Although living at bare subsistence, the family ended the year with a debt of fifty-seven lire, owed to their landlord, to the local doctor, and to the pharmacist.

Tassinari's wife had been sickly since the birth of their first child, and their eldest daughter had to take responsibility for the housework. Along with several other *braccianti* families, they lived in an isolated building in the countryside. Their apartment, for which they paid forty-seven lire per year, had two small rooms, both with low ceilings, one on top of the other. The first floor room, with dirt floor, consisted of a kitchen and the parents' bed. Since the room was too small for a table, a dresser served in its place, with Angiolo's farm tools leaning against the wall. The five children slept in two beds in the upstairs room, alongside a supply of firewood and potatoes, a gift from some sharecroppers.

Angiolo had not always lived in such miserable circumstances. He had been born in 1838 to two *braccianti*, but his father soon succeeded in renting a hectare of land on which he grew vegetables and raised two calves. Despite their large family—five boys and a girl—they were doing well until disaster struck. The great flood of 1843 destroyed their home, their crops, and their animals. Their father, distraught, had to find work as a *bracciante* while Angiolo and his siblings went door to door among the sharecroppers begging for bread. When his father soon died, Angiolo, aged twelve, found a position as *garzone* for a sharecropper.

Angiolo moved from sharecropper to sharecropper as he grew older, seeking those who needed the most help and were thus willing to hire an older and hence more expensive *garzone*. He sent part of his wages back to his mother, while his younger siblings eventually became of age to take positions as *garzoni* themselves. Finally Angiolo became a *bracciante* and even acquired sufficient savings to support himself through periods of illness. In 1859, at the age of twenty-one, he was fortunate enough to find a position as a *bracciante obbligato*, thus providing himself with secure employment. Angiolo then spent the next seventeen years living with his married brother and his family, before getting married at the age of thirty-eight. He looked back upon those years nostalgically as carefree, in contrast with the woes subsequently brought about by his sick wife and numerous small children.

Rural Living Conditions

The distinction in status between the sharecroppers and the *braccianti* was clearly reflected in their housing conditions and their diet. Sharecroppers lived in the houses provided by the proprietor as part of the sharecropping contract. These houses, often quite large, lay at the center of the farm and combined living quarters for the family with the headquarters of an agricultural firm. These often imposing two-story brick buildings not only housed humans but also either housed or were attached to the quarters for animals. Typically, the ground floor consisted of a large kitchen, which was the center of family life, a cellar in which wine and various cured meats and other produce were stored, a room for the loom that was used by the women in the winter, and a storage room for animal fodder and rubbish. Just outside, often attached to the house, were the stable, the oven, and the shack housing the farm equipment. On the second floor were the bedrooms, each holding four or five individuals, plus one or more storage rooms. The building was inevitably cold and damp, good for the heat of the summer but nasty in the winter, when evenings were spent in the stable, sharing the warmth given off by the livestock (Nardi 1957; Broccoli 1979: 271; Gambi 1977).

Although these housing conditions may have been far from ideal—animals crowding humans, little privacy, and cold and damp—they were far better than those found among the *braccianti*. The most reliable account of their housing is provided by the Agrarian Inquiry, published in 1881, which states that the majority of *braccianti* lived in decaying brick buildings that housed several to a hundred or more families, each with a one or two room apartment. These buildings were the "most decrepit, the most lurid, the most unhygienic. . . . The space assigned to the family is always the minimum possible." Floors were often of clay and the wind and rain frequently whipped through the living quarters. The landlords showed no interest in improving housing conditions, for such was the demand for housing that they could rent the apartments despite their miserable state. For the benefit of this housing the *braccianti* had to pay from thirty to sixty lire per year, and it was not rare for families to be driven to steal from neighboring farms at night to be able to pay their rent and avoid eviction (Tanari 1881: 10–11, 235; Preti 1955: 55).

The sharecropper ideal had long been to raise the main items needed for subsistence, and in fact crops raised on the farm provided the sharecroppers with the bulk of their diet. The major portion of the diet was composed of bread and polenta made from the wheat and corn grown on the farm, with small amounts of meat, especially pork, eaten as a condiment. Wine and, more commonly, wine diluted with water were drunk, made from grapes grown on the farm.

Aside from their use as condiments, meat and chicken were eaten only on Sundays or special holidays. Eggs, available from the henhouse, were regularly used but were considered precious. Milk, butter, and cheese were also produced and eaten, and in the summer the diet became much richer with the harvest of fruits and vegetables (Toscanelli 1861: 259–260; Comizio Agrario 1881; Goretti 1882: 145, 1883: 55–56; INEA 1931: 17).

Much less satisfactory was the diet of the *braccianti*. During the summer and harvest months they were usually able to acquire sufficient food to feed their families, often being paid in kind by their employers and being given meals while at work, but in the winter they often faced malnutrition. In these months the staples of their diet consisted of polenta made from corn, with only water to drink. This diet, along with their housing conditions, led to a high incidence of disease during the winter months. Yet even though they ate so poorly, they were forced to spend a large part of their income on food. According to Somogyi's analysis of Pasolini's data, the Ravenna *braccianti* of the late nineteenth century were spending 73 percent of their income on food (Tanari 1881: 233–234, 443; Nardi 1980: 173).

Sharecropper-*Bracciante* Social Relations

Given the greater living standard and status enjoyed by the sharecroppers, and the fact that the *braccianti* often had to work for them, it is hardly surprising that tension and distrust existed between the two. The livelihoods of the *braccianti* were partially dependent on the sharecropper's needs to hire wage laborers on their farms. However, as already discussed, it was in the interest of the sharecropper to minimize such wage labor. In addition to the maximization of family labor, this traditionally took the form of the sharecropper labor exchange (*zerla*). In peak periods of activity sharecroppers requested the aid of other sharecroppers, who in turn could expect reciprocation. This also served to reinforce social ties among participating sharecroppers.[6] The *zerla* was always resented by the *braccianti* and, by the latter part of the nineteenth century, it became one of the foci of *bracciante* organization. In many areas the *zerla* was prohibited; *braccianti* had to be employed in its place (Schiavi 1904: xxvii; Poni 1977: 108).

But it would be a mistake to portray sharecropper-*bracciante* relations in purely hostile terms. Sharecroppers served both as patrons and friends to *braccianti* and sometimes also kinsmen. It was customary for the sharecroppers to leave some of the grain harvest in the fields to allow the *braccianti* to glean the remains, and it was customary too for sharecroppers to open their door to *braccianti* children who came to request a piece of bread. Indeed, there was the custom of the *zirudelle* on the day of the winter carnival, when children of *braccianti* put on masks and costumes and went from home to home among sharecroppers, receiving specially prepared food (Pasolini 1892a: 320; Broccoli 1979: 119).

The sharecroppers not only provided food for the *braccianti* but shelter as well. During the winter, when evenings were spent in the only warm space, the barn, *braccianti* friends of the sharecropping family were invited to drop in regularly. With the men telling stories and the women spinning their thread, these evenings were among the major sources of sharecropper social contact beyond the family. In exchange for this opportunity for warmth and companionship, the *braccianti* offered a full day of work to the sharecropper during the following agricultural season, at a time of the sharecropper's choosing (Poni and Fronzoni 1979: 34; Broccoli 1979: 34, 120–121).

The Moral Question

The literate elite of central Italy devoted countless pages to decrying the change in morality that had come upon the rural population in the latter half of the nineteenth century. In this romanticized view, formerly obedient and hard-working sharecroppers, ever thankful for what they received, were being replaced by an increasingly godless and presumptuous body of sharecroppers alongside a rapidly growing number of openly hostile *braccianti*. We will later examine developments that magnified this class antagonism in the last two decades of the nineteenth century and the beginning of the twentieth. Here we look at the situation as it existed in the years immediately following Unification.

The old landed nobility blamed much of these perceived changes on the *Risorgimento* itself and on the replacement of papal authority with the new secular state. Whereas in the past religous teachings had given legitimacy to the subordination of the sharecroppers and *braccianti*, with the struggle against the church that was such a major part of the *Risorgimento*, church authority waned and the moral underpinnings of *padrone* ascendancy eroded (Scarselli 1890: 28; Grabinski 1892: 166; Ramponi 1892: 115; Urtoller 1898: 224).

The state affected the rural population in another way, through universal male conscription, which not only robbed sharecropping families of prime labor power but also exposed the rural youths to urban life and to ideologies emanating from urban and foreign centers. Conscription was fiercely opposed by sharecroppers, who were often faced with the necessity of trying to replace lost manpower with *garzone* or wage labor. In some extreme cases, the loss of a son to the military could mean loss of the farm to a larger family. And even when the son returned, in many cases the old relationship of patriarchal authority came to be challenged by the youth who believed his knowledge superior to that of his elder and who had seen a larger world he wanted to be a part of (Tanari 1881: 246–247; Società Agraria 1883: 71).

The *padroni*, however, saw the *braccianti* as the primary force of moral decay and insubordination in the countryside. The *braccianti* came to be referred to as *proletari*, proletarians, and they were blamed for widespread and continuous theft of crops. The *padroni* blamed their moral decline on the spread of socialist ideology, on increasing laziness, and on a weakness for alcohol and gambling (Tanari 1881: 250–251, 442; Goretti 1883: 61; Pasolini 1891: 7).

Moral decline among the sharecroppers was largely portrayed by the elite as the fault of the rebellion of the younger generation against patriarchal authority. With the younger men and women unwilling to be totally dependent on the *reggitore* and *reggitrice* of the household and wanting to have some money of their own to buy factory-made clothes or other luxuries, it was not unusual for them to expropriate furtively some part of the crop. A special target for such theft was the hemp harvest, which was vulnerable for three reasons: it had the highest value per unit volume, making it valuable to steal; it was cured by the sharecroppers before being taken from the farm, and consequently it was in the sharecroppers' hands longer than other crops, allowing easier access; and unlike the subsistence crops that were divided on the farm, the hemp crop was consigned in its entirety to the *padrone*, who only later paid back the sharecroppers, after deducting debt payment. Thus, as early as 1875 a special commission was established by the Società Agraria and the Comizio Agrario of Bologna to draft provisions to cope with the theft of hemp by sharecroppers (Bandera et al. 1875; Goretti 1882: 146; Crispolti 1894: 124; Rabbeno 1899: 46).

As we have seen, rural Bologna in 1880 showed both the continuity of a social order based on sharecropping and the legacy of political and economic developments that had brought about changes in rural life. Although in later years this period would be seen by many as the time of tradition and conservatism, in fact continuous changes had been taking place throughout the nineteenth century, as they had through previous centuries. The search for the static social order of the past is a vain one. Yet it is also true that a series of events, rooted in part in economic and political forces long beyond Italy's borders, would bring about accelerated social change in the closing decades of the century.

Agricultural Crisis and Economic Development in Bologna

Italy's transformation from a peasant society to a modern capitalist society followed a lengthy and uneven path. For centuries the rural masses had been tied into a world market economy, the romantic image of an isolated peasantry working in a purely subsistence economy notwithstanding. Yet, as we have seen, important vestiges of the former feudal order remained: the economy was dominated by agriculture, and the agriculture was run not on a modern capitalistic basis but on a mixed feudal/market system. Manufacturing had an ancient history in Italy, experiencing booms and declines in conjunction with world market forces. Yet the manufacturing was linked to artisanal methods rather than capital-intensive production.

The beginning of the modern capitalist transformation of this system took place in the latter part of the nineteenth century when large-scale factories and capitalist agricultural businesses began to spread in the north (Zangheri 1969).[7] Bologna was soon affected by these developments, though some other areas were affected even more in this period. The case of Bologna shows just how complex and mixed the process of the spread of capitalism actually was, with the decay of the old economic order under way before a new order could take its place (Masulli 1980: 5).

The economic transition that began to be felt in Bologna in the 1880s brought with it tremendous political pressures, as the victims of the distintegration of the old system—principally the sharecroppers and *braccianti*—showed themselves unwilling to accept quietly their desperate situation. Beginning in the 1880s and continuing into the twentieth century, a series of militant protests convulsed the countryside, as an expanding number of impoverished rural proletarians lashed out against their conditions and organized to improve their lot. They were too numerous to be supported by the agricultural system, and the inroads made by industrialization were not yet sufficient to absorb them in the nonagricultural economy (Sereni 1968: 349).

In these pages we examine just what this period of transition meant for the people of rural Bologna in order to understand the effect of these changes on their domestic situation. In chapter 4 we will consider current theories regarding the effect of proletarianization on coresidence and look at the evidence from Bertalia to see what the Bolognese case has to tell us about the presumed demise of the complex family household.

Population Growth

From the end of the eighteenth century to the beginning of the twentieth the population of Emilia-Romagna grew substantially, with an increase of over one and a third million people producing a 50 percent larger population. This rate was similar to the other sharecropping regions (Anselmi 1980:36). The population of the diocese of Bologna, excluding the city, had remained relatively constant from the middle of the sixteenth to the middle of the eighteenth century but had then begun to climb, from 190,000 in 1770 to 360,000 in 1880. The population of the entire province of Bologna grew in the last four decades of the nineteenth century from 417,000 to 530,000. During the same period, the population of the commune of Bologna grew from 113,000 to 148,000. Although the city was growing at a somewhat faster rate than the province as a whole, the difference was not great (31 percent versus 27 percent). Over the next decade, though, from 1901 to 1911, the pace of urbanization accelerated, and the city increased in size by 17 percent, whereas the rest of the province increased by just 8 percent (Comune di Bologna 1971: 26; Bellettini 1978: 12; Cazzola 1980a: 41–42).

This substantial population growth in the province was largely a result of the excess of births over deaths, a differential that was becoming particularly notable at the turn of the century with the decline of mortality. However, the population growth of the city of Bologna can only be explained on the basis of immigration from the rural hinterland and not from any so-called natural increase. Indeed, throughout the nineteenth century there were more deaths than births in the city, for the city had both a higher deathrate and a lower birthrate than did the rural parts of the province. Of particular importance to us is the fact that the increase in the population of the commune of Bologna was not the result of any large increase in the size of the population within the walls of the old city; rather, it was a result of the progressive expansion of the urban center beyond the walls of the city. The walls would only be torn down in the first years of the twentieth century, after this suburban growth process had long been under way; the population of the suburbs of the city had already grown by 93 percent in the first eight decades of the nineteenth century, making it the area of greatest population growth in the province.

By 1881, there were 46,670 people living in the suburbs (including Bertalia), and 92,241 living within the city's walls (Bellettini 1978: 9–14).

The Agrarian Crisis

The rural social order experienced a tremendous upheaval in the 1880s with the onset of the agrarian crisis and the national economic depression that accompanied it. This period marked an era of "profound transformation in the body of Italian society" provoked by changes taking place well beyond Italy's border (Cazzola 1980a: 54). At the bottom of the agrarian crisis lay alterations in the world economy resulting from the development of extra-European agricultural production and export. Not only was vast new fertile agricultural terrain being exploited in the Americas, but technological advances in transportation meant that the cost of transporting crops across the seas was drastically reduced. Cheaper grains began to flow into Western Europe from the United States and Russia; rice from India and silk from China and Japan were also imported. Wheat that sold on the Italian market in 1880 for 33.1 lire per quintal (220 pounds) sank to just 22.8 lire five years later. Corn fell in the same period from 23.6 to 14.7 lire per quintal, and rice fell from 47 lire in 1880 to 36 in 1886. Domestic agricultural production decreased sharply, with exports of the principal agricultural products falling nationwide by almost 30 percent between 1880 and 1885 (Masulli 1980: 58–59). Nor was the nascent industrial sector unaffected; certain sectors of industrial employment were jeopardized and work conditions threatened by the deep national depression of 1889–1893 (Clough 1964: 12).

Bologna was greatly affected by the crisis, not only by the precipitous decline in grain prices but also by the disaster that hit the principal commercial crop, hemp. A quintal of hemp had sold in 1880 for 103 lire on the market in Bologna; three years later it sold for 75 lire (Camera di Commercio 1888: 20; Luzzatto 1968: 170–171).

What effect did the crisis have on Bolognese agriculture? One of the major results was the quickening of the tempo in the mechanization of agriculture, for major increases in efficiency had to be made if Bologna was once more to become competitive in the world market. Thus landowners, after a period of retrenchment, began to invest in machinery and in chemical fertilizers (Masulli 1980: 104–105). Another result of the crisis was the development of commercial crops that had not been adversely affected by changes in the world market. Principal among these was the sugar beet, which Bolognese proprietors had experimented with for decades but did not begin to produce on a large scale until the turn of the twentieth century. By 1910, sugar beet cultivation occupied 22,540 hectares of land in Emilia Romagna, constituting 45 percent of the national crop. Moreover, sugar refineries were built to convert the crop into the finished form. In this way an agricultural innovation had direct and rapid consequences for Bolognese industrialization. Constructed at the end of the nineteenth century, the sugar refinery of the city of Bologna was located in the parish of Bertalia and was one of the most important in the country. The refinery was owned by a national sugar company based in Genoa, as were the other two refineries in the province. At the height of the season, the Bertalia factory employed hundreds of workers (Consiglio Provinciale 1932: 635, 776; Evangelisti 1980: 102).

Sharecroppers and *Braccianti* in the Years of Crisis

The agrarian crisis had a disastrous effect on the sharecroppers of Emilia and central Italy. As prices of their crops declined, they fell increasingly into debt to proprietors who themselves were suffering financial losses. The result was that in many cases the proprietor began taking more than half of the crop, for the sharecropper was no longer able to provide half the capital, as contracted. The proprietors, moreover, came increasingly to believe that to be competitive in the world market they would have to modernize their agricultural operations and that the sharecroppers were a barrier to modern capitalist enterprise. Thus to render their operations more profitable, some proprietors began to substitute salaried *boari* and foremen for the sharecroppers, relying on *braccianti* for the bulk of their labor force. This tendency, it should be noted, was partially offset by the belief that the sharecroppers provided the proprietors with greater stability and loyalty. Relying entirely on *braccianti*, by contrast, meant entrusting one's operations to a group known for their propensity to revolt and to strike (Commissione per lo Studio 1883; Goretti 1883: 59–60; Sereni 1968: 299–301; Masulli 1980: 106–107).

The transformation of sharecroppers into wage laborers was spurred on by a basic demographic movement as well, for even if the number of farms run by sharecropping families had not changed in this period, the increase of births over deaths among the sharecroppers meant that over time excess sons would have to be expelled from the sharecropper ranks.

The Bolognese sharecropper family system was based on either a population that did not grow or on a population growth rate that did not exceed the rate at which new land was placed into sharecropping cultivation. By the late nineteenth century these conditions no longer prevailed and the result was a crisis in the ranks of sharecroppers and a sharp increase in the tensions found within sharecropping families.[8]

Although these economic and demographic factors account for the push from sharecropper ranks, there was also a "pull" that attracted young sharecroppers to the ranks of the *braccianti*. For many years, young sharecroppers, living with their spouses in the patriarchal home, had asked themselves if they would not be happier on their own, rather than in a household in which they could not expect to be head until well into middle age. Jacini wrote of just such a phenomenon among the sharecroppers of Lombardia at mid-century (1860: 70–78). Perhaps characteristic of his time, he blamed the in-marrying women for these disloyal sentiments, citing the proverb: "*Suocera e nuora, tempesta e gragnuola*" (mother-in-law and daughter-in-law, storm and hail). The men asked themselves, according to Jacini, "Why should we forever remain children along with our wives and our own children, under the authority of an older brother, or a father, or an uncle?" Writing of the Bolognese situation, Evangelisti (1980: 67) maintains that many sharecropper youths became *braccianti* as a conscious choice rather than as a necessity, choosing the uncertainty and poverty of agricultural wage labor in order to achieve personal liberation from patriarchal and *padrone* authority.

In the last decades of the nineteenth century the ranks of the *braccianti* grew rapidly, not only as a result of their own fertility and the influx of those coming from sharecropping families but also because of the addition of impoverished refugees from the nonagricultural sector. These included small landowners in the mountains, failed artisans, fishermen, and even hunters (Pagani 1931: 53–54; Sereni 1968: 342). They faced difficult conditions, for though wage rates had risen, there was not nearly enough work to keep them all employed for much of the year. The winter, in particular, was a time of great hardship. And by 1900 the situation in the countryside had in many respects worsened rather than improved, for the decline in the rice production that had employed so many Bolognese *braccianti*, along with increased mechanization and other changes, meant a decline in the need for wage laborers in the fields (Conti 1905: 394–395; Pagani 1931: 58–60; Sereni 1968: 345).

Social Unrest

In a nation known for the strength of its socialist movements, Emilia-Romagna stands out as one of the foremost grounds of rural revolt and socialist organization. The last two decades of the nineteenth century and the first two decades of the twentieth were marked by a tremendous amount of rural agitation and by the spread of socialism. The chief participants in this movement were the *braccianti* who, in the face of overwhelming displays of political and economic force on the part of the landowners, nevertheless continued to organize themselves and take militant action.

In the commune of Molinella, in the plain of Bologna, for example, where 69 percent of the *braccianti* belonged to an agrarian league, the final years of the century saw one strike after another (Schiavi 1904: xxv–xxvi). In 1904 a general provincial strike was called in which 70,000 peasants were reported to have participated (Masulli 1980: 246). Strike after strike took place throughout the province, with the *braccianti* demanding that the proprietors recognize the authority of the *braccianti* leagues that were being established. Shouting *"pane e lavoro,"* hundreds of protestors were arrested as police forces sought to break the strikes and demonstrations. These leagues established minimum pay scales and insisted that the proprietors hire their workers directly through the league's local offices, rather than on the free market. For its part, the league would insure that what work there was would be divided fairly among the *braccianti*. Attempts at increased agricultural mechanization were resisted, and demands were made to limit the work day to nine hours (Urtoller 1898; Schiavi 1904: xxxiv; Arbizzani 1961: 88; Ciuffoletti 1980: 101; Evangelisti 1980: 107).

The social center of these movements was often found in the local taverns, which provided a meeting place for the *braccianti* who had no fixed work place. There socialist ideas were spread and the first actions and groups organized. The influence of the Socialist Party and allied rural organizations was reflected not only in a rapidly increasing socialist vote but also in the increasing number of *case del popolo*, local cooperative social centers that began to dot the countryside (Arbizzani 1961, 1977).

The propensity of the *braccianti* to organize and to revolt, in contrast with the more quiescent sharecroppers, was not only a result of their desperate poverty and insecurity but also a product of their relationship to the means of production. They were a mobile population, moving in search of work and working with a different group of fellow *braccianti* from day to day or week to week. Contact among *braccianti* throughout the province was great. Moreover, for the most part they had no relationship of clientage with any particular proprietor and were thus freer to act on behalf of their class interests against the proprietors as a class rather than be bound by personalistic, feudal ties (Preti 1955: 58).[9]

Although the sharecroppers were generally in no position to strike, for such action would risk both their crop and their contract, they were certainly affected by the rural movements led by the *braccianti*, and they occasionally joined in. Such was the case, for example, in Baricella and Minerbio in the Bologna plain when, in 1902, 2,000 *braccianti* and sharecroppers converged to strike for higher salaries and better contractual terms (Masulli 1980: 229). However, such actions were no guarantee of success, as the proprietors were often willing to forego their crops rather than cede better terms to their workers.

The development of an urban proletariat and urban unrest in this period was closely linked to the changing circumstances of the rural *braccianti* of the countryside, for many of the urban workers themselves came from the ranks of the *braccianti*. As we will see in our later discussion of migration, there was a continuous interchange between the rural and the urban populations, in the never-ending search of the poor for work. Those sectors of the economy employing the greatest number of former *braccianti* were those that had the highest incidence of strikes and worker action (Masulli 1980: 230–233, 247; Evangelisti 1980: 88–89).

3

Sharecropping and Coresidence

Family life in the sharecropping areas of Italy revolved around the multiple family household, the preferred form of coresidence among sharecroppers. The reasons for this preference, as we argued in chapter 2, are to be found in the economic relations that characterize a sharecropping economy. Our goal in this chapter is to document the fact that sharecroppers did indeed prefer multiple family coresidence. We do this in two ways. First, by investigating one particular parish in detail, we are afforded a close view of coresidential processes among sharecroppers and their neighbors in nineteenth-century Bologna. However, this case alone can hardly allow us to generalize confidently about household composition throughout sharecropping Italy. To provide a firmer basis for such generalization, we then examine all the available historic evidence on households in Emilia-Romagna, Tuscany, Marche, and Umbria. Finally, we examine evidence from sharecropping areas of France to demonstrate that the family system we describe for Italy is not unique but is found in other areas that have a similar economy.

Marriage, Birth, and Death

Until the 1880s, Italy had a relatively stable demographic regime typical of a nonindustrial, predemographic transition society. The Italian crude birthrate hovered around 36 per 1,000, with a crude deathrate of about 30. Although the deathrate began to fall in the 1880s, declining to 20 per 1,000 around 1910, the birthrate declined at a much slower pace and did not show a comparable decline until the 1930s. In Emilia-Romagna, a similar pattern pertained (Tanari 1881: 242–243; Consiglio Provinciale 1932: 169; Livi-Bacci 1977: 49–50, 62–65).

Like most of Western Europe (Hajnal 1965), Italy was characterized by relatively late marriage for both men and women and a relatively high proportion of never marrieds, a pattern that was found in Emilia-Romagna as well. Mean women's age at first marriage long remained at twenty-four to twenty-five years, with men marrying about three years later. In 1881, 12.1 percent of Italian women aged fifty to fifty-four (and 10.2 percent of women in Emilia-Romagna) had never been married. These figures were considerably higher in the cities, which tended to attract unmarried women in service and other occupations. In the city of Bologna in 1871, for example, 17 percent of all women age fifty to fifty-four were spinsters (Livi-Bacci 1977: 106–107, 119).

Some of these marital characteristics can be illustrated by our data from Bertalia. In the 1880s, median age of men at first marriage as 27.4, compared to 23.8 for women. Over the next two decades women's age at marriage remained the same, while men's age fell (to 25.9 for the marriages in the first decade of the twentieth century). One implication of this relatively late age of marriage and sexual differential in marital age bears directly on household composition. This is the likelihood that the parents of the newlyweds are alive and thus available for coresidence. Least likely to be alive was the groom's father. In the 1880s, the groom's father was alive at only 53 percent of the weddings, with the groom's mother being alive at 68 percent. The bride's father was alive in 69 percent of the cases, and her mother was alive in 79 percent. The slight decline in men's age at marriage, combined with a decrease in mortality, meant that the parents of newlyweds, and especially those of the groom, were more likely to be alive in the early 1900s than they were in the 1880s. In that latter decade, 60 percent of the grooms' fathers and 76 percent of their mothers were alive, and 72 percent of the brides' fathers and 81 percent of the brides' mothers were living at the time of their marriage.

It is likely that the sharecroppers married at a younger age than the *braccianti*, for marriage of a son meant an increase in the labor power of the household through the addition of the son's wife, and the children of the marriage promised one day to aid the family work force and to guarantee a continued high level of production. But from the perspective of the *bracciante*, as Pasolini's sketches demonstrate, marriage represented a significant threat to one's standard of living, for the resulting children were a great burden.

The custom of dowry (*dote*), prevalent throughout sharecropping Italy in the nineteenth century, acted to postpone marriage. For a woman to marry properly, she should bring with her a trousseau consisting of furniture, household furnishings, clothes, and, among the more prosperous, cash. Although some *braccianti* undoubtedly were forced to marry without an adequate dowry, this was a mark of their low status and was perceived as such. The value of the sharecropper's dowry was considerable, apparently in the range of 400–500 lire in this period. This is the equivalent of a year's income for the poorer *braccianti* families. Providing the dowry was the responsibility of the entire household (Goretti 1882: 145; Pasolini 1891: 21; Priore 1906: 618; INEA 1931: 70; Marangoni 1948: 12, 87; Broccoli 1979: 249).[1]

The dowry undoubtedly functioned as part of the social mechanism that encouraged endogamous marriages among sharecroppers and among the wage laborers. However, it was considered even less desirable for a sharecropper daughter to marry a *bracciante* man than for a sharecropper son to marry a *bracciante* woman. In the former case the girl would suffer not only a loss in status but also a loss in living standard. In the latter case, the son's life would be less affected, though her lack of a generous dowry and her unfamiliarity with women's duties in a sharecropping household made the *bracciante* woman less desirable.[2]

Unlike other parts of Europe, in sharecropping Italy there was no cultural norm limiting the number of sons of a family who could get married and remain on the farm. Yet though the norm accommodated the wives of each successive son, the farm they lived on was often unable to absorb the extra labor and extra consumption demands. Thus where a household had several sons, either a larger farm had to be found as more sons married, or the later marrying sons had to go off on their own. It was not uncommon in such situations for two or more married siblings and their families to branch off and together acquire another sharecropping farm.

One of the most intriguing questions about family life in this area concerns the difference in fertility between the sharecroppers and the *braccianti*. This of course relates to the larger debate regarding the extent of birth control in the premodern period. Each newborn in the *bracciante* family represented a major burden, one that promised to be felt for at least a decade. Since both mother and father worked away from the household, and since the nuclear family household was prevalent, care of small children threatened the earning power of the family by forcing the mother to stay home. Conditions in sharecropper households were quite different. There the future of the family's economic well-being rested in replacing older members of the family with a new generation. Moreover, women worked in the same place that they lived, and the multiple family household offered the mother considerable aid in child care.

Unfortunately, adequate studies have not yet been undertaken to document differential fertility in sharecropping Italy. What studies we do have use the indirect method of measurement of number of small children (e.g., four years old or less) residing with each mother (Angeli and Bellettini 1979). Although it can be shown that sharecropping women have larger numbers of coresiding children, this may be due to greater infant mortality among the children of *braccianti* or the greater likelihood that *braccianti* give up their children for adoption.[3]

Epidemic diseases had long been a major source of mortality and a major influence on Italian society. Some notion of the way these epidemics were dealt with can be gleaned from accounts of the last major outbreak of cholera, which struck much of Italy in 1884 but which did not reach Bologna until 1886.

The site of the first outbreak of cholera in Bologna, and the center of the epidemic, was none other than the parish of Bertalia. The initial outbreak was blamed on the railway employees who lived there and who had come into contact with people from the afflicted areas of northeastern Italy. Indeed, for the first month of the epidemic, it was limited to Bertalia and two neighboring parishes. When each case was discovered, municipal officials oversaw the burning of the personal effects of the sick individual and the boarding up of his or her rooms. Although a hospital was available in Bologna, city officials did not want to alarm the population or risk spread of the disease by transporting the patients across the city; hence, a communal school in Bertalia was transformed into an emergency infirmary. In a two month period in the summer of 1886, the Bertalia infirmary treated seventy-seven individuals, forty-eight of whom died. Another 138 cases, outside Bertalia, were treated in another hospital, where 106 of the patients died (Commissione Sanitaria 1887).

Aside from that epidemic year, Bertalia's mortality rate was not espe-

Table 3.1. *Crude Deathrate in Bertalia, 1880-1889*

Year	Number of Deaths	Total population	Crude deathrate
1880	43	1,756	24.5
1881	49	1,860	26.3
1882	42	1,848	22.7
1883	39	1,945	20.1
1884	45	1,949	23.1
1885	44	2,008	21.9
1886	114	2,138	53.3
1887	56	2,219	25.2
1888	63	2,175	29.0
1889	60	2,240	26.8

SOURCE: The number of deaths is taken from parish death records, archives of San Martino di Bertalia; the total population is based on the *status animarum* of the parish and is taken from Bellettini and Tassinari (1977: 476).

cially high for Italy in the 1880s, averaging in the mid-twenties (see table 3.1). It is notable, though, that there was no sign of mortality decline through the 1880s. Another characteristic of pretransition mortality is its great concentration on infants and small children, and this factor must be considered in any discussion of family life in Europe of this period. The age distribution of Bertalia deaths in the 1880s shows that over one-third of all deaths involved infants (under a year old) and virtually one-half of all deaths involved children under age five (see table 3.2). To translate this better into the life experience of the people of Bertalia in this period, we can estimate that approximately 28 percent of all babies born to women of the parish died before reaching their first birthday.[4]

Household Composition in Bertalia

Given this economic and demographic background, just what did households in sharecropping Italy look like, and what changes in coresidential experiences were typical for the people of this period as they passed through their life course? We begin our discussion by looking at the case of Bertalia in some detail, examining the 1880 parish census, the *status animarum*, to see how this still overwhelmingly agricultural population

Family Life in Central Italy

Table 3.2. *Age Distribution of Deaths in Bertalia, 1880-1889*

Age at death	Number of deaths		Percentage of deaths		Cumulative percentage of deaths	
	Male	Female	Male	Female	Male	Female
under 1	92	100	31.7	37.9	31.7	37.9
1–4	50	31	17.2	11.7	48.9	49.6
5–9	6	7	2.1	2.7	51.0	52.3
10–14	4	4	1.4	1.5	52.4	53.8
15–19	5	9	1.7	3.4	54.1	57.2
20–24	8	8	2.8	3.0	56.9	60.2
25–29	16	10	5.5	3.8	62.4	64.0
30–34	4	11	1.4	4.2	63.8	68.2
35–39	2	3	0.7	1.1	64.5	69.3
40–44	8	10	2.8	3.8	67.3	73.1
45–49	7	6	2.4	2.3	69.7	75.4
50–54	16	8	5.5	3.0	75.2	78.4
55–59	9	4	3.1	1.5	78.3	79.9
60–64	12	8	4.1	3.0	82.4	82.9
65–69	14	9	4.8	3.4	87.2	86.3
70–74	17	15	5.9	5.7	93.1	92.0
75–79	12	13	4.1	4.9	97.2	97.0
80 +	8	8	2.8	3.0	100.0	100.0
Total N	290	264				

SOURCE: Parish death records, found in parish archives.

lived on the eve of the expansion of the nearby city of Bologna. The census was taken each spring, just before Easter, by the parish priest, as part of his annual visit to bless the parishioners' homes. It was divided by household, listing all individuals and their characteristics, as well as indicating who owned the building in which the household lived.[5]

The parish priest was under instructions to list first the name of the household head. This is generally the eldest married male in the household, but in some cases a married male of the second generation is listed as head. Women, invariably widows, are found as household heads only when there is no married male in the household. Although kin relationship to household head is not always indicated by the priest, the parental information provided for each individual allows us to deduce kinship

Table 3.3. *Composition of Bertalia Households, 1880*

Household composition	Number of households	Percentage
Solitary	7	2
No family		
Siblings only	1	0
No kin relations	1	0
Simple family		
Married couple	29	8
Married couple with child(ren)	165	48
Widow(er) with child(ren)	28	8
Extended family		
Patrilateral	40	12
Matrilateral	16	5
Other	1	0
Multiple family		
Patrilateral	51	15
Matrilateral	5	1
Other	1	0
Two families		
Not kin related	2	1
Total	347	100

connections where these are not directly recorded in the census.

The method used for analyzing these households is discussed in detail in the Appendix, and readers interested in methodological issues in historical household analysis should read that chapter before proceeding further. We have used the method of household categorization made famous by Peter Laslett (Laslett 1972a; Hammel and Laslett 1974) in order to maximize the comparability of our findings. However, to permit greater detail we have altered and expanded some of the subcategories employed by Laslett. The five principal categories used by Laslett are defined as follows:

Solitaries: People who live by themselves.
No family: Coresidents who are not kin related, or a collection of unmarried siblings.
Simple family: A married couple, with or without children, or a

widow or widower with a child or children.

Extended family: A simple family (or CFU—conjugal family unit) with the addition of one or more kinsmen, there being, however, no more than one CFU present.

Multiple family: Two or more kin-related CFUs coresiding.

In what kinds of households were the people of Bertalia living in 1880? A first approach to this problem is to categorize all the households and determine how many fall into each category. If we do this, we see that most fall into the simple family type, with 48 percent consisting of parents and children, 8 percent of a married couple living alone, and another 8 percent of a widow or widower with children (see table 3.3). The extended and multiple family households, about equally numerous, together constitute just one-third of all households. These show a strong patrilateral bias. That is, the kinship extension of the household is along the male line rather than through the female.

Further analysis of the extended family households shows them to be rather evenly divided between three and two generations in composition. The three-generation households are composed of a simple family with the addition of one of the widowed parents of the husband or wife. Two-generation extended households are most often formed by the coresidence of a sibling of the husband with the husband's conjugal family. In contrast, about 80 percent of the multiple family households contained three generations, generally including an elderly couple along with one or more married sons and the sons' children.

What can we conclude from these data about the prevalence of complex family coresidence in Bertalia? At first glance, they appear to show the predominance of the simple family household and thus undermine our earlier contention that the multiple family household typified the sharecropping area of Italy. However, the analysis of coresidential data is not well served by simple tallies of household frequencies, even apart from the fact that the population is occupationally heterogeneous and such data may conceal important differences in household composition among different occupations.

If our goal is to understand the nature of people's family experiences in past times, it is more relevant to look at coresidence in terms of individuals, rather than in terms of household units.[6] Hypothetically, for example, half the households of a community might be solitary in composition, yet the great majority of community residents may never live in such a household. We avoid this problem if we look at coresidence as an attribute of individuals. Another cautionary note is relevant here as well. If our interest is in the individual, and thus the coresidential experiences an individual has through his or her life course, it is clear that the age of the individual may make a great deal of difference in affecting the kind of household in which he or she lives.[7] It could be, for example, that though all males remain in their parental home after marriage, bringing their wives to live with them there, mortality in the older generation results in a minority of the population living in such three-generation households at any one time. We could not, then, go from a cross-sectional description of household composition to make statements about norms favoring the simple family household.

The only way that this problem can be addressed using cross-sectional data from a single year is by breaking the population down into age groups and seeing how coresidential experience varies by age. This is the classic demographic method for viewing the developmental cycle of the family, but it must be used with the greatest caution. The tendency is to make the assumption that the life course can be reconstructed by arranging data on successive age groups to yield a composite of what happens to people as they age. The problem with this is that it assumes absence of historical change in life course experiences. In the absence of such change, it is true that the prior coresidential experience of fifty-year-olds in 1880 can be derived from looking at the coresidential experience of younger age groups in 1880. But we are rarely safe in assuming an absence of historical change, and certainly such an assumption would be erroneous in examining nineteenth-century Europe. The coresidential experience of children under four years old in 1880 was probably different from that of the same age group a half century before. If that is so, data on children under age four in 1880 cannot be used to describe the earlier life course experience of fifty- to fifty-four-year-olds in 1880.[8]

However, this is not to say that we should throw out the age variable or the notion of changes across the life course. If coresidence is to be a useful historical subject, it must be understood as a process, an experience of individuals through time, rather than as a static attribute of household units. Ideally, we would want to have longitudinal data that follow all individuals through their entire life course, but this is rarely possible. As a practical alternative, we must glean what we can from age-grouped cross-sectional data and supplement these data by what limited forms of longitudinal data are available. In this section we focus on the data from

Table 3.4 *Coresidence of All Bertalia Residents by Age and Sex, 1880*

	<5	5–9	10–14	15–19	20–24	25–29	30–34	35–39
Solitary and no family (%)								
M	0	0	0	0	1	1	2	1
F	0	0	0	1	1	2	2	2
MF	0	0	0	1	1	1	2	2
Simple family (%)								
M	51	65	70	66	65	41	44	44
F	47	56	63	61	47	43	54	58
MF	49	60	67	64	57	42	49	50
Extended family (%)								
M	23	16	14	14	6	15	24	25
F	17	22	20	16	12	19	19	22
MF	20	19	17	15	9	17	21	24
Multiple family (%)								
M	24	19	16	20	26	42	31	27
F	37	22	17	20	37	36	24	17
MF	30	21	16	20	31	39	27	23
Two families unrelated (%)								
M	2	0	0	0	1	1	0	3
F	0	0	0	1	3	0	2	2
MF	1	0	0	1	2	1	1	2
Total N								
M	96	74	94	103	85	76	59	77
F	90	81	84	80	73	67	67	59
MF	186	155	178	183	158	143	126	136

SOURCE: Copyright 1977 by the National Council on Family Relations. Reprinted by permission.

1880, though in subsequent chapters we will make use of some longitudinal data to overcome partially the limitations of the cross-sectional approach.

Examining coresidence as an attribute of all individuals, and dividing the population of Bertalia into five-year age groups, we see that age is indeed an important variable in coresidence (table 3.4). We also see the impact made by using the individual as the point of reference in measuring the prevalence of complex family households. Since complex family households are larger than simple family households, a larger proportion

40–44	45–49	50–54	55–59	60–64	65–69	70+	Total
0	0	2	0	8	0	0	0
0	0	2	0	3	0	0	1
0	0	2	0	6	0	0	1
63	68	64	68	56	29	24	57
72	73	63	55	35	35	25	54
67	70	64	62	44	32	25	56
14	20	13	8	4	29	36	17
18	8	11	7	24	41	33	18
16	14	12	8	15	34	35	18
24	12	18	24	28	42	39	25
10	20	20	38	38	24	42	26
17	16	19	30	33	34	40	25
0	0	2	0	4	0	0	1
0	0	4	0	0	0	0	1
0	0	3	0	2	0	0	1
59	41	45	37	25	24	33	937
50	40	46	29	29	17	24	843
109	81	91	66	54	41	57	1,780

of Bertalia residents actually lived in complex households than is evident from the household frequency figures provided earlier. In fact, in 1880 fewer than 56 percent of all Bertalia residents lived in simple family households, and almost 43 percent lived in complex family households, with the majority of these living in multiple family units.

The age-grouped data, moreover, give us reason to believe that most of the people of Bertalia lived a portion of their lives in a complex family household. The opportunity to live in a complex family household, following the patrilateral norm of coresidence, depends on the simultane-

Table 3.5. *Household Composition by Age of Household Head, Bertalia, 1880*[a]

Household composition	≤29	30–34	35–39	40–44
Solitary (%)	—	4	2	—
	(0)	(1)	(1)	(0)
Simple family (%)	65	74	63	76
	(11)	(20)	(32)	(28)
Extended family (%)	29	15	25	16
	(5)	(4)	(13)	(6)
Multiple family (%)	—	4	8	8
	(0)	(1)	(4)	(3)
No family (%)	6	4	—	—
	(1)	(1)	(0)	(0)
Other (%)	—	—	2	—
	(0)	(0)	(1)	(0)
Total	100	101	100	100
	(17)	(27)	(51)	(37)

SOURCE: Copyright 1977 by the National Council on Family Relations. Reprinted by permission.

NOTE: Discrepancies due to rounding cause some totals to be more or less than 100%.

[a] Figures in parentheses are *N*s.

ous existence of grandparents, parents, and children. These three generations are most likely to be alive when the grandchildren are very young and the parents are in their early childbearing years.[9] Thus, even in a society in which patrilocal residence at marriage is the invariant rule, we would not expect all households to be complex in composition at any single time. People of different ages, consequently, have different likelihoods of living in complex family households. Very young and very old people show considerably greater frequencies of complex family coresidence than adolescents, whose grandparents are probably dead and whose brothers (if any) have not yet married, or middle-aged individuals, whose children have not yet come of marital age. This is indeed the pattern that emerges from our age-grouped data for Bertalia. The proportion living in complex family households shows three peaks: among those un-

	45–49	50–54	55–59	60–64	65+	Total
	—	5	8	11	—	3
	(0)	(2)	(3)	(3)	(0)	(10)
	79	70	68	54	31	63
	(30)	(28)	(27)	(15)	(16)	(207)
	13	10	8	4	25	16
	(5)	(4)	(3)	(1)	(13)	(54)
	8	13	18	32	43	16
	(3)	(5)	(7)	(9)	(22)	(54)
	—	—	—	—	—	1
	(0)	(0)	(0)	(0)	(0)	(2)
	—	2	—	—	—	1
	(0)	(1)	(0)	(0)	(0)	(2)
	100	100	102	101	99	100
	(38)	(40)	(40)	(28)	(51)	(329)

der five years old, among those twenty-five to twenty-nine, and among those over seventy. In all, half the small children, 56 percent of those twenty-five to twenty-nine years old, and three-quarters of the elderly lived in extended or multiple family households.

This life course effect is also evident from a look at household heads (see table 3.5). Since multiple family households are formed patrilaterally, and the patriarch is the household head unless he is infirm, we would expect there to be a relationship between age of household head and type of household. In those households headed by men old enough to have married sons (i.e., heads over age sixty), only a minority preside over simple family households. Of the fifty-one household heads over sixty-five years old, 43 percent headed multiple family households, and another 25 percent headed extended family households. Households headed by young and middle-aged men, by contrast, are rarely multiple in composition, though they often contain relatives outside the simple family unit. This reflects the fact that few married brothers succeed in living together for very long after their father has died.

Our discussion to this point has dealt with the population as an undifferentiated mass, yet we are especially interested in the coresidential behavior of the sharecroppers and how this contrasts with that of the other major agricultural group, the wage laborers. We would expect that the sharecroppers show much higher frequency of multiple family coresidence than do the *braccianti*, for reasons discussed in chapter 2. This is just what we find. If we divide households by the occupation of the head (table 3.6), we see that though the *braccianti* live in complex family households at about the same frequency as the parish population as a whole, the households of the sharecroppers are strikingly different. Indeed, the frequency of multiple family households among the sharecroppers is over three times that found among the *braccianti* (40 percent to 12 percent).

When we take individuals rather than households as our unit of analysis, the predominance of the multiple family household among the sharecroppers of Bertalia becomes even clearer (see table 3.6). Just over a third of all sharecroppers lived in a simple family household, while a majority (52 percent) lived in multiple family households. Although the proportion of *braccianti* who lived in multiple family households is considerably less, the proportion (22 percent) is far from negligible. Indeed, 39 percent of the *braccianti* lived in either an extended or a multiple family household. This pattern is borne out again in the *status animarum* of ten years later. In 1890, 60 percent of wage laborers and just 26 percent of sharecroppers lived in simple households; 14 percent of wage laborers and 15 percent of sharecroppers lived in extended family households; and 59 percent of sharecroppers compared with 24 percent of wage laborers lived in multiple family households.

Nor was this pattern of complex sharecropper households new. Examination of the *status animarum* for 1821 provides us with a glimpse of family life in Bertalia in the early part of the century. In that year there were seventy-three sharecropper households, containing 601 individuals. Of these households, 42 percent were multiple, and 57 percent of the people in these households lived in multiple family units; just over a quarter lived in simple family households. The structure of the complex family households, moreover, reflected the patrilateral ideal seen again

Table 3.6. *Household Composition of Wage Laborers and Sharecroppers, Bertalia, 1880*[a]

	Wage Laborers		Sharecroppers	
Household composition	Household heads (%)	All (%)	Household heads (%)	All (%)
Solitary and no family	4	3	0	0
Simple family	68	58	43	37
Extended family	15	17	18	11
Multiple family	12	22	40	52
Other	1	1	0	0
Total N	138	203	40	98

[a] Youths under age 15 were excluded from these figures, as are females (for whom data are unreliable).

in 1880. Eleven of the fourteen extended sharecropper households and all thirty-one of the multiple sharecropper households were extended patrilaterally. In contrast, *bracciante*-headed households were largely (78 percent) simple in composition.[10]

The 1821 data also permit us to know whether the parents of the household head were alive and to determine the possibility that a sharecropper living in a simple family household could have lived in a three-generation complex family household. As we might expect, simple family households were headed by relatively young men whose own parents were dead but whose sons were not yet old enough to marry. Of these twenty-seven household heads, just one had a living father. The mean age of these heads was 46.4, with a range of from 29 to 61. All of the thirty-one multiple sharecropper family households were headed by men of the senior generation; their mean age of 63.1 and age range of from 44 to 80 were much higher than those of the simple family household heads.

Related to the high proportion of complex family households among the sharecroppers of Bertalia is the high proportion of three-generation households. The typical experience for sharecroppers was to spend significant portions of their life in such a household, with all that this implies in terms of interpersonal relations and lines of authority in the family. Over a third (38 percent) of all sharecropper households con-

Table 3.7. *Number of Generations in Bertalia Households as an Attribute of All Residents, by Age, 1880*

					Number of	
	1		2		3	
Age	N	Percentage	N	Percentage	N	Percentage
<5	0	0	110	59	73	39
5–9	0	0	111	72	44	28
10–14	0	0	134	75	44	25
15–19	2	1	130	71	48	26
20–24	4	3	101	64	41	26
25–29	4	3	83	58	53	37
30–34	12	10	74	59	38	30
35–39	10	7	77	57	45	33
40–44	8	7	78	72	23	21
45–49	4	5	62	77	14	17
50–54	8	9	61	67	19	21
55–59	8	12	40	61	16	24
60–64	6	11	27	50	20	37
65–69	2	5	19	46	20	49
70+	3	5	19	33	33	58
Total N	71	4	1,127	64	531	30

SOURCE: Copyright 1977 by the National Council on Family Relations. Reprinted by permission.

tained three generations, over two and a half times the rate found among *bracciante*-headed households.[11]

Again, when we take individuals rather than households as our basic unit, and when we consider age, the prevalence of three-generation coresidence becomes even clearer (see table 3.7). These data closely correspond with those on household composition found in table 3.4, for they reflect the same basic facts of mortality and family cycle in relation to the life course. Children in the first years of their lives are likely to live in three-generation households because they are the ones most likely to have their paternal grandparents still alive. The initially high proportion (40 percent of those under age five) diminishes through the older ages of childhood as the grandparents are more likely to die but then increases to about one-third when the individual is old enough to have his or her own children. This proportion again diminishes through

Generations					
4		Other		Total	
N	Percentage	N	Percentage	N	Percentage
1	1	2	1	186	100
0	0	0	0	155	100
0	0	0	0	178	100
2	1	1	1	183	100
1	1	10	6	158	100
1	1	2	1	143	100
0	0	2	2	126	101
0	0	4	3	136	100
0	0	0	0	109	100
1	1	0	0	81	100
0	0	3	3	91	100
2	3	0	0	66	100
0	0	1	2	54	100
0	0	0	0	41	100
2	4	0	0	57	100
10	1	25	1	1,764	100

middle age as the likelihood of having living parents declines, only to rise once more in old age with the birth of grandchildren. The majority of people over age sixty-five live in three-generation households.

Household Size

Household composition can be seen, in part, as a strategy for establishing a household of a certain size. This is especially true where, as in the case of sharecropping, the household is the unit of production and must cope with certain capital constraints. We have already seen in chapter 2 why there was considerable pressure on sharecroppers to have large households, for the most desirable farms required having more than two adult workers, and families having only two adults might be en-

Table 3.8. *Mean Size of Households of Different Composition, Bertalia, 1880*

Household composition	Mean household size	Range of sizes	Number of households
Solitary	1.0	1	7
No family	3.5	3–4	2
Married couple	2.0	2–3	29
Parents with child(ren)	5.0	3–12	165
Widow(er) with child(ren)	3.8	2–9	28
Extended family	5.5	3–11	57
Multiple family	8.0	4–17	57
Unrelated families	7.5	6–9	2
All households	5.1	1–17	347

SOURCE: Copyright 1977 by the National Council on Family Relations. Reprinted by permission.

tirely excluded from sharecropping by landowners eager to maximize production with optimum capital efficiency. We have also seen why different constraints affected wage laborers, for the household was not their unit of production.

Before looking directly at these occupational differences, it is worth documenting the link between household composition and household size in Bertalia of 1880 (table 3.8). Although the mean size of all households in the parish was 5.1, the mean size of multiple family households was 8.0. Perhaps less obvious is the fact that extended family households are not that much larger than households that contain just parents and their children (5.5 in the former and 5.0 in the latter). This suggests that the extended family household is a much less effective mechanism for increasing the labor power of the household than is the multiple family household. Indeed, the extended family household is better seen in most cases as a social security device, embedded in the kinship system, through which widowed parents are able to coreside with their married children and unmarried adults are provided with lodging by their married siblings.

As we would expect, sharecroppers live in much larger households than do the wage laborers. In Bertalia in 1880, the mean size of sharecroppers' households was 7.6, compared to only 4.4 for *braccianti*. A third of a decade before, in 1847, sharecropper households in Bertalia and the other outlying areas of the city of Bologna had been even larger, twice the size of *braccianti* households. In Bertalia in that year sharecropper households had a mean size of 9.1 (Bellettini 1971: 341). In the province of Bologna as a whole in 1847, though over three-quarters of the *bracciante*-headed households were under five in size, just one-quarter of the sharecropper households were that small (Bellettini 1971: 179).[12] This pattern lasted well into the twentieth century, with mean sharecropper household size in the province of Bologna in 1921 being 8.2, compared with a mean size of 4.8 among *braccianti* (Consiglio Provinciale 1932: 473).[13]

There was, however, important variation in household size among the sharecroppers related to the size of the farm they had.[14] Proprietors selected sharecroppers for their farms, as we discussed in chapter 2, according to their size. As we noted there, since the larger farms generally meant the highest standard of living, there was considerable pressure on the sharecroppers to do what they could to maximize adult labor force in the household and hence to form multiple family units. Some of our best available data on this point were gathered in the mid-nineteenth century by Berti Pichat for farms just to the west of the city of Bologna, within a few kilometers of Bertalia. We find a clear and large correlation between farm size and size of sharecropper household, ranging from a mean household size of 4.8 for the smallest farms to 18.7 for the largest.[15] Similarly, Balugani and Fronzoni (1979) recently followed a series of Bolognese farm units over the period 1715–1770, using data on household membership and data on size of farm units and amount of production per farm. They show a strong relationship between size of farm and complexity of households. All of the largest holdings are farmed by sharecroppers having multiple family households; all of the smallest holdings are farmed by simple family households.

Household Composition in Sharecropping Italy

We have argued that complex family household organization was the norm in the sharecropping areas of Italy, and that this constrasts with the relative rarity of multiple family households in many other parts of Western Europe. However, the empirical data on Italian household organization we have presented to this point is largely limited to a single parish,

Table 3.9. *Sharecropper and* Bracciante *Household Composition in the Suburbs of Bologna, 1847*

Household composition	Households (by occupation of head)		Residents	
	Sharecropper (%)	Bracchianti (%)	Sharecropper (%)	Bracchianti (%)
Solitary	—	3.2	—	0.7
Simple family	41.6	73.9	28.2	69.2
Extended family	11.9	11.5	10.3	13.3
Multiple family	46.2	10.7	61.4	16.3
Other	0.3	0.7	0.2	0.5
Total *N*	1,052	1,249	9,256	5,501

SOURCE: Angeli and Bellettini (1979: 160, 168).

Bertalia, and thus provides us with a weak basis for generalization. Our intention in this section is to establish the fact that the pattern found in Bertalia is representative of that found throughout this part of Italy. This task would have been impossible a few years ago. However, due in no small measure to the catalyzing influence of Peter Laslett, a number of studies of household organization in this part of Italy have been made in the past decade. We draw on these studies, many of them unpublished, in these pages.

We first ask the question of how typical Bertalia is of the immediate area in which it is found, the rural zone surrounding the city of Bologna. Fortunately, Angeli and Bellettini (1979) have recently examined the coresidential situation of the 21,715 inhabitants living in twenty-eight parishes of this area in 1847, dividing them by occupation of household head (table 3.9). They discovered that over three-fifths of all sharecropper family members were living in multiple family households, and just over a quarter were living in simple family households. In contrast, over two-thirds of the *braccianti* coresidents were living in simple family households, with the remaining third divided between extended and multiple family households. That this is not a classic stem family system in which just one son marries and remains on the farm with his parents is made clear by the fact that a full 28 percent of all members of sharecropper families were living in households that contained at least three conjugal family units. Indeed, over 11 percent of sharecropper coresidents lived in households containing four or more such conjugal

Table 3.10. *Household Composition for All Individuals Living in Households Headed by Sharecroppers and* Braccianti, *in Two Communes of the Province of Bologna, 1881*

Household composition	Casalecchio		San Giovanni in Persiceto	
	Share-cropper (%)	Braccianti (%)	Share-cropper (%)	Braccianti (%)
Solitary	0	2	0	5
No family	2	0	0	2
Simple family	15	73	19	69
Extended family	14	13	15	12
Multiple family	69	12	65	10
Unknown	0	0	1	2
Total N (households)	88	126	344	1,291
Total N (individuals)	919	507	—	—

SOURCES: Data on Casalecchio are from Proietti (1980: 241, 244). Data from San Giovanni in Persiceto are unpublished figures based on manuscript censuses, kindly made available to the author by Marzio Barbagli.

family units (1979: 168). Clearly, there was no restriction on the number of sons who could bring their wives to live in the parental household.

Temporally even more comparable to our Bertalia data is the situation in Casalacchio, a commune bordering the city of Bologna on the west. In 1881, over two-thirds of all those living in sharecropper households were residing in multiple family units, with only 15 percent living in simple family households. As expected, the family situation of the *braccianti* was dramatically different, with almost three-quarters living in simple family households and 12 percent living in multiple families. In that same year in the commune of San Giovanni in Persiceto in the plain of Bologna, 65 percent of all sharecroppers lived in multiple family households compared to 10 percent of the *braccianti* (table 3.10).

A similar examination of sharecropper and *braccianti* households in the province of Bologna focuses on the commune of Granarolo, a few kilometers to the northeast of the city of Bologna, and reveals an even

Table 3.11. *Sharecropper Household Composition in Three Communes of Ravenna, Emilia-Romagna, 1811*

Household composition	Bertinoro (1811)		Faenza (1811)		Ferrara (1881)[a]	
	Households (%)	Residents (%)	Households (%)	Residents (%)	Sharecroppers (%)	Braccianti (%)
Solitary	0.9	0.1	0.1	0.0	1	5
No family	1.8	0.7	2.7	1.4	2	1
Simple family	54.5	43.8	46.3	35.7	13	60
Extended family	14.2	15.4	17.1	16.6	8	13
Multiple family	28.6	40.0	33.8	46.2	73	21
Unknown	—	—	—	—	3	—
Total *N*	563	3,625	1,225	8,773	63	592

SOURCES: Data on Bertinoro and Faenza (province of Ravenna) come from Barnabè (1977: 129–130). Data on Ferrara, in the province of Ferrara, are previously unpublished and have been kindly made available to the author by Marzio Barbagli. They are based on manuscript census forms.

[a]Data on the commune of Ferrara refer to all individuals living in households headed by sharecroppers and *braccianti*. The total number refers to number of households.

greater proportion of complex family households. In Granarolo in 1881, of the 2,046 people living in sharecropping households, 87 percent lived in complex family units, in contrast to 30 percent of the 1,061 *braccianti* (Sardi 1973: app. pp. 9–12). This makes Granarolo one of the most extreme cases of complex family household composition in Western Europe.[16]

A similar pattern of high frequency of multiple family households is found in the other provinces of Emilia-Romagna, though here the data are thus far less abundant. In Ravenna, in the eastern portion of the region in 1811, a majority of sharecroppers in two communes lived in complex family households. Of the 8,773 sharecropper coresidents living in the large commune of Faenza in that year, little more than a third lived in simple family households. Also in the east, in the provincial capital of Ferrara, virtually three-quarters of the sharecroppers were living in multiple family households as late as 1911. Just a fifth of the *braccianti* lived in such households (table 3.11). To the west of Bologna, in the parish of Corniglio (province of Parma) in 1858, 40 percent of the households were complex in composition (Anelli, Siri, and Soliani 1979: 181). When we realize that this includes the entire parish population and not just the sharecroppers and that the figure refers to household units rather than to the residents, we can appreciate the weight of the complex family households in this population.[17]

Nor is this pattern confined to Emilia-Romagna. From all we can tell a similar pattern characterizes the rest of central Italy as well. Silverman, in her study of the hill town of Montecastello in Umbria, shows not only that multiple family coresidence characterized sharecroppers in the past but that this pattern persisted as late as 1960 when the sharecropping contract was becoming obsolete. In that year, just 40 percent of the 213 sharecropping households were simple family units; 24 percent were extended; and 35 percent were multiple (1975: 182).[18] Silverman argues that multiple family coresidence was the norm for sharecroppers in Umbria, and she attributes this to the land tenure and economic system, a system very similar to that found in Bologna.

In Tuscany the fullest nineteenth-century data on coresidence are found in Pesciullesi's study of the commune of Sesto Fiorentino, ten kilometers from the city of Florence. Here again we find the predilection of sharecroppers for multiple family households, with 52 percent of such *households* being of this kind in 1861, 17 percent extended, and 29 percent simple. In contrast, almost three-quarters (73 percent) of the *braccianti*-headed households were simple, 15 percent extended, and 10 percent multiple (1978: 164–165). Again it should be noted that these data refer to household units and not to the total number of residents in the households of each type. Pesciullesi gives us a further breakdown of the multiple family households by kinship type. Of the 411 such households in Sesto Fiorentino, 384 (93 percent) are extended patrilaterally (1978: 118).[19]

Eighteenth-century data on three communities of rural Tuscany have been reported by Laslett (1977a: 97). These are notable in showing the highest proportion of multiple family households of all the communities he lists in Western Europe. In all three Tuscan communities a majority of households were complex, with the proportion of multiple family households ranging from 39 to 45.

Tuscany also provides us with the earliest well-documented material on sharecropper households that we have for Italy, a product of the long-term study directed by David Herlihy and Christine Klapisch, based largely on a tax-related census done in 1427. Their results give us reason to believe that the pattern of pressure toward multiple family living among the Italian sharecroppers is an ancient one. Of the thousands of sharecropper households examined, nearly a third were multiple family units, with 55 percent of the simple family type. Undoubtedly more than half of these people were living in complex family dwellings.[20]

As we would expect, the sharecropper households were also larger than those of their rural neighbors. For example, in rural Pisa in 1427, nearly half (47 percent) had six or more residents (Klapisch and Demonet 1972: 883). Household extension was along the patrilateral line, with married women rarely coresiding with their parents (Klapisch and Demonet 1972: 876, 879). Although many of the multiple family households were composed of three generations, a large number consisted of married brothers, their wives, and children (Klapisch 1972: 280). In the countryside of Pisa, one quarter of all households consisted of three or more generations, whereas in rural Tuscany in general, Herlihy tells us three-generation households were "the most common of all types" in "the last phases of the developmental cycle" (Herlihy 1972: 11; Klapisch and Demonet 1972: 879).[21]

The reasons given for this pattern echo those we have already provided to explain the high frequency of sharecropper multiple families in nineteenth-century Bologna. Fifteenth-century Tuscan sharecroppers traveled from parish to parish in search of better farms, and the proprietors who controlled these farms selected from these competing families those that offered a "complete unit of production." Once having hired such a family, the proprietors sought to do everything possible to prevent any breaking off of its component kinship units (Klapisch and Demonet 1972: 885–887).

France

More than the case of Italy, which to date has been little known by European family historians, it has been the recent evidence from France that has undermined the claim that the extended family in Western Europe's past is but a myth. In this section we gather together these new studies to establish the fact that the complex family household was the norm among a sizeable proportion of the rural population of southern France. Sharecropping Italy was not an anomalous case in southern Europe but part of a larger pattern.

These French studies have led scholars to conclude that there were two Frances as far as coresidential processes are concerned: the north

Table 3.12. *Household Composition in Northern France*

Household composition	Longuenesse 1778 (%)	Villages around Valenciennes 1693 (%)	Treil/ Seine 1817 (%)	Grissy-Suisnes[a] 1861 (%)
Solitary	1	1.5	17.9	15.6
No family	6	1.8	1.1	1.5
Simple family	76	85.8	76.9	79.0
Extended family	14	10.6	4.1	} 3.9
Multiple family	3	0.3	0	
Total N	75	330	541	334

SOURCES: Data for Longuenesse, the Valenciennes area, and Treil/Seine are taken from Flandrin (1979: 71); data for Grissy-Suisnes come from Blayo (1972: 258).

[a] Blayo's catagories differ from the Laslett typology. I have reorganized them to fit as well as possible into that typology to facilitate comparison.

and the south. In the north, as in northern Europe generally, the simple household was the norm and multiple family households were rather rare. In much of the center and south, complex family households were the norm, with a high frequency of multiple family living (Parish and Schwartz 1972; Collomp 1974; Fine-Souriac 1977: 478; Flandrin 1979: 73–74). As yet, French scholars have not fully clarified the relationship between these different household norms and differences in land tenure and economic systems. However, it is in southern France that the sharecropping system most similar to the Italian was found, and reports suggest that here too proprietors sought out families containing several adult members to maximize their profit (Mendels 1978: 789–790).[22]

The pattern of household composition characteristic of northern France can be gleaned from table 3.12, where the results of a number of studies are presented. Complex family households are generally a small minority; multiple family households are rare.[23]

But in southern France the situation is very different. Scholar after scholar proclaims the dominance of the complex family household (table 3.13). In the southeastern area of Provence, Collomp (1972: 974) castigates Laslett for writing of the complex family as foreign to Western Europe. Collomp concludes, on the contrary, that through the eighteenth century the nuclear family household in Haute Provence was more uncommon than the complex households that grouped together parents and

Table 3.13. *Household Composition in Central and Southern France*

Household composition	Central France	Southwest France		Southeast France
	Rural Ussel 1806 (%)	Bessède 1851 (%)	Aunat 1872 (%)	Mirabeau 1745 (%)
Solitary	4.9	7	4	7
No family	3.0	3	4	—
Simple family	59.5	59	54	59
Extended family	10.8	13	25	13
Multiple family	23.5	18	13	220
Total *N* (households)	166	111	106	1

SOURCES: For Ussel, Lemaitre (1976: 223); for Bessède and Aunat, Fine-Souriac (1977: 480); for Mirabeau, Collomp (1974: 785).

their married children.[24] The structure of these households, moreover, follows the patrilateral line of extension found in Italy, with 90 percent of the complex households being of this kind (1972: 971). The households were, also like Italy, patriarchically run, and fathers relinquished control to their married sons only if they became infirm.

The same case has now been made for the southwest, especially in studies of the Pyrenees. Fine-Souriac (1977: 481–482) forcefully contends that for this region, as late as the nineteenth century, "it is the stem family that is the rule." He cites mortality as responsible for the fact that a small majority of households at any one time are simple in composition, offering a complex family household rate of 25 to 30 percent as "statistical proof" of the "predominance of the stem family."

The reasons for the predominance of the complex family household in the Pyrenees, though, are somewhat different than those responsible for the Italian situation. In the Pyrenees small landholdings rather than sharecropping characterized the farmers. The important goal was to keep the family holding intact, rather than have it fragmented. According to Poumarède (1979), the stem family system, in conjunction with small landholding, had been dominant in this region since the Middle Ages. Similar forces seem to have been at work in central France, where high rates of stem family households are also found (Lemaitre 1976: 221). Citing the need to keep the patrimony of land intact, Lemaitre reports that nearly half (43 percent) the population of rural Ussel in 1806 lived in complex family households. In the department of Nièvre, also in central France, Berkner (1977: 162) found that 46 percent of the almost ten thousand peasants studied lived in complex family households in 1820.

What evidence we have for the sharecroppers of southern France suggests that their coresidential norms were similar to those found in Italy. The best available data come from Peyronnet's study of three communities scattered within a sixty-kilometer radius from the city of Limoges. Peyronnet provides data on both sharecroppers and agricultural day laborers. The large majority of sharecroppers in 1836 lived in complex family households, with almost three-fifths living in multiple family units and less than a quarter living in simple family households. In sharp contrast, the day laborers lived overwhelmingly (83 percent) in simple family households, with multiple family living rare indeed (1 percent).[25] Although the mean size of day laborer households was 4.4, the sharecroppers lived on the average in households having 8.5 residents (1975: 581). Peyronnet, too, accounts for the predominance of multiple family households among the sharecroppers of southwestern France by the economic system that drove people to try to augment the number of family workers on their land (1975: 570). Flandrin makes the same point about French sharecroppers we have had occasion to make about Italy, writing that "those who offered themselves for employment as managers of a share-cropping holding, accompanied by a family which was numerous and included people of working age, had more chance of obtaining the concession than a married couple on their own" (1979: 87).

Conclusions

In his discussion of household composition in the various parts of Europe, Laslett (1977b: 24) expresses his perplexity at the Italian case, referring to it as a "rather confused and irregular situation." It is hoped that this chapter has served to lift some of that confusion by documenting the strength of the multiple family household in central Italy and the necessity for distinguishing between the coresidential situation of the sharecroppers and that of others. When the common method of lumping together all individuals who live in a particular parish or commune is employed, these differences among component social formations are often obscured. Moreover, we are robbed of any way of explaining the pattern of household composition that we find, for we cannot isolate factors that do not characterize the community as a whole.

Unlike the agricultural wage laborers, who were the second largest category in much of rural central Italy, the sharecroppers were under great pressure to maintain a sizeable adult labor force within the household. The tensions between the component conjugal family units that nevertheless often made life difficult suggest that there would have to be a powerful incentive to keep such composite units together. In the absence of such an incentive, we would expect the simple family household to be the rule, as it is among the wage laborers.

The principle underlying sharecropper coresidence was that sons should bring their wives into the parental household. Unlike the classic French stem family norm, in Italy there was no rule of primogeniture nor any notion that just one son was entitled to marry and remain in the household. This can be explained, in part, by the fact that the sharecroppers did not own their own land and thus did not face the problem of partibility that was at the heart of the stem family system.[26] Landowning peasants who had more than one son marry and remain on the land confronted a lower per capita yield and the eventual fragmentation of the land into impossibly small parcels upon the death of the father. The Italian sharecroppers had much more flexibility, for they could move to a larger, more productive farm if their adult labor force grew. Moreover, not owning any land, they did not need to worry about its division. Yet tensions within the household increased when the parents died, for the authority wielded by the father could not so easily be wielded by one brother over another. Moreover, there was a limit in size to a household, determined not just by interpersonal family relations but also by the nature of the farm organization, including the size of the house provided by the proprietor. Thus, by the time the following generation married and had children, the married brothers commonly divided their household, having worked to build up enough capital to allow the segment that branched off to acquire another sharecropping farm.

Of course this ideal was often not reached in practice, as a result of both idiosyncratic factors of ability, inclination, and fortune, and of demographic factors such as the birth of sons and their survival. The sharecropper whose only son died in childhood might never preside over a multiple family household. If he and his wife were hard-working and skillful, they might have been able to remain on a small farm as sharecroppers, with the aid of daughters and servants. Yet it was com-

Sharecropping and Coresidence

mon in such cases for the family to be forced out of sharecropping altogether and replaced by one offering the proprietor a greater work force, hence, a larger harvest to divide.

Sharecropping was part of an ancient system of agricultural and family organization. But the system was continually subject to changing pressures emanating from the larger economy and the larger political system. These pressures began to build in the nineteenth century, first with the Napoleonic invasion and later with the demise of the old political order and the birth of the new Italian state. Not long after the Italian state was born a series of economic changes began to make themselves felt. These involved the expansion of capitalism in the countryside and the growth of the cities beyond the walls that had long enclosed the urban populations. Just what effect these changes had on the people of this area, and especially what effect they had on the processes of coresidence described in this chapter, are the subject to which we now turn.

4

Urbanization and Coresidence

Among the central issues of modern European social history is the impact that the forces of urbanization and industrialization have had on family life. Curiously, though, this topic had received little research attention until recent years, for scholars had long assumed that they knew what the relationship between these classic forces of modernization and the family was. With industrialization and urbanization came the nuclearization of the household and the liberation of the young from their kinship bonds. A formerly traditional social order, in which extended family ties were of great importance, gave rise to a modern society in which more universalistic principles reigned.

This picture of European family life was undermined by Peter Laslett and his associates when they demonstrated that even before industrialization had begun the simple family household was the overwhelming norm in England. In this revisionist view, the "pre-industrial west European family pattern" consisted of "a separate household at marriage," and "small households comprising only a single conjugal family" (Wrigley 1977: 76). Thus, industrialization and urbanization could hardly have been responsible for the erosion of an extended family system, as none had previously existed. Once this was accepted, the central theoretical question was no longer how economic change brought about family change, but, rather, did the preexisting nuclear family system found in Western Europe preadapt that society for industrialization? Perhaps it was the European family system that explains why industrialization first took place in Western Europe, rather than in other parts of the world where extended family systems were the norm.

The case of sharecropping Italy, little considered to date in this debate, casts these arguments in a different light. Rather than deny the link between recent economic changes and the nuclearization of the family on the grounds that the family system was nuclear to begin with, we are faced with the case of a society in which complex families were common if not dominant. In this chapter we ask what impact these economic changes had on coresidence in such a setting, and ask what this impact tells us about the interaction of family nuclearization, urbanization, and industrialization.

The Household Nuclearization Debate

The nuclearization thesis has been simply stated by Goode: "Wherever the economic system expands through industrialization, family patterns change. Extended kinship ties weaken, lineage patterns dissolve, and a trend toward some form of the conjugal system generally begins to appear" (1963: 6). He cites a number of reasons for this family change: the increased rate of migration accompanying industrialization reduces kin contact; class differential mobility within families creates barriers among kinsmen; nonkin agencies take over political, economic, and social welfare functions from the kin group; there is movement toward a value system that emphasizes individual achievement; and there is a decreasing likelihood of finding employment through the efforts of kinsmen (1963: 369–370). Industrialization creates new job opportunities that free young adults from dependence on their elder kinsmen, thus enabling them to make their own decisions regarding marriage and setting up a household (Smelser and Halpern 1978: 294).

This position has been supported by a number of prominent social scientists, such as Litwak (1965) and Firth (1964). It is not in any sense new; it has been with us for over a century in scholarly form (LePlay 1871) and is even older in more popular form. In the early part of this century, Livi, a prominent Italian demographer voiced his belief in this thesis, writing of the Italian rural zones that were then experiencing early industrialization:

In the peasant families of these places two economic forces are at work, one determined by agricultural exigencies, the other by the requirements of big industry; the first acts to promote greater family cohesion, the second acts in the opposite direction. It is the latter which is normally victorious, for it is the one which offers the people greater income. (1915: 93)

Laslett's assault on this formulation grew out of his examination of British parish census data for the past few centuries. Not only did Laslett conclude that the nuclear family household had been the prevalent form in preindustrial England, but he also suggested the possibility of proving "the exact reverse of the conventional proposition about industrialization and the structure of the household." Where communities were compared before and after industrialization took place, "it can be shown that households became more, not less, extended" with industrialization (1973: 23). Further empirical support for this revisionist position was provided for England by Anderson (1972b: 223) and Armstrong (1972: 213–214), and for very different historical and cultural contexts as well, such as contemporary India (Owens 1971; Conklin 1974; Freed and Freed 1982) and Latin America (Carlos and Sellers 1972).

Wrigley, along these lines, argues that the impact of industrialization on the family may have been "anti-'modern.'" Whereas in the past the individual peasant could rely on a certain amount of capital and community organization for aid in times of economic adversity or infirmity, with early industrialization the worker was at the mercy of wages and, hence, in a more precarious position. According to Wrigley, "In circumstances such as these, a web of informal relations with kin and neighbors may be the only resort against disaster, and they may tend to produce changes in family structure and behavior which appear regressive when compared with later changes." Only when the state later began to take over the social welfare functions from the family did family structure begin to "move once more in a 'modern' direction" (1977: 82). Early industrialization did not always liberate young people from their kinsmen; often it had the opposite effect, at least in England. In peasant society young people were commonly sent out of the parental household at an early age to go into service or to become an apprentice. Indeed, a recent study of early modern England reveals that the great majority of youths left their parental household at the time of puberty or shortly thereafter and became resident servants. They were primarily involved in husbandry and moved frequently from farm to farm over a period of ten to fifteen years before marrying and establishing a household of their own (Kussmaul 1981). Industrialization and urbanization lessened the need to leave home, for young people could find jobs in some of the same factories as their parents, and the concentration of job opportunities in the city meant the entire family could find jobs while remaining in the same home (Anderson 1978: 11).[1]

Our view of the impact of industrialization on European family life has also been influenced in recent years by the substantial scholarly energy being devoted to the study of protoindustrialization. It is now clear that industrial production was not something new to Europe in the late eighteenth and nineteenth centuries, nor was it confined to factories. An earlier form of industrial production for the international market, based on household units of production and the putting-out system, had marked portions of rural Europe for many decades. As many of the first factory workers were apparently drawn from these ranks, we begin to see the impact of industrialization on family life in a different way. Since extended family coresidence characterized some of these protoindustrial populations, we must be even more wary of broad generalizations about *the* effect of industrialization on *the* rural European family (Mendels 1972; Medick 1976). Furthermore, as we have already pointed out, we cannot simply divide the masses into a rural peasantry and an urban proletariat. Much of the rural population of Western Europe had already become proletarianized before the impact of industry was ever felt (C. Tilly 1979: 29).[2]

In this debate, there has been a general equation of industrialization with urbanization, though it should be obvious that industrialization can take place without urbanization and vice versa. Although some studies have distinguished between industrial and commercial cities (e.g., Katz 1975), the implications of this distinction for a theory of coresidence have not been fully explored. The guiding question must ask what it is about urbanization or industrialization that affects the makeup of the coresidential family unit.[3] If the key factors are migration, abandonment of agriculture, and bureaucratization, then urbanization and industrialization should have similar effects. On the other hand, if it is thought that the household of a factory worker is subject to different pressures than the household of a bricklayer, we would be remiss in lumping together the effects of urbanization and industrialization.

In the period under study, from 1880 to 1910, Bologna was a commercial center rather than an industrial city, and in Bertalia more people worked in the railroad system and other facets of the urban trade center than worked regularly in large factories. However, by the end of the period the parish did have a sizeable number of factory workers, and this chapter will explore whether their coresidential experience was any different from that of their urbanized but nonindustrial neighbors.

Industrialization and Urban Expansion

Modern factories were slow to develop in Bologna, though some medium-sized factories connected with agricultural products had long been operating. The pace of industrialization began to quicken around the turn of the twentieth century: the proportion of the provincial work force engaged in agriculture gradually fell and the proportion engaged in industry and transportation rose. This happened despite the fact that the formerly important textile industry suffered a sharp decline in this period, falling by 50 percent in its share of the work force between 1881 and 1901. Industries closely tied to agriculture, such as flour mills and pasta factories, began to increase their exports in the first years of the century, and the chemical industry began to expand as well. From 1901 to 1911, the number of workers in the food and chemical industries in the city of Bologna increased from 4,300 to 5,900. In the province as a whole, the proportion of the male work force engaged in agriculture fell from 49.1 percent to 44.6 percent in that same decade (Masulli 1980: 16–17, 193–201). Notable too was the rise of the metalworking industry, which employed 7,900 workers in the city of Bologna in 1911, representing a 100 percent increase in ten years (1980: 195–196).

Of special importance to the larger pattern of economic change taking place in this period were the changes being made in transportation and communications, facilitating regional, national, and international commerce. The number of employees in transportation and communication more than doubled between 1881 and 1901, with major expansion in railroad lines, in the urban tram, and in the roads throughout the province (1980: 140–141).

Bertalia was greatly affected by these forces, for along with the other outlying rural areas of the commune of Bologna it was the site of urban expansion and early industrial development. In addition to the large sugar refinery built there at the end of the nineteenth century, there were several brick-making plants, providing the building blocks for Bologna's expansion, along with a number of hemp-processing establishments. Of particular importance was the fact that Bertalia was the site of a large railroad depot that serviced the city, and railroad-owned housing provided quarters for many families.

Bertalia had long been an agricultural outpost of the city of Bologna, but in these years it began to be increasingly incorporated into the urban structure. Its population between 1880 and 1910 increased at almost twice the rate of the population of the city as a whole, rising from 1,780 to 3,080, and its occupational structure was greatly altered as well. In 1880, over half those in the labor force had tilled the soil,[4] primarily as *braccianti*, who constituted almost a third of the work force, and sharecroppers, who were 15 percent. Thirty years later, agricultural workers constituted under a third of the work force. In the same period, those in urban occupations (factory, railroad, and construction) increased from just 15 percent of the work force to 41 percent. And where there had only been fourteen merchants in Bertalia in 1880, by 1910 there were sixty-eight.

Thus, over this thirty-year period the number of people in agriculture in Bertalia remained almost stationary while the total population increased sharply. With the opening of the sugar refinery along the border of the parish, and the expansion of other factories outside Bertalia, the number of factory workers in the parish population rose from 7 to 251. Evidence for this transformation is also provided by the sharp rise in construction and other unskilled nonagricultural laborers (from 49 to 143), as well as the increase in the number of railroad workers (from 44 to 92).

Economic Change and Coresidence in Bertalia

Sharecropping Italy represents a good opportunity for verifying the process of nuclearization that scholars had traditionally associated with the economic convulsions of the nineteenth century in Europe. After all, the fact that urbanization and industrialization did not bring about household nuclearization in Britain says little about the effect of these forces on complex household family systems, for Britain had long had a nuclear family household organization. But just what did happen in those areas of Europe where the complex family household was common? In Bertalia

Table 4.1. *Composition of Households in Bertalia, 1880–1910*

Household composition	1880 N	1880 Percentage	1890 N	1890 Percentage	1900 N	1900 Percentage	1910 N	1910 Percentage
Solitary	7	2.0	9	2.1	11	2.2	18	3.0
No family								
Kin	1	0.3	4	0.9	6	1.2	5	0.8
No Kin	1	0.3	2	0.5	5	1.0	4	0.7
Total		(0.6)		(1.4)		(2.2)		(1.5)
Simple family								
Married couple	29	8.4	45	10.5	41	8.2	45	7.5
Conjugal family	165	47.6	182	42.3	243	48.4	284	47.2
Widow(er) and child(ren)	28	8.1	32	7.4	42	8.4	51	8.5
Total		(64.1)		(60.2)		(65.0)		(63.2)
Extended family								
Patrilateral	40	11.5	64	14.9	63	12.5	71	11.8
Matrilateral	16	4.6	11	2.6	14	2.8	18	3.0
Other	1	0.3	0	—	0	—	1	0.2
Total		(16.4)		(17.5)		(15.3)		(15.0)
Multiple family								
Patrilateral	51	14.7	77	17.9	66	13.1	88	14.6
Matrilateral	5	1.4	2	0.5	8	1.6	10	1.7
Other	0	—	0	—	2	0.4	2	0.3
Total		(16.1)		(18.4)		(15.1)		(16.6)
Unrelated families	3	0.9	2	0.5	1	0.2	4	0.7
Total	347	100.1	430	100.1	502	100.0	601	100.0

NOTE: Discrepancies due to rounding cause some totals to be more than 100%.

in 1880, just before urban expansion and the agricultural crisis were to bring about major changes in the parish's occupational structure, over 42 percent of the people were living in complex family households. What happened to them, their children, and the migrants who came into Bertalia in the ensuing three decades?

Following the traditional argument, we should certainly expect to find that the considerable economic change experienced in Bertalia brought with it an equally dramatic change in coresidential arrangements, with nuclear family households becoming much more frequent and complex families dying out. Yet a comparison of the household composition data from 1880 with those from 1910 shows virtually no aggregate change in

Table 4.2. *Coresidence of All Bertalia Residents, 1880–1910*

Household composition	1880 N	1880 Percentage	1910 N	1910 Percentage
Simple family				
Solitary	7	0.4	19	0.6
No family	7	0.4	29	0.9
Married couple	60	3.4	92	3.0
Conjugal family	822	46.2	1,434	46.5
Widow(er) and child(ren)	107	6.0	187	6.1
Total		(55.6)		(55.6)
Extended family				
Patrilateral	224	12.6	424	13.7
Matrilateral	82	4.6	115	3.7
Other	5	0.3	5	0.2
Total		(17.5)		(17.6)
Multiple family				
Patrilateral	413	23.2	665	21.6
Matrilateral	34	1.9	70	2.3
Other	0	—	23	0.7
Total		(25.1)		(24.6)
Unrelated families	19	1.1	22	0.7
Total	1,780	100.1	3,085	100.0

NOTE: Discrepancies due to rounding cause some totals to be more than 100%.

the coresidential pattern of the people of Bertalia (table 4.1) and certainly gives no support to the nuclearization thesis. Although the number of households had increased from 347 to 601, the proportion that were simple family households remained unchanged (64 percent in 1880 compared to 63 percent in 1910); the proportion of multiple family households, in which two or more nuclear families were coresiding, likewise was unchanged (16.1 percent in 1880 versus 16.6 percent in 1910).

The almost uncanny similarity in coresidential situation of the people of Bertalia over the thirty years of economic change is also evident if we look at data on all individuals rather than just household units (table 4.2). Even in 1910, only a slender majority of people were living in

Table 4.3. *Coresidence of All Bertalia Residents by Age and Sex, 1910*

	<5	5–9	10–14	15–19	20–24	25–29	30–34	35–39
Solitary and no family (%)								
M	0	0	0	0	0	3	0	1
F	0	0	0	1	1	2	2	4
Simple family (%)								
M	54	66	61	63	61	54	56	50
F	50	59	61	60	55	45	57	56
Extended family (%)								
M	18	12	19	18	15	8	19	23
F	21	28	21	18	14	12	16	25
Multiple family (%)								
M	26	22	20	20	24	34	26	27
F	29	14	18	22	30	39	24	16
Unrelated families (%)								
M	1	0	0	0	0	1	0	0
F	0	0	0	0	0	1	0	0
Total N								
M	178	160	140	164	137	141	102	101
F	174	167	153	144	138	127	129	84

simple family households; 42 percent lived in some kind of complex family household. A quarter of Bertalia residents in 1910 lived in households containing two or more nuclear family units, which continued to show a strong patrilateral bias. The occupational structure of Bertalia may have been greatly altered in this period, but this appears to have had no impact on people's living arrangements.

The relationship between people's age and the kind of household they live in similarly shows little change when we compare 1880 with 1910 (comparing table 4.3 with table 3.4). The same life course curve discussed in chapter 3 with respect to 1880 characterizes the people of Bertalia in 1910.[5] In both cases, the highest frequency of complex family coresidence is found for individuals in their first years of life, in their young adulthood, and when they grow old. As this closely relates to the

40–44	45–49	50–54	55–59	60–64	65–69	70+	Total
0	2	2	2	8	6	8	2
0	1	4	0	4	3	2	1
57	56	67	64	62	38	26	57
62	69	62	51	46	35	7	54
17	21	13	12	11	9	18	16
19	11	11	8	15	32	47	20
24	20	18	23	19	47	47	25
19	18	22	41	33	29	44	25
1	0	0	0	0	0	0	1
0	0	0	0	2	0	0	0
89	84	87	61	37	34	38	1,562
79	71	71	49	48	34	55	1,523

demographic opportunity people have of living in a three-generation household, it supports the view that a norm of complex family living was operative in 1910 just as it was in 1880.

One of the key aspects of coresidential norms regards the experience of the elderly. What kind of position do the elderly find themselves in, and how does this change with urbanization? If we look at the experience of the Bertalia residents over sixty-five years old in 1880 and 1910, we find that their coresidential situation, as we would expect, is related to their marital status (table 4.4). Approximately equal numbers of old folks with living spouses live in simple and multiple family households in both years. A majority of those who have married sons live with one of those sons. But what about widows and widowers? In the great majority of cases, they live with a married child, not uncommonly with one or

Table 4.4. *Household Composition of the Elderly, by Sex and Marital Status, Bertalia, 1880 and 1910*[a]

	Marital status							
	Single		Married		Widower		Total	
Household structure	1880 (%)	1910 (%)	1880 (%)	1910 (%)	1880 (%)	1910 (%)	1880 (%)	1910 (%)
	Men (age 65 and over)							
Solitary	—	[b]	—	—	—	4	—	3
	(0)	(1)	(0)	(0)	(0)	(1)	(0)	(2)
No family	—	[b]	—	—	—	—	—	4
	(0)	(3)	(0)	(0)	(0)	(0)	(0)	(3)
Simple family	—	—	42	46	4	18	26	32
	(0)	(0)	(14)	(18)	(1)	(5)	(15)	(23)
Extended family	[b]	[b]	12	3	64	30	33	14
	(1)	(1)	(4)	(1)	(14)	(8)	(19)	(10)
Multiple family	[b]	[b]	46	51	32	44	40	46
	(1)	(1)	(15)	(20)	(7)	(12)	(23)	(33)
Other	—	—	—	—	—	4	—	1
	(0)	(0)	(0)	(0)	(0)	(1)	(0)	(1)
Total N	(2)	(6)	(33)	(39)	(22)	(27)	(57)	(72)
	Women (age 65 and over)							
Solitary	—	—	—	—	—	3	—	2
	(0)	(0)	(0)	(0)	(0)	(2)	(0)	(2)
No family	—	—	—	—	—	—	—	—
	(0)	(0)	(0)	(0)	(0)	(0)	(0)	(0)
Simple family	[b]	—	47	44	17	8	29	18
	(1)	(0)	(7)	(11)	(4)	(5)	(12)	(16)
Extended family	[b]	[b]	7	4	52	57	37	43
	(2)	(1)	(1)	(1)	(12)	(36)	(15)	(38)
Multiple family	—	—	47	52	30	32	34	37
	(0)	(0)	(7)	(13)	(7)	(20)	(14)	(33)
Other	—	—	—	—	—	—	—	—
	(0)	(0)	(0)	(0)	(0)	(0)	(0)	(0)
Total N	(3)	(1)	(15)	(25)	(23)	(63)	(41)	(89)

SOURCE: Kertzer, *Urban Anthropology*, 6 (1978): 1–23.

[a] Figures in parentheses are base *N*s for adjacent percentages.

[b] Small *N* renders percentage meaningless.

more of their unmarried children as well. Virtually no widows or widowers live in households without at least one of their children, a striking statistic when it is considered that some people must have had no living children, thus accounting for the rare cases of widows and widowers living alone. The extended or multiple family household was as likely to care for the elderly in 1910 as it was in 1880.

But so far we have been dealing with an economically undifferentiated population. Since our primary concern is the impact of occupational change on coresidence, we need to compare the portion of the population in the more traditional rural sector of the Bertalia economy with that engaged in the expanding urban and industrial sector. Does the fact that there was no aggregate change in household composition over these years mean that the coresidential experience of the urban/industrial population was the same as that of the agricultural population?

When we examine the population in terms of occupation, important differences in coresidential behavior are found. If we first divide all households for 1880 and 1910 by the occupation of the head, we see the continuation of the distinction in coresidential norms within the agricultural category between *braccianti* and sharecroppers (table 4.5). In both years the sharecroppers ran multiple family households at a much greater frequency than any other occupational group. In 1910, as in 1880, the *braccianti* had complex family households somewhat less frequently than did the parish population as a whole. The pattern of household composition of the urban/industrial heads in 1910 is rather similar to that of the *braccianti*. The primary exception to this similarity is the low frequency (6 percent) of multiple family households among the railroad workers. This may be a special case, though, for, alone among the nonfarm workers of Bertalia, the railwaymen were provided with housing by their employer. It may be hypothesized that rules prohibiting or discouraging multiple family occupation of these apartments were in effect, though no historical documentation on this point has yet been unearthed.

This pattern is further evident from data on the coresidential situation of all Bertalia residents (table 4.6). The sharecroppers and other nonwage farm workers generally lived in complex households in 1910, whereas the wage workers, including both those in agriculture and in the urban/industrial sector, lived more commonly in simple family households. However, a substantial proportion of these wage laborers were living in complex family households (roughly 30 percent of the

Table 4.5. *Household Composition by Occupation of Household Head, Bertalia, 1880 and 1910*[a]

Household structure	Bracciante 1880 (%)	Bracciante 1910 (%)	Sharecropper 1880 (%)	Sharecropper 1910 (%)	Other agricultural 1880 (%)	Other agricultural 1910 (%)	Railroad 1880 (%)	Railroad 1910 (%)
Solitary	3 (4)	1 (2)	— (0)	— (0)	— (0)	— (0)	— (0)	1 (1)
No family	1 (1)	1 (2)	— (0)	— (0)	— (0)	3 (1)	— (0)	— (0)
Simple family	68 (94)	64 (93)	42 (17)	21 (7)	66 (19)	50 (18)	69 (18)	75 (54)
Extended family	14 (20)	14 (21)	18 (7)	18 (6)	17 (5)	22 (8)	19 (5)	18 (13)
Multiple family	12 (17)	18 (26)	40 (16)	61 (20)	17 (5)	25 (9)	12 (3)	6 (4)
Other	1 (2)	1 (1)	— (0)	— (0)	— (0)	— (0)	— (0)	— (0)
Total *N*	(138)	(145)	(40)	(33)	(29)	(36)	(26)	(72)

SOURCE: Kertzer, *Urban Anthropology*, 6 (1978): 1–23.

[a] Figures in parentheses give the *N* found in each cell.

[b] Small *N* renders percentage meaningless.

urban/industrial workers and 43 percent of the agricultural wage laborers in 1910).

The Bertalia case provides little evidence of any difference in household characteristics between the industrial workers and the nonindustrial urban workers in this early period of urban/industrial development. We can compare the factory workers with the nonagricultural unskilled and construction workers (e.g., bricklayer, day laborer, porter). Of the factory worker household heads, 26 percent had complex families, compared to 29 percent of the unskilled and construction workers. In all, 29 percent of the factory workers and 33 percent of the unskilled and construction workers lived in complex family households.

According to the traditional wisdom, urbanization entails a decline in household size. The revisionist view, expressed by Laslett and others, hypothesizes that just the opposite is often the case, at least in the initial

	Factory		Construction		Artisan		Merchant		All households	
	1880 (%)	1910 (%)	1880 (%)	1910 (%)	1880 (%)	1910 (%)	1880 (%)	1910 (%)	1880 (%)	1910 (%)
	—	—	—	2	—	3	—	—	2	3
	(0)	(0)	(0)	(1)	(0)	(1)	(0)	(0)	(7)	(18)
	—	—	—	—	—	3	—	—	1	1
	(0)	(0)	(0)	(0)	(0)	(1)	(0)	(0)	(2)	(9)
	—	72	87	69	74	62	b	67	64	63
	(0)	(47)	(13)	(44)	(23)	(24)	(5)	(28)	(222)	(380)
	b	12	13	12	13	18	b	19	16	15
	(1)	(8)	(2)	(8)	(4)	(7)	(3)	(8)	(57)	(90)
	b	14	—	17	13	15	—	14	16	17
	(2)	(9)	(0)	(11)	(4)	(6)	(0)	(6)	(56)	(100)
	—	2	—	—	—	—	—	—	1	1
	(0)	(1)	(0)	(0)	(0)	(0)	—	(0)	(3)	(4)
	(3)	(65)	(15)	(64)	(31)	(39)	(0)	(42)	(347)	(601)

stage of urbanization. The changing size of households is obviously linked to household composition, but a number of other social factors are involved here, all presumably sensitive to the changes brought about by urbanization and industrialization. These include fertility, age at marriage, child mortality rate, and frequency of servants and boarders (cf. Berkner 1977).[6]

If we compare the Bertalia of 1880 with the Bertalia of thirty years later, we find a striking similarity in distribution by household size (table 4.7). Roughly a quarter of the households are small (one to three persons), one-half are of medium size (four to six), and another quarter large (seven or more). Yet though change in household size did not take place at the parish level, important differences are found among the various occupational groups in household size. As we would expect, sharecroppers had the biggest households, with a majority in both 1880 and

Table 4.6. *Coresidential Situation of All Bertalia Residents by Occupation, 1880 and 1910*[a]

Household structure	Bracciante 1880 (%)	Bracciante 1910 (%)	Sharecropper 1880 (%)	Sharecropper 1910 (%)	Other agricultural 1880 (%)	Other agricultural 1910 (%)	Railroad 1880 (%)	Railroad 1910 (%)
Solitary	2	1	—	—	—	—	—	1
	(4)	(2)	(0)	(0)	(0)	(0)	(0)	(1)
No family	1	2	—	—	—	2	—	1
	(2)	(3)	(0)	(0)	(0)	(1)	(0)	(1)
Simple family	57	53	38	24	64	38	57	67
	(117)	(109)	(39)	(25)	(25)	(24)	(25)	(62)
Extended family	17	17	11	14	15	19	16	15
	(34)	(35)	(11)	(15)	(6)	(12)	(7)	(14)
Multiple family	21	26	51	62	20	41	25	14
	(42)	(53)	(52)	(64)	(8)	(26)	(11)	(13)
Other	2	1	—	—	—	—	2	1
	(5)	(2)	(0)	(0)	(0)	(0)	(1)	(1)
Total *N*	(204)	(204)	(102)	(104)	(39)	(63)	(44)	(92)

SOURCE: Kertzer, *Urban Anthropology*, 6 (1978): 1–23.

[a] Figures in parentheses are base *N*s for adjacent percentages.

[b] Small *N* renders percentage meaningless.

1910 having large households. Small households were rare among sharecroppers in 1880 and absent in 1910. In contrast, roughly one-third of the *bracciante*-headed households were small in these years. Among the urban and industrial workers, the medium-sized households were most common. Very large households (ten or more in size) were almost entirely limited to the sharecroppers and other nonwage agricultural workers.

The Impact of Urbanization

Why does Bertalia show virtually no change in household composition during a period in which there was so much economic change? From 1880 to 1910 there can be no question that Bertalia moved substantially

	Factory		Construction		Artisan		Merchant		Total population	
	1880 (%)	1910 (%)	1880 (%)	1910 (%)	1880 (%)	1910 (%)	1880 (%)	1910 (%)	1880 (%)	1910 (%)
	—	—	—	1	—	1	—	—	0	1
	(0)	(0)	(0)	(1)	(0)	(1)	(0)	(0)	(7)	(19)
	—	—	—	—	—	1	—	6	0	1
	(0)	(0)	(0)	(0)	(0)	(1)	(0)	(4)	(7)	(29)
	b	70	74	65	56	58	43	57	56	56
	(2)	(176)	(36)	(93)	(45)	(52)	(6)	(39)	(989)	(1,713)
	b	14	18	11	16	14	36	18	17	18
	(2)	(35)	(9)	(16)	(13)	(13)	(5)	(12)	(311)	(544)
	b	15	8	22	25	26	21	19	25	25
	(3)	(37)	(4)	(32)	(20)	(23)	(3)	(13)	(447)	(758)
	—	1	—	1	2	—	—	—	1	1
	(0)	(3)	(0)	(1)	(2)	(0)	(0)	(0)	(19)	(22)
	(7)	(251)	(49)	(143)	(80)	(90)	(14)	(68)	(1,780)	(3,085)

in the direction of the urban and industrial from its formerly rural and agricultural position. What is the theoretical lesson in this?

Perhaps one of the most important lessons to be learned is the fallacy of a simple rural/urban or agricultural/industrial dichotomy. Coresidence is less a function of such lines of division than a function of access to the means of production. Why should rural or agricultural families be characterized by more complex households than urban or industrial families? The answer, in good part, is that in the rural/agricultural economy the household is more typically the basic unit of production. As the unit of production, it is governed partially by economic considerations of maximization of production (or, more precisely, maximization of production relative to demand for consumption). Such a pattern is often found where the farmers own their land, particularly where land is a scarce good or requires intensive investment of labor or capital. It is also found

Table 4.7. *Household Size by Occupation of Household Head, Bertalia, 1880 and 1910*[a]

Household size	Bracciante 1880 (%)	Bracciante 1910 (%)	Sharecropper 1880 (%)	Sharecropper 1910 (%)	Other agricultural 1880 (%)	Other agricultural 1910 (%)	Railroad 1880 (%)	Railroad 1910 (%)
1–3	33 (46)	29 (42)	10 (4)	— (0)	21 (6)	8 (3)	23 (6)	32 (23)
4–6	53 (73)	44 (64)	32 (13)	39 (13)	43 (12)	47 (17)	62 (16)	50 (36)
7–9	13 (18)	23 (33)	35 (14)	24 (8)	21 (6)	28 (10)	15 (4)	14 (10)
10+	1 (1)	4 (6)	22 (9)	36 (12)	14 (4)	17 (6)	— (0)	4 (3)
Total N	(138)	(145)	(40)	(33)	(28	8	23	32

SOURCE: Kertzer, *Urban Anthropology*, 6 (1978): 1–23.

[a] Figures in parentheses give the N found in each cell.

[b] Small N renders percentage meaningless.

where sharecropping predominates, as the Italian case shows. Here it is in the interest of the landowner to maximize the adult labor power on his land, thus favoring access to the land by large and complex households. Other kinds of land tenure arrangements, however, are less conducive to the formation of complex households in rural areas. Where the relationship to means of production is a simple wage labor affair, the household is not the unit of production, and there is much less impetus for the formation of complex households.

In the case of Bertalia at the turn of the century, the shift in relationship to the means of production is not nearly so dramatic as the shift from rural to urban or from agricultural to industrial. As discussed above, through the nineteenth century the once predominant sharecropping system declined in Emilia, while the agricultural wage labor force grew substantially. By 1880, there were twice as many *braccianti* as sharecroppers in Bertalia. Insofar as the agricultural sector of the population was composed of *braccianti*, we would not expect a shift to urban/industrial wage labor to diminish the frequency of complex households.

If we divide the agricultural workers into those who share directly in

	Factory		Construction		Artisan		Merchant		Total population	
	1880 (%)	1910 (%)	1880 (%)	1910 (%)	1880 (%)	1910 (%)	1880 (%)	1910 (%)	1880 (%)	1910 (%)
	b	22	13	25	18	33	b	19	27	27
	(1)	(14)	(2)	(16)	(5)	(13)	(3)	(8)	(95)	(163)
	—	55	67	58	63	54	b	55	50	49
	(0)	(36)	(10)	(37)	(17)	(21)	(5)	(23)	(174)	(293)
	b	20	20	17	11	13	—	21	16	18
	(1)	(13)	(3)	(11)	(3)	(5)	(0)	(9)	(57)	(110)
	b	3	—	—	7	—	—	5	6	6
	(1)	(2)	(0)	(0)	(2)	(0)	(0)	(2)	(21)	(35)
	(3)	(65)	(15)	(64)	(27)	(39)	(8)	(42)	(347)	(601)

what they produce and for whom the household is the unit of production, and those who work for a wage, this distinction becomes quite clear. In addition to the *braccianti*, other agricultural occupations performed on an individual, wage basis include salaried farm worker and gardener. Along with the sharecropper, the farm renter's household is a basic unit of production. In table 4.8 we contrast household composition among these three categories in 1910.

As we see here, there is a great contrast between households headed by wage laborers (urban or rural) and those in which the household itself is the unit of production. The agricultural wage laborers do live more commonly in complex households than do the urban wage laborers (34 percent to 26 percent), but the difference is minor compared to the difference between them and the sharecroppers/farm renters (72 percent of whose households are complex).

This distinction is significant in determining what our expectations should be for changes in household composition for the parish in this period of urbanization. If we follow the traditional dichotomy, pitting agricultural workers against urban/industrial workers, we see a drastic shift

Table 4.8. *Household Composition by Occupation of Household Head, Bertalia, 1910*

Household structure	Urban proletarian		Farm wage/ farm salaried		Sharecropper/ farm renter	
	N	Percentage	N	Percentage	N	Percentage
Solitary	2	1	2	1	0	—
No family	0	—	2	1	1	2
Simple family	145	72	106	63	11	26
Extended family	29	14	27	16	7	16
Multiple family	24	12	31	18	24	56
Other	1	1	1	1	0	—
Total N	201	100	169	100	43	100

SOURCE: Kertzer, *Urban Anthropology*, 6 (1978): 1–23.

in the population taking place, from one in which there are almost five times as many agricultural as urban/industrial household heads (60 percent to 13 percent) to one in which there is a rough parity (36 percent to 33 percent). If we divide these same households into those that are headed by wage workers and those that are themselves units of production, we find a much less dramatic shift taking place in the thirty-year period. Agricultural households in which the household itself is the unit of production were never a large proportion of the total and, though the percentage diminishes over the period, the numbers are small (13 percent in 1880 and 7 percent in 1910). We would not expect such a small shift to have much impact on the household characteristics of the parish as a whole.

With the bulk of its agricultural labor force already working on a wage labor basis by 1880, Bertalia was preadapted to an urban proletarian economy. From this perspective, what is surprising about the experience of the parish is not that there was so little change in coresidential characteristics over this period but that the proportion of complex family households was so high in a largely proletarian population. Given the thesis that wage labor fosters the nuclear family household, the approximately one-third of all households having complex family composition is anomalous. More than 40 percent of the 1910 population lived in such complex households and, when life cycle and demographic constraints on the formation of complex family households are considered, the Bertalia case flies in the face of the traditional urban/simple family household thesis.

One key to the interpretation of the Bertalia case lies in the characteristics of the complex family households. They are overwhelmingly extended patrilaterally. This is most pronounced in the case of multiple family households, where the characteristic arrangement is the coresidence of father, mother, married son, son's wife, and son's children. Married daughters are rarely found in their parents' homes. In the case of extended families, the patrilateral pattern is somewhat less pronounced but still strong. A widow or widower is much more likely to live with a married son than a married daughter. This pattern follows from the sharecropper heritage, where sons' wives were brought into the household; the man and his sons formed the core of the productive unit throughout the life of the elder generation. The strong patrilateral bias among the wage laborers (both agricultural and industrial) cannot be explained on the grounds of economic forces alone. What we see is a cultural element (postmarital residence) that evolved in response to one set of economic conditions, continuing for many years under altered circumstances. This is certainly not to argue that the customs were dysfunctional, for ways were certainly found to adapt the patrilateral postresidence system to the problems people faced in the new economic and social conditions.

The high frequency of complex family households in the urbanizing community is also linked to the universal practice of coresidence of the elderly with their children, regardless of their children's marital status. This raises the familiar issue of security for the aged in societies lacking public old age assistance programs. In Bertalia there must have been strong normative pressure on the younger generation to provide for their aging parents, and this care entailed coresidence. This is not to say that such coresidence provided no material rewards to the younger generation; it is likely that the elderly provided important household services (see Anderson 1972b: 229–230). But it is not obvious that the rural/urban distinction is terribly significant here; the need for social security and the limited availability of church funds for the elderly would differ little along rural/urban lines. It is reasonable to hypothesize that in later stages of economic and political development, with the institution of an efficient state welfare system, the proportion of complex family households would decline (cf. Anderson 1972b: 228). This decline would affect rural and urban areas alike.

The fact that the proportion of complex family households did not decline with early urbanization is also related to an aspect of the urbanization process itself, namely, rapid population influx without a concomitant increase in housing. In the case of Bertalia, though good data are lacking, it does not appear that the erection of new housing kept pace with the rate of population increase. If this is so, and to the extent that it is a phenomenon more generally encountered in urbanization, there is an added impetus to the coresidence of kinsmen. The effects of this would be most likely felt at certain points in the life course, particularly upon marriage, when newlyweds were forced to live with their parents as a result of unavailability of affordable housing. Likewise, elderly individuals whose wage earning capacity was reduced found it difficult to afford to live by themselves.

Urbanization encourages larger and more complex households in another way as well. In rural areas a youngster living in a poverty-stricken family was often forced to find employment outside the community in which his parents lived. In Europe, this often meant becoming a servant, a common stage in the life of poorer young people in many areas (Anderson 1971: 84–85; Laslett 1977b). For the young person living in the urban area, though, there was a greater variety of economic opportunities, and these did not entail leaving one's parents' residence.[7]

In examining the changes in household composition that occurred in this period, perhaps the most striking change involves the increase in multiple family households among the sharecroppers. We do not know if this increase in proportion of multiple family households reflects a more general historical process during this period of early industrialization and the decline of sharecropping. One explanation for this trend seems plausible, though it needs to be tested in a larger sample of sharecropping areas. With the increasing emphasis on cash crops and economies of scale, landowners were finding it more productive to hire seasonal labor than to be tied to a single family of farmers who resisted hiring outsiders whom they would have to pay (in whole or in part). From the point of view of the sharecroppers themselves, heavier capital investment in the farms together with dependence on the world market price of cash crops were increasingly leading to bankruptcy and failure. Given this economic picture, it may be that productive units (i.e., households) having few laborers (adults) were no longer considered viable by the landowners and, where established, had a high rate of failure. As the number of farms available for sharecropping decreased, the simple family households were the most vulnerable to eviction.

Comparative Perspectives

Before drawing any theoretical conclusions from the case of urbanization in Bertalia it is useful to consider briefly what happened in the city of Preston and the surrounding area of Lancashire, England, in the mid-nineteenth century. Preston provides us with an instructive comparison in that it represents a case of urban and industrial development in a northern European context, one in which the complex family household had not been a common part of the preexisting rural social system. Moreover, Michael Anderson's study of family structure in nineteenth-century Lancashire remains one of the best historical works to date on urbanization and the household.

Anderson found that, contrary to the nuclearization theory, in England "there apparently has been a massive *increase* over the past two centuries in co-residence of married couples and their parents" (1972b: 216). Over much of North America and Western Europe, "industrialization meant that more children stayed home for longer" and in many areas three-generation households became more common (1979a: 69).

The touchstone of these generalizations is the situation described by Anderson for the textile-producing communities of Lancashire in the nineteenth century. In the city of Preston in 1851, 10 percent of the households consisted of parents living with their married children, a markedly higher proportion than found in the sample of preindustrial communities collected by Laslett (Anderson 1972b: 222–223). Moreover, unmarried children were considerably more likely to remain living with their parents in the city than in the rural areas of Lancashire. Children of urban dwellers could find jobs in the city and almost all who did so remained coresident with their parents. Indeed, in many of the British textile centers parents were able to find jobs for their children in their own factories, thus reinforcing the tendency for the urban children to remain living with their parents (1976: 320). But in the rural areas, barely half of the young people remained in the parental home, being forced to migrate to other rural areas or to the city to find work (1971: 84, 125–126, 1972b: 233–234).

Old people were also more likely to be living with their children in the city than in the rural areas. In his rural sample of 1851, just 48 percent of people over sixty-five years old were living with their children (1972b: 225). In Preston in 1851, "no fewer than 32% of old people aged 65 and over lived with a married or widowed child, and a further 36% with unmarried children." Anderson concludes that "there were few old people who could not find one among their children prepared to give them house room in old age, if they actually had any children alive" (1971: 139, 1972a).[8]

In a study of the Canadian commercial city of Hamilton, Ontario, during this period, Katz found a different pattern of coresidence. Few of the elderly lived with their married children; 87 percent of those 60 years and older lived in simple family households or as solitaries in 1851 (1975: 250). However, at the other end of the life course a similar pattern to that found in Preston was uncovered, with early industrialization making it more likely for youths to remain in the parental home. In the period 1851–1871, when industrial growth was taking place in Hamilton, the proportion of fifteen- to nineteen-year-olds living in the parental home rose from 49 to 76 percent (1975: 260). Indeed, Katz and Davey (1978: S116) make the claim that "during early industrialization ties between parents and their teenage children actually grew stronger." However, though unmarried children lived longer with their parents, Katz (1978) argues on the basis of the Hamilton evidence that coresidence of kinsmen beyond the simple family declined with industrialization.[9]

Urbanization, Industrialization, and Coresidence

The Bertalia case suggests some of the complexities in making theoretical generalizations about the impact of urbanization or industrialization on coresidence. It should be clear by now that any simple statement that relates these processes to household nuclearization is unsatisfactory. We now know that in some cases urbanization and industrialization bring about the diminution of complex family households but that in other historical contexts there is either no apparent change in coresidential behavior or, in fact, there is an increase in household complexity. We now need to work toward replacing our traditional, comfortable nuclearization theory with a more complex model that relates the historical developments of the past two centuries with changes in coresidence (Mendels 1978: 782).

To understand the relationship, we clearly need to specify just what aspects of urbanization and industrialization are related to coresidence and how they are related. Urbanization is not a uniform process the world over, nor is industrialization. Moreover, even where identical macrosocial processes are operating, the impact on coresidence is partially a product of what the preexisting system of coresidence was.

Owens (1971), in his study of households in India, argues that the most economically "rational" coresidential strategy varies from person to person, even within the same general industrializing context. As he puts it: "industrialization is not a homogeneous process but rather one which creates a variety of opportunities which may be exploited by diverse strategies" (1971: 247). If this is admitted, the microeconomic context of the individual must be understood before any statements can be made about the impact of industrialization on the person's choice of coresidential arrangement. Although we can profitably operate at a more abstract level of generalization than that of the individual, no generalization about the relationship between industrialization or urbanization and household composition is satisfactory unless it specifies diverse and potentially conflicting variables. Our generalizations must also recognize that the impact of industrialization and urbanization on household composition depends upon the characteristics of the particular socioeconomic context in which they occur. Moreover, even within such a specific context, the effects of industrialization and urbanization on individuals differ according to the individuals' socioeconomic position.

We must also resist the temptation to see coresidence as simply a dependent variable, a complex function of independent economic forces. As a number of recent studies have argued, prevailing coresidential and kinship norms do have an impact on the course that industrialization takes as well as on the likelihood that new industrial enterprises will be successfully established (Hareven 1975: 256, 1977, 1978; Anderson 1979b: 51). Louise Tilly has written that though the household was no longer the unit of production in the industrial city, "it remained the mediating unit between the economy and individual workers" (1979c: 110). Coresidential and kinship norms are not simply abandoned with changing economic conditions; rather, they are reworked to serve people's interests better in their changed environment.

The rural population in Westen Europe that encountered the developing capitalist world of the nineteenth century was itself diversified, and the differences among and within regions must be part of any account of the impact of industrialization and urbanization on coresidential experience. As we have already noted, in many areas the people were already proletarianized, making for a far different situation than in those areas where sharecroppers or small farmowners were swept into the urban or industrial world.

Stone has recently argued that the evidence of industrialization and urbanization taking place in harmony with complex household coresidence and extended kin ties "casts some doubt on the causal model which posits economic development as the key variable in family change" (1981: 65). We can agree with Stone that simple models of economic determinism have been shown to be wrong in describing the nuclearization of coresidence. However, this does not mean that economic variables are of minor importance. Rather, economic changes and kinship and coresidential changes must be seen as two phenomena that are reciprocally related and interacting. The high frequency of complex family households in urbanizing Bertalia cannot simply be understood by reference to prevailing economic forces but must be placed within a historical context, a context that includes both an economic heritage and a cultural legacy.

5

Migration

In trying to explain the impact of industrialization on family life and coresidence, scholars often cite migration as a key factor (Goode 1963: 369). Many claim that high rates of migration, brought about by the development of capitalism, are incompatible with complex family coresidence. Increased migration, particularly of a rural-urban kind, brings about household nuclearization (LePlay 1871; Parsons and Bales 1955). These generalizations were first formulated with Europe in mind, but they have been applied more universally as well. Nimkoff and Middleton, using cross-cultural and historical data, compare the industrial family with that found in hunting and gathering societies:

> The modern industrial society, with its small independent family, is then like the simpler hunting and gathering society and, in part, apparently for some of the same reasons, namely, limited need for family labor and physical mobility. The hunter is mobile because he pursues game; the industrial worker his job. (1960: 225)

In recent years this simple link between economic development, migration, and household composition has come under serious attack on several points. The widely assumed geographical stability of European peasants has failed to bear up under historical scrutiny. Laslett (1963, 1968), Schofield (1970), Anderson (1971), and others have shown that many rural areas of Great Britain in the preindustrial period had high rates of population movement, though often involving only short distances. Similar results have been found for France (Poussou 1970) and elsewhere in Europe.

The assumption that European peasants lived in complex households has, as already discussed, come under even more sustained attack, principally by Peter Laslett (1972c) and associates. Recent evidence suggests that rural-urban migration, rather than being a destructive force leading to the decline of complex family households, is itself facilitated by extended family systems (e.g., Wilkening, Pinto, and Pastore, 1968). Kinship ties provide communication links and assurance that there will be lodging and other forms of assistance available at the migrant's destination.[1]

Migration in Europe

Migration is one of the least understood aspects of European social history, though it is certainly of great importance for understanding the nature of life among the masses (Blayo 1970; Bouchard 1977: 350; Rozat 1977: 21). Our knowledge of rural and urban social organization is hampered by our ignorance of how geographically stable people were and by our uncertainty regarding the social implications of high rates of mobility where these are known to have existed. The meaning of community to the people of Western Europe, the extent to which social life was based on long-term interpersonal ties of neighbor, friend, and patron, can only be interpreted with reference to the extent to which people were mobile. The importance of kinship must be seen in this light as well, for in a highly mobile population kin ties may provide the only ongoing social bonds many people have.

The image of the traditional European peasantry, bound to their place of birth, is surely wrong. Macfarlane, for example, provides evidence on the fourteenth through the seventeenth centuries to show just how mobile the English peasantry was (1978: 73–74, 152–153). Most mobile of all were the adolescents and the young adults who spent part of their lives as servants. Each year over half of these changed masters and often villages as well (Kussmaul 1981: 54). Similarly, in portions of Austria the annual turnover of servants was over 50 percent in the eighteenth and nineteenth centuries (Mitterauer and Sieder 1979: 261, 282–283). In

France, even before industrialization, the city drew large numbers of adolescent girls from the countryside to work as domestic servants (Moch 1981a, 1981b).

The meaning of all this migration remains in doubt. The nature of local social organization certainly depended on differences in mobility among the various parts of the population. But we do not know the answer to such questions as whether those who lived in a community all their lives enjoyed more political or economic power than those who were more transient. Did high levels of migration, by acting as a safety valve in areas of periodic unemployment, bolster the position of the regional elite by decreasing the likelihood of revolt and attenuating claims of the workers to the land? The study of migration in European social history has barely begun (Tilly and Tilly 1971: 194).

Method

Little European research on the impact of rural-urban migration on coresidence has been done outside Britain. To provide an Italian test for the theoretical propositions linking migration to changes in coresidence, we examine the case of Bertalia. Obviously, before we can make any generalizations about Italy as a whole, many other such studies must be undertaken. But the limited case of Bertalia does permit us to examine the migration-household relationship in a very different social environment than that found in northern Europe and consequently provides us with an enlightening comparison.

In testing the traditional theory that links rural-urban migration to household nuclearization, we ask whether migration either inhibits the formation of complex family households or whether it preselects as immigrants those people coming from simple family households. In either case, if this theory is correct, we would expect the proportion of immigrants living in complex family households in Bertalia to be significantly lower than the proportion of the nonmigratory population living in complex family households. If the evidence does not support the traditional nuclearization thesis, we will want to test the adequacy of the revisionist thesis. According to this view, immigrants to the city often live in complex family households because they join the households of already resident kinsmen.

As we examine these questions in light of the Bertalia data, it is important to realize that though central Italy in this period had high rates of migration, movements were of relatively short distances. These hypotheses then are being examined for a situation of short-distance migration, a distinction that could bear on the validity of the hypotheses themselves. It is certainly conceivable that long-distance migration has a different effect on household composition than short-distance migration. However, the relationship between distance of migration and patterns of household structure is far from obvious. In the case of some long-distance migration, individuals make the move first, only later to be joined by their kin. On the other hand, where migration means confronting a radically different cultural environment, immigrant kinsmen from one's homeland may be especially valued as coresidents for the social, psychological, and economic support they provide.

We have two ways in which to discover migration characteristics of the Bertalia population. The simplest is the information provided for each individual on place of birth. This gives us some idea of the range and direction of migration, though it does not provide information on the frequency with which people move or on the proximate causes for that movement. In addition, we cannot assume that just because an individual was born in Bertalia and currently lives there, he or she never lived outside of the parish.

The second indication we have of mobility, and the method most commonly used in historical migration studies, is the persistence of an individual from census to census (Katz 1975; Segalen 1976). In any given ten-year period, for example, we can ask who left the locality, who migrated into it, and who remained there, by comparing the census of the earlier year with the census of ten years later. Although this method provides considerable detail on patterns of migration, it does have a number of weaknesses. It tends to underestimate the amount of population flux, for all those individuals who come and go in the intercensal years are lost from view (Hollingsworth 1970: 88). Moreover, this method does not provide us with the destinations of the emigrants or the places from which the immigrants come. Not knowing exactly when in an intercensal period a family arrived or left, we are also not in a good position to link the move to its contemporary circumstances. For example, though we may know a man was living alone in 1880 and that he had left the parish by 1890, we cannot say that at the time he left the parish he was living alone. It is clearly preferable to follow individuals throughout their life

Migration

course, tracing all moves over time regardless of where these may be. However, even when this approach is possible, it requires a great deal of time and a large amount of research funding. The method of measuring persistence is second best, but it does permit us to draw some preliminary conclusions.

Each Bertalia resident found in the parish censuses of 1880, 1890, 1900, and 1910 was assigned a migration status through census linkage. For example, to assign a migration code to an individual in 1900, the 1880, 1890, and 1910 censuses were checked to see if the person was present in the parish at those times. An individual present in every census received one code, a person present in just 1890 and 1900 received another code, and so on. The coding was further refined by birthplace and mortality data. Thus, a youth age six in 1900 received one code if he or she were born in the parish and another code if he or she were born elsewhere and had moved into the parish. A person who appeared in one census but not the next was checked against the parish's death records for each year between the censuses. People who died in the parish were given different migration codes than those who had left the population through emigration. In conformity with the notion of migration implicit in the theories linking migration to household composition, migration is operationally defined in terms of moves into and out of the parish; it does not include movements within the boundaries of the parish.

The distinction we make between immigrants and persisters is a relative one. All those who had migrated into the parish within the past ten years of the date in question are considered to be immigrants, whereas all those who had been present in the parish during the census of ten years before are considered persisters.[2] In fact, since there was a substantial preindustrial rate of migration, most of the older persisters were not born in the parish; they were migratory at one time. It should also be noted that given our retrospective definition of migration (characterizing the individual by his or her experience over the past decade), we do not deal with individuals under ten years old, for they are not comparable with the other age groups.[3] Our analysis concentrates on the residents of the parish for the first and last years for which we have ten-year retrospective data (1890 and 1910).

Family Life in Central Italy

Migration in Bertalia

Preindustrial Bologna, far from representing the stationary, locally bound populations of popular history, in fact had great population flux. Sharecroppers were moving to upgrade their farm or to find a new farm after having been evicted from the old. *Braccianti* moved to find new public works projects or to work on land recently brought into agriculture in the wake of reclamation. Small artisans traveled through the countryside selling their wares. Even the nobility and large landowners traveled from their winter home in the city to their summer and harvest home in the provincial countryside amidst their fields.

Nor was the movement between countryside and city limited to the elite. Our image of an urban versus a rural population notwithstanding, much of the city's population was composed of people who grew up in the countryside and who were to return to the countryside. A corollary of this, of course, is that a considerable portion of the rural population had spent part of their lives in the city. A study of one area of the city of Bologna, for example, showed that 59 percent of the families living in the area in 1816 had moved out of that area by 1820. Although some of these people moved elsewhere in the city, many left the city for outlying areas, to be replaced by rural immigrants (Giusberti 1982). A similar phenomenon is reported for the medieval period as well (Dal Pane 1969: 7–8). As we have already noted, the city had long been dependent on this migration to keep from losing population. The important point is that this was never a one-way process; city dwellers had been streaming into the countryside for centuries.

As the city began to expand in the latter part of the nineteenth century, this process of rural-urban interchange continued. Bertalia, formerly a part of the rural hinterland, gradually began to be a place where people working in the old city could live and where people employed in the new urban jobs—from the railroad depot to the sugar refinery—could both live and work. In the thirty years in which this transition was fully underway, from 1880 to 1910, rates of both immigration and emigration were high. But the migration pattern found in these years cannot easily be distinguished from that found in the earlier period. If we look at the birthplace of the adult population of 1880, when Bertalia was still basically agricultural, we see how common movement among communities was. Of all people over twenty years old, just 14 percent had been born

Migration

Table 5.1. *Birthplace of Persisters and Immigrants over Age Ten, Bertalia, 1890 and 1910*

Birthplace	Persisters (%)		Migrants (%)		Total (%)	
	1890	1910	1890	1910	1890	1910
Bertalia	43.2	36.5	5.8	6.4	22.0	20.5
Commune of Bologna (excluding Bertalia)	19.8	17.7	23.5	19.4	21.9	18.6
Province of Bologna (excluding the commune of Bologna)	33.4	40.9	58.7	62.7	47.7	52.5
Region of Emilia-Romagna (excluding the province of Bologna)	0.4	1.2	3.2	3.1	2.0	2.3
Outside Emilia-Romagna	1.4	2.3	4.3	4.6	3.0	3.5
Unknown	1.9	1.3	4.5	3.8	3.4	2.6
Total percentage	100.0	99.9	100.0	100.0	100.0	100.0
Total *N*	739	1,121	968	1,270	1,707	2,391

NOTE: Discrepancies due to rounding cause some totals to be less than 100%.

in the parish and another 18 percent born in other parts of the city of Bologna and its suburbs; 59 percent were born in other communes of the provinces of Bologna.

The volume of migration was high, but its scope was local, confined largely to intraprovincial moves. The expansion of the city and the development of industry at the turn of the twentieth century did little to change this pattern. The national census of 1911 reveals that both in the city of Bologna and in the rest of the province a majority of the adult population lived in a different commune from the one they had been born in (Ministero di Agricoltura 1915: 63, 103).

Some idea of the extent and range of migration in Bertalia in this period can be gleaned from looking at the birthplaces of the population in 1890 and 1910 (table 5.1). Just a fifth of the over ten-year-old population had lived in the parish all their lives, with another fifth having come to Bertalia from other parts of the city of Bologna, including the other ru-

Family Life in Central Italy

Table 5.2. *Birthplace of Persisters in Bertalia, by Age, 1910*

Birthplace	10–19 (%)	20–29 (%)	30–39 (%)	40–49 (%)	50–59 (%)	60–69 (%)	70+ (%)	Total (%)
Bertalia	72.1	48.5	33.0	11.0	11.7	14.9	10.7	36.5
Commune of Bologna	10.9	14.5	19.9	19.0	22.7	27.6	21.4	17.7
Province of Bologna	14.7	33.0	43.8	63.2	56.5	50.6	62.5	40.9
Region of Emilia-Romagna	0.4	0.4	1.1	3.1	1.3	2.3	1.8	1.2
Outside Emilia-Romagna	1.2	2.2	1.1	2.5	3.9	4.6	3.6	2.3
Unknown	0.8	1.3	1.1	1.2	3.9	—	—	1.3
Total percentage	100.0	99.9	100.0	100.0	100.0	100.0	100.0	99.9
Total *N*	258	227	176	163	154	87	56	1,121

NOTE: Discrepancies due to rounding cause some totals to be less than 100%.

ral suburbs. The great majority of the rest came to Bertalia from other parts of the province of Bologna; not one in ten had been born outside the province.

When we divide the population into those who had been living in Bertalia for at least the past ten years and those who had immigrated into the parish within the past decade, we see that even among the persisters a majority had been born elsewhere. Although relatively stable in their residence, they too experienced migration at some point in their lives.

The older a person is, of course, the more chance he or she has had to move. The likelihood of having been born in the parish where one lives should be inversely related to an individual's age. From this perspective, aggregate data on birthplace give a misleadingly low estimate of population flux, for they do not fully take into account the likelihood that an individual will move at some point in his or her life course.

In this light it is revealing to examine age differences in birthplace for the persisters, those who had lived at least ten years in Bertalia (table 5.2). If we look at the proportion that had been born in the parish, we find, as expected, that this declines with age. Whereas almost three-quarters of the persisters age ten to nineteen had been born in Bertalia, just 12 percent of those age forty and over were born locally. Few were the middle-aged and older individuals who had spent their entire life in the parish.

Table 5.3. *Proportion of Bertalia Population Having Entered Parish within Previous Decade, by Age, 1890 and 1910*

Age	Percentage of immigrants		Number of immigrants	
	1890	1910	1890	1910
10–19	52.1	56.9	197	340
20–29	62.3	58.3	285	317
30–39	68.9	57.1	210	234
40–49	48.6	50.2	120	164
50–59	50.0	42.1	84	112
60–69	50.0	43.1	67	66
70+	47.5	39.8	32	37
Total	56.7	53.1	968	1,270

Bertalia's migrants, like those described in most of the migration literature (Jansen 1970: 14; Shaw 1975: 18), tend to be young. However, age is a much less pronounced factor in Bertalian migration than in the migration experience studied elsewhere. In Bertalia, rates of migration are high at all ages (table 5.3). Although those most prone to migrate are those in their teens and twenties, the difference between the migration rate of these young people and the middle-aged and elderly adults is modest. Over half of all residents of Bertalia (over ten years of age) in 1890 and 1910 had immigrated to the parish within the previous decade, and in no age category was the proportion of immigrants less than 48 percent in 1890 or less than 40 percent in 1910. Rate of immigration was higher during the 1880s, a time of severe agricultural crisis in the province, than it was in the first decade of the 1900s, despite the fact that the urbanization of Bertalia was proceeding more rapidly in the latter decade. However, since there was a larger total population in the latter period, the actual number of immigrants in most age categories had increased in the early 1900s compared to the 1880s.

Women in Bertalia were somewhat more migratory than men, though the difference is modest.[4] In 1890, the women immigrated at a 6 percent higher rate than did the men, and this differential was 8 percent in 1910. The sexual differential was greatest during the years of marriage, reflecting patrilocal norms of postmarital residence. This is accentuated in the twenty to twenty-nine-year-old age group by the later age of mar-

Table 5.4. *Migration Characteristics of Various Occupations in Bertalia, 1890 and 1910*

Occupation	Percentage who immigrated in decade		Number of all males in designated occupation	
	1890	1910	1890	1910
Agricultural wage laborer	60	56	298	190
Sharecropper	44	39	94	79
Other agricultural	69	53	32	53
Railroad	65	54	69	91
Factory	a	51	6	160
Construction	54	35	43	119
Artisan	29	34	48	50
Merchant	31	48	13	44
Elite	73	65	33	43
All other	50	57	76	82
Total	55	50	712	911

[a] Small *N* renders percentage meaningless.

riage of men. In this age group, women were 26 percent more migratory than men in 1890 and 17 percent more migratory in 1910.

As we would expect, occupation was also related to the likelihood of migration (table 5.4). Those occupations that involve control over local capital—the sharecroppers, merchants, and artisans—were less migratory than their neighbors. The agricultural wage laborers, on the other hand, were among the most migratory. Perhaps less to be expected, though, is the fact that in 1910, when urbanization was taking hold, those in the most characteristically urban occupations—the factory, construction, and railroad workers—were not drawn disproportionately from the migrants.[5]

In short, during early urbanization Bertalia experienced high rates of population flux, but these represent a continuation of a long heritage of population movement. Urban development and industrial expansion did not entail an immigrant population employed in the new sector alongside a more traditionally employed local population. Bertalia was but part of a larger field of migration, in which the people of the province had long been accustomed to move in search of a living.

Table 5.5. *Composition of Households Headed by Persisters and by Immigrants, Bertalia, 1890 and 1910*

	1890		1910	
Household Composition	Persisters (%)	Immigrants (%)	Persisters (%)	Immigrants (%)
Solitary	2.6	1.7	2.2	3.5
No family				
Kin	0.5	1.3	1.4	0.3
Not kin	—	0.8	1.1	0.3
Total	(0.5)	(2.1)	(2.5)	(0.6)
Simple family				
Married couple alone	10.0	10.6	5.8	9.1
Conjugal family	40.0	44.9	46.8	48.4
Widow(er) and child(ren)	8.9	6.4	2.2	7.9
Total	(58.9)	(61.9)	(61.9)	(65.4)
Extended family				
Patrilateral	14.2	14.8	12.9	10.7
Matrilateral	4.2	0.8	3.6	2.5
Other	—	—	—	0.3
Total	(18.4)	(15.7)	(16.5)	(13.5)
Multiple family				
Patrilateral	18.4	17.8	16.2	13.2
Matrilateral	1.1	—	0.7	2.5
Other	—	—	—	0.9
Total	(19.5)	(17.8)	(16.9)	(16.7)
Unrelated families	—	0.8	—	0.3
Total percentage	99.9	100.0	100.0	100.0
Total *N*	190	236	278	318

NOTE: Discrepancies due to rounding cause some totals to be less than 100%.

Table 5.6. *Coresidential Situation of Persisters and Immigrants in Bertalia, by Age, 1890*

Age	Simple family		Extended family	
	Persisters (%)	Immigrants (%)	Persisters (%)	Immigrants (%)
10–19	61.9	64.0	13.8	18.8
	(63.0)[a]		(16.4)	
20–29	47.4	45.0	15.4	14.7
	(45.9)		(15.0)	
30–39	44.7	48.8	20.2	15.9
	(47.5)		(17.3)	
40–49	58.3	68.3	22.0	15.0
	(63.2)		(18.6)	
50–59	63.1	53.6	13.1	14.3
	(58.3)		(13.7)	
60–69	29.9	22.4	22.4	17.9
	(26.1)		(20.1)	
70+	34.5	28.1	37.9	34.4
	(31.1)		(36.1)	
Total	51.6	51.3	18.4	16.7
	(51.4)		(17.5)	

[a] Figures in parentheses refer to totals of the entire parish population, undifferentiated by persistence.

[b] Percentage of the entire parish population over age ten who are persisters and percentage who are immigrants.

Migration and Coresidence in Bertalia

Is migration a significant variable linking urbanization to historical changes in household composition? Specifically, is there any evidence of incompatibility between migration and complex family coresidence? Or, to the contrary, do we find that migrants to the city often take up residence with kinsmen?

Multiple family		Other		Total N	
Persisters (%)	Immigrants (%)	Persisters (%)	Immigrants (%)	Persisters	Immigrants
23.8	16.2	0.6	1.0	181	197
(19.8)		(0.8)		(378)	
35.9	37.2	1.3	3.1	156	258
(36.7)		(2.4)		(414)	
34.0	30.0	1.1	5.3	94	207
(31.2)		(4.0)		(301)	
17.3	14.2	2.4	2.5	127	120
(15.8)		(2.4)		(247)	
22.6	29.8	1.2	2.4	84	84
(26.2)		(1.8)		(168)	
46.3	59.7	1.5	—	67	67
(53.0)		(0.7)		(134)	
27.6	31.2	0	6.2	29	32
(29.5)		(3.3)		(61)	
28.7	29.0	1.4	2.9	738	965
(28.9)		(2.2)		(1,703)	
				43.3%[b]	56.7%[b]

The evidence from Bertalia lends no support to the traditional view of migration as promoting household nuclearization. Comparing households headed by recent migrants with those headed by longer-term residents, we see little difference between them (table 5.5). Moreover, what little difference there is can be explained by the difference in age between the household heads who are recent immigrants and those who are not. Since the migrants are younger, and since younger individuals are

Table 5.7. *Coresidential Situation of Persisters and Immigrants in Bertalia, by Age, 1910*

Age	Simple family		Extended family	
	Persisters (%)	Immigrants (%)	Persisters (%)	Immigrants (%)
10–19	62.4	59.1	20.2	18.2
	(60.5)[a]		(19.1)	
20–29	67.8	44.2	9.7	13.9
	(53.9)		(12.3)	
30–39	48.3	58.5	21.0	17.9
	(54.1)		(19.3)	
40–49	61.3	59.1	19.0	17.7
	(60.2)		(18.3)	
50–59	64.3	60.7	11.7	9.8
	(62.5)		(10.9)	
60–69	47.1	39.4	13.8	21.2
	(43.8)		(17.0)	
70+	17.9	10.8	39.3	29.7
	(15.1)		(35.5)	
Total	58.0	53.0	17.3	16.8
	(55.3)		(17.0)	

[a] Figures in parentheses refer to totals of the entire parish population, undifferentiated by persistence.

[b] Percentage of the entire population over age ten who are persisters and percentage who are immigrants.

less likely to head complex family households, it is not surprising that proportionately fewer recent migrants head complex family households.

When we look at the coresidential situation of *all* Bertalia residents, we see a difference between the 1890 pattern and that found twenty years later. Although in the earlier year immigrants and persisters displayed virtually identical distributions of household situations, in the later year the immigrants were considerably less likely to live in simple

Multiple family		Other		Total N	
Persisters (%)	Immigrants (%)	Persisters (%)	Immigrants (%)	Persisters	Immigrants
17.1	22.4	0.4	0.3	258	340
(20.1)		(0.3)		(598)	
21.6	38.2	0.9	3.7	227	317
(31.2)		(2.7)		(544)	
30.1	20.5	0.6	2.9	176	234
(24.6)		(2.0)		(410)	
19.0	20.7	0.6	2.4	163	164
(19.9)		(1.5)		(327)	
20.1	28.6	3.9	0.9	154	112
(24.0)		(2.6)		(266)	
29.9	36.4	9.2	3.0	87	66
(32.7)		(6.5)		(153)	
35.7	59.5	7.2	—	56	37
(45.2)		(4.3)		(93)	
22.7	28.1	2.1	2.1	1,121	1,270
(25.6)		(2.1)		(2,391)	
				46.9%[b]	53.1%[b]

family households than were the persisters. The amount of this difference in coresidential behavior, moreover, is linked to age (tables 5.6 and 5.7). Individuals in their young adult years and the elderly were more likely to live in multiple family households if they were immigrants than if they had been living in the parish for at least a decade.

What accounts for this age-related pattern and, specifically, why are old folks more likely to live in complex family households if they are immigrants? The answer is linked to the lesser propensity of older people to migrate compared to their juniors. An older person is less likely to give up work he has done all his life to seek a new job and he is probably less eager to alter radically his social environment (Katz 1975: 144). In the case of an urbanizing area like Bertalia, where immigrants came from overwhelmingly rural outposts, this means that an older person is less likely to abandon agricultural employment to seek urban employment (the opportunities available in this direction being much less for older people than for the young). Older people who migrated to Bertalia from the countryside were migrating not because of their own career aspirations but because of those of their adult sons. Looked at from the viewpoint of coresidence in the countryside, an older person living with an adult son would be more likely to migrate to the city than an older person living only with a spouse or preadult children. In many of these cases the adult son was married; in others he married soon after arriving in Bertalia; hence the disproportionate number of complex family households found among the older migrants to the parish.

Another possible explanation for this pattern, linked to the alternative to the traditional nuclearization hypothesis, is also worth considering. Perhaps the older migrants did not move with their children but rather came to Bertalia in order to move in with one of them. In this scenario, as a couple became old or as individuals became widowed, they became less self-sufficient and sought the aid of their adult children through coresidence. Thus, many of the older migrants could have been moving into Bertalia to take up residence with one of their married children who had moved to the parish years before.

To judge the viability of this hypothesis, we need to know the extent to which members of a complex household entered the parish together. We are limited here by not having annual data to work with, but given any substantial time lag, for example, between the entry into the parish of a man and his father, we would expect to find a considerable number of households headed by persisters having migrant members or vice versa (depending on which person was considered head of the household). The data from comparisons between the migration status of the members of each household and the migration status of their household head strongly support the thesis that migration is a family affair (table 5.8). That is, families seem to migrate as a unit; individuals seldom strike off on their own. Looking first at the extended family households, we see that in 1890, 87 percent of the nonhousehold heads living in households

Migration

Table 5.8. *Migration Characteristics of Nonhousehold Heads Linked to Migration Characteristics of Their Household Heads, Bertalia, 1890 and 1910*

Nonhousehold heads (over age ten)	1890			1910		
	Household head			Household head		
	Persisters (%)	Immigrants (%)	Total (%)	Persisters (%)	Immigrants (%)	Total (%)
	Simple family households					
Persisters	88.3	3.7	42.0	93.8	7.1	50.7
Immigrants	11.7	96.3	58.0	6.2	92.9	49.3
Total N	290	350	640	481	476	957
	Extended family households					
Persisters	86.7	6.0	47.0	88.3	7.9	48.8
Immigrants	13.3	94.0	53.0	11.7	92.1	51.2
Total N	120	116	236	145	140	285
	Multiple family households					
Persisters	77.3	5.6	40.4	79.5	10.9	43.1
Immigrants	22.7	94.4	59.6	20.5	89.1	56.9
Total N	203	215	418	229	258	487

headed by a persister were themselves persisters; only 13 percent differed from their household head in migration status. Of the nonhousehold heads living in households headed by immigrants, 94 percent were themselves immigrants, with just 6 percent being unlike their household head in migration status. A similar pattern pertains for extended family households in 1910.

Some evidence favoring the thesis that accounts for complex family formation among immigrants in urban situations on the basis of joining already established kinsmen in the city, appears to be provided by the data on multiple family households. We see that 23 percent of the nonhousehold heads living in households headed by persisters in 1890 were themselves *migrants*. This contrasts with the modest 6 percent of the nonhousehold heads living in households headed by immigrants who were themselves persisters.

On the face of it, this suggests the merit of the hypothesis discussed above, in which older people are moving into the parish to take up resi-

Table 5.9. *Age, Marital Status, and Sex of Immigrants Living in Multiple Family Households Headed by Persisters, Bertalia, 1890 and 1910*

Age	1890							
	Unmarried		Married		Widowed		Total	
	Male	Female	Male	Female	Male	Female	Male	Female
20–29	2	2	4	18	0	0	6	20
30–39	1	1	4	5	0	0	5	6
40+	0	0	1	7	0	1	1	8
Total	3	3	9	30	0	1	12	34
	1910							
20–29	3	4	2	17	0	0	5	21
30–39	0	0	0	8	0	0	0	8
40+	2	0	4	5	1	1	7	6
Total	5	4	6	30	1	1	12	35

dence in the homes of their married children. To see if this is indeed the case, we can look more closely at just who these immigrants are who move into households of their kinsmen already established in the parish (see table 5.9). If multiple family households are formed by the elderly moving in with their married children who had already settled in the parish, we would expect to find a large proportion of the immigrants in these households to be old; however, this is not the case. Those 40 years of age or older compose just 30 percent of the immigrants in 1890 and 28 percent in 1910. The great majority of the immigrants living in multiple family households headed by persisters are young, a majority being in their twenties. Most of these people are married females. The implication is clear: the significant proportion of households headed by persisters that have immigrant residents simply reflects the norm of patrilocal postmarital residence.

Before leaving Bertalia, one other aspect of migration in this period of urban expansion should be mentioned, the fact that adults migrated either with their families or in order to marry into the parish. Despite the great social dislocations in the countryside, we do not find single men coming to Bertalia by themselves in search of work. Unlike what we find in other societies, boarding was not part of the Italian culture. People lived with their own families or they lived as servants; they did not live with nonkinsmen and few lived alone.[6]

Migration, Coresidence, and the Social Order

The extensive migration that characterized industrializing Europe must be seen in light of the large volume of migration that characterized the preindustrial period. If industrialzation and urbanization brought about anomie, or rootlessness, it was not because people were for the first time being forced to move out of their native communities. Through much of Western Europe, migration had long been a way of life, tied to the economic order. The social organzation served as a mechanism for providing for people's needs in a context of geographical mobility; the countryside did not consist of a set of locally based social systems. Indeed, no one has questioned the fact that the upper classes were regional in scope; it should not be surprising that the lives of the working classes were similarly organized. The migration that accompanied nineteenth-century industrialization was not the frightful experience it has often been seen as, with peasant bumpkins arriving in urban centers, torn from their families and friends. The previous social order rested on such transiency, with kinship networks and domestic groups nurturing the migrants in their movements. Darroch (1981) has recently argued that migration in this world of economic change should be seen as an attempt to keep the old social order intact, to allow domestic groups and kin networks to survive the shock of economic dislocation. Migration did not tear individuals away from their families and from their kinsmen but rather was a way in which individuals could keep their previous social world alive.

A similar reevaluation of the role of migration in the nineteenth century is taking place among American historians. High rates of migration, particularly in the expanding cities of that era, were traditionally seen as indications of a breakdown in the social and moral order. Mobility was contrasted with stability, and migrants were characterized as alienated and socially and politically invisible. Stephenson has perceptively criticized this view, which portrays working-class communities as "no more than a gathering of strangers" (1979: 32). Physical mobility and social stability are not mutually exclusive.

It is in this context that we see the relationship between rural-urban migration and coresidence. The social organization of the Italian rural population had long been based on high rates of mobility. Part of the mobility involved children moving by themselves to work as servants in the homes of others, but these children remained in touch with their parents and siblings and often took up residence with them when they were later able to work on their own. A second aspect of the mobility involved young women who, at marriage, went to live in the home of their husband. A third aspect involved entire domestic groups, who moved for economic reasons, searching for improved work conditions or to regain work situations that had been lost.

It should not be surprising, given this background, that people's strategies in confronting the economic changes accompanying early industrialization represented a continuation of their long-time strategy (Lehning 1980). Traditional kinship obligations were not quickly broken; rather, they took on new import as they were refashioned to cope better with the changing environment. Families migrated to the city in this period, but many of these migrants later migrated back to the countryside (cf. Stearns 1967: 121–122). Insofar as urban migration meant leaving sharecropping and taking up wage labor, there was reason for multiple family households to disband. However, most of the rural-urban migration involved people who were already wage laborers, albeit in the agricultural sector. For them, there is no reason to expect any change in coresidential arrangements.

In Bologna, early industrialization and urban expansion did not mean a radical alteration in migration levels or even in the geographical scope of migration. Migration continued to occur at a high rate, and it continued to be largely confined within the borders of the province. The interchange of population between the city and the hinterland continued as it had for centuries, though with gradually increasing net benefit to the city and population loss to the countryside. The city represented less a new world to the rural population than one of life's old and familiar options.

6

Coresidence in Life Course Perspective

Historical household study has suffered from its heavy reliance on cross-sectional data. Each person's coresidential experience—the constellation of other people with whom the person lives—changes through time, and these changes reflect both processes of individual aging and historical processes that change the society and the social environment. It is indicative of the crucial importance of this issue that, in the heated debate between Laslett and Berkner, each accuses the other of the fatal flaw of not adequately dealing with longitudinal, life course data (Berkner 1972, 1975; Laslett 1978: 98).

There have been few attempts to follow individuals through time in historical coresidential research, and most of these have been limited to tracing individuals from one population listing to the next, comparing their characteristics at the beginning and end of the period (see Katz 1975; Otterbein and Otterbein 1977). Such studies have demonstrated the inadequacy of the cross-sectional approach in interpreting the coresidential experience of individuals. However, they are severely constrained by the fact that they miss so much of the flux of social life through time.[1]

The ideal historical study of coresidence would follow individuals continuously through time, illuminating the interplay among the social, demographic, economic, and personality factors that condition coresidential choices.² To conduct such a study, however, fully longitudinal data must be available, and they are available in only few places in the world and for limited historical periods. Moreover, such study means forsaking the relatively simple techniques used in cross-sectional data analysis and confronting the much more complex conceptual and methodological problems inherent in longitudinal analysis.³ In part for these reasons, even where historical longitudinal data exist, as they do in the population registers of many European countries, they have been little used. Those who have pioneered their use, most notably Van de Walle's (1976) use of the Belgian population register, have, however, quickly attracted a great deal of attention (Bradley and Mendels 1978: 381n; Mitterauer and Sieder 1979: 258).⁴

In studying Bertalia, for practical reasons of available financial and human resources, a compromise was made between use of an entirely cross-sectional approach and a fully longitudinal approach. Controlling for age and occupation, cross-sectional data can provide significant, if limited, insight into coresidential processes. Yet, as a result of life course factors and the existence of historical change, by itself the cross-sectional approach is flawed. In an attempt to complement our cross-sectional material, two paths were followed. First, all individuals in Bertalia were linked from one decade to the next, enabling us to contrast the characteristics of each nonmigratory resident at ten-year intervals. This approach made possible the characterizing of residents by migration history that formed the basis of chapter 5. It also allows us to gain more insight into the changes in coresidential arrangements that individuals experience during their life course. Rather than having to manufacture synthetic cohorts through use of age-controlled cross-sectional data, we are able actually to follow individuals through portions of their life course.

To provide richer material on coresidential processes, we supplemented this "panel study" approach by following a sample of individuals *continuously* through the years they resided in Bertalia. This was accomplished by using the Bertalia parish censuses for *each single year* from 1880 through 1910, along with the parish marriage and death records, and by examining the record of each individual in the municipal population register (*l'anagrafe*) of the city of Bologna. Because individuals often moved into and out of Bertalia from other parts of the municipal area of Bologna, this enabled us to trace people for a greater period of time than was possible through use of the parish register.⁵ However, use of these *anagrafe* records for a city the size of Bologna is an exceedingly time-consuming process, and we thus limited the sample to a modest size. The nature of the sample drawn, as well as the results of this inquiry, are discussed later in this chapter.

Occupational Mobility

Although our primary concern in tracing individuals through time is to understand coresidential processes better, by following individuals we are also in a position to throw light on a related problem of social history: the nature of people's occupational changes through their life course. This is of particular interest in the Bertalia context, where we may gain insight into the effect of urbanization on people's career patterns. Although full consideration of this question is beyond the scope of this book, a few observations are in order.

For individuals who remained in Bertalia from one decade to the next we are able to compare their earlier occupation with their later occupation.[6] We do this for each of the three decades under study and find that though occupational change was substantial in the 1890s, it was considerably more modest in the 1880s and the first decade of the twentieth century (table 6.1). The occupational flux of the 1890s can be linked with the continuing agrarian crisis of those years, together with the beginning of the expansion in the urban job sector. The difference among decades may be best illustrated by the case of the *braccianti*. Just 5 percent of the *braccianti* in 1880 had changed occupation by 1890, and just 12 percent of those in 1900 had changed occupation by 1910. Yet of the *braccianti* in Bertalia in 1900, 42 percent had changed occupation ten years later. The most plausible explanation of this pattern is that large numbers of displaced rural workers were crowding into Bertalia with the mounting agricultural crisis of the 1880s. They first searched for the most familiar job, that of *bracciante*, and were likely to be listed as such in 1890. However, over the ensuing decade they sought out any wage labor they could find, often passing into more urban occupations.

The fact that a large majority of residentially stable sharecroppers remained sharecroppers over each ten-year period is obviously linked to the fact that those sharecroppers who were unable or unwilling to renew their sharecropping contract were not only deprived of a job but were evicted from their homes as well. Yet, in this context, it is notable that a

Table 6.1. *Occupational Mobility of Nonmigrant Males, Ages 20–59 at Initial Year: Percentage Switching Occupation*

Occupation in initial year	1880–1890		1890–1900		1900–1910	
	N	Percentage	N	Percentage	N	Percentage
Bracciante	62	5	95	42	67	12
Sharecropper	47	26	37	35	44	14
Boaro	3	67	4	25	9	22
Railroad	13	23	26	38	30	13
Factory	3	33	1	0	9	0
Service	11	18	5	60	12	16
Artisan	26	15	21	19	24	8
Construction	9	11	16	50	54	9
Merchant	6	17	6	50	19	11
Other	24	46	36	39	36	53
Total	204	16	247	38	304	12

significant minority of the residentially stable people who were sharecroppers in 1880 and in 1890 changed occupation within ten years. Of these, about half suffered the characteristic downward mobility of the period, becoming *braccianti* (five out of twelve in the 1880s, and eight out of thirteen in the 1890s).

It appears that following the period of economic and social dislocation suffered in the 1890s, a period of relative stability returned in the early 1900s. In both the agricultural and the urban sector, the residentially stable inhabitants of Bertalia were remarkably stable in occupation.

No consideration of the subject of occupational mobility would be complete without considering the significance of age. It is often noted that some age categories (particularly the young) are more occupationally mobile than others (the middle-aged). In a situation of structural economic change, such as we find in Bertalia in this period, this issue becomes particularly important. As the economic structure of a locality alters, does this have a differential impact on people of different ages?

A summary of the shifts in occupation of the residentially stable population by ten-year age category, based on age at the beginning of the decade (those age ten to nineteen are dealt with separately below), shows that in both the 1890s and in the first decade of the 1900s, the younger men changed occupation more often than the middle-aged and older men

Table 6.2. *Occupational Mobility by Age: Percentage of Nonmigrant Males Switching Occupation*

Age in initial year	1880–1890	1890–1900	1900–1910
20–29	17	50	16
30–39	13	40	16
40–49	15	26	5
50–59	21	29	5
Total (ages 20–59)	16	38	12

(see table 6.2). In the 1880s, before urbanization was felt much in Bertalia, there was relatively little difference among the cohorts in propensity for occupational change. The contrast between the magnitude of occupational mobility between the 1890s and the following decade is dramatic for each of the cohorts considered. It was the young men who were most likely to respond to the dislocations of the 1890s by changing their occupations, with the rate of occupational mobility for the two youngest cohorts shown here three times greater in the 1890s than in the early 1900s.

What about the occupational experience of the people in the two youngest cohorts, many of whom were entering their first jobs? What jobs did the children who grew up in Bertalia take during this period of economic change? If we look at the boys under age ten at the initial point of observation, focusing on those who had entered the work force ten years later, we have a good synopsis of the economic changes taking place in Bertalia (see table 6.3). Whereas 70 percent of the youngsters of 1880 became *braccianti* or sharecroppers by 1890, of the same aged cohort of 1900, just 16 percent were found in these occupations ten years later. Most strikingly, though 41 percent of the 1880 youngsters became *braccianti* by 1890, this proportion among the comparably aged population of the following decade fell to 11 percent, falling to a mere 1 percent in the first decade of the 1900s.

Where then were the young people finding employment? Many were going into the more urban occupations, particularly factory work, that specialized in youth labor (see table 6.3). Indeed, the proportion of youths going into factory work for the three decades rose from 2 percent to 29 percent to 34 percent respectively. Looking at those age ten to

Table 6.3. *Occupations of Male Youths Ages 0–9 at Initial Year, Ten Years Later*

Occupation	1890		1900		1910	
	N	Percentage	N	Percentage	N	Percentage
Bracciante	23	41	11	11	1	1
Sharecropper/ farm renter	16	29	17	17	17	15
Boaro	0	—	2	2	0	—
Railroad	2	4	1	1	0	—
Factory	1	2	29	29	38	34
Construction/ service	8	14	24	24	43	39
Artisan	2	4	6	6	6	5
Servant	0	—	1	1	0	—
Merchant	1	2	7	7	3	3
Other	3	5	2	2	3	3
Total number in work force	56		100		111	
Total number not in work force	38		25		31	
Total	94		125		142	

*a*Percentages are based only on those in the work force.

nineteen in each of our three ten-year periods, a similar pattern emerges. Whereas 55 percent of the ten- to nineteen-year-olds in 1880 had become *braccianti* and sharecroppers at the end of that decade, the comparable proportion for the 1890 cohort of the same age was 31 percent; 16 percent for the 1900 cohort.

We are left with a portrait of a population that experienced dramatic economic dislocation in the 1890s, but which, by the early 1900s, had found a new occupational stability. The young people of the first decade of the twentieth century were entering the urban sector of the economy, but the urbanization did not mean a change in occupation for the parents.

Coresidence through Time

We now can turn back to our central interest in this chapter: how do people's coresidential experiences change through time? We first address this question by comparing people's coresidential situation at one

Table 6.4. *Stability and Change in Household Composition of Nonmigrants, 1880–1890 and 1900–1910*

Household composition		Percentage	
At beginning of decade	*At end of decade*	*1880–1890*	*1900–1910*
Simple	Simple	33.2	44.9
Simple	Extended	6.5	4.3
Simple	Multiple	10.9	8.1
Extended	Simple	10.8	6.8
Extended	Extended	6.1	8.7
Extended	Multiple	3.2	3.4
Multiple	Simple	6.9	6.0
Multiple	Extended	5.5	4.2
Multiple	Multiple	14.3	11.1
Other combinations		2.6	2.5
Total percentage		100.0	100.0
Total N		741	1,121

point in time with their situation ten years later. As previously discussed, this approach misses considerable variability in the intervening ten-year period; however, it does provide some idea of the extent to which people's coresidential constellations change over time and the nature of that change.

As Berkner and many others have pointed out, the fact that a person lives in a simple family household at one time is no indication of what sort of household he or she lives in at any other time. Indeed, given certain cultural norms and demographic factors, we would expect many of those living in simple family households at one time to be living in complex family households ten years later. Likewise, we might predict, given certain features of household formation, that many individuals living in complex family households in one year would be living in simple family households a decade later.

An aggregate view of the changes people in Bertalia experienced in the composition of the household in which they lived is provided in table 6.4. In the first decade, just over one-half (53.6 percent) of the residentially stable population was found at the end of the decade in a household of the same composition as they had been in at the beginning of the decade. In the latter period, this proportion rose to nearly two-

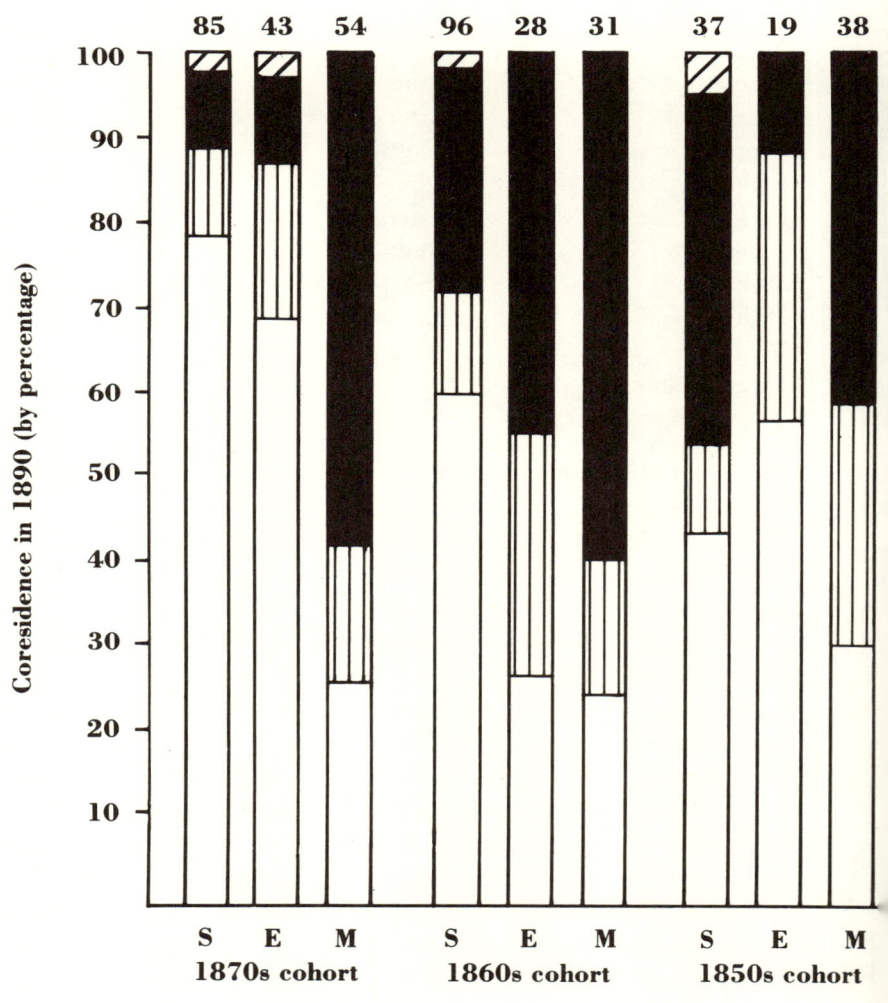

Figure 6.1. *Individuals' Coresidential Situation in 1890 as a Function of Their Coresidential Situation in 1880, by Ten-Year Birth Cohorts*

S = simple family household
E = extended family household
M = multiple family household

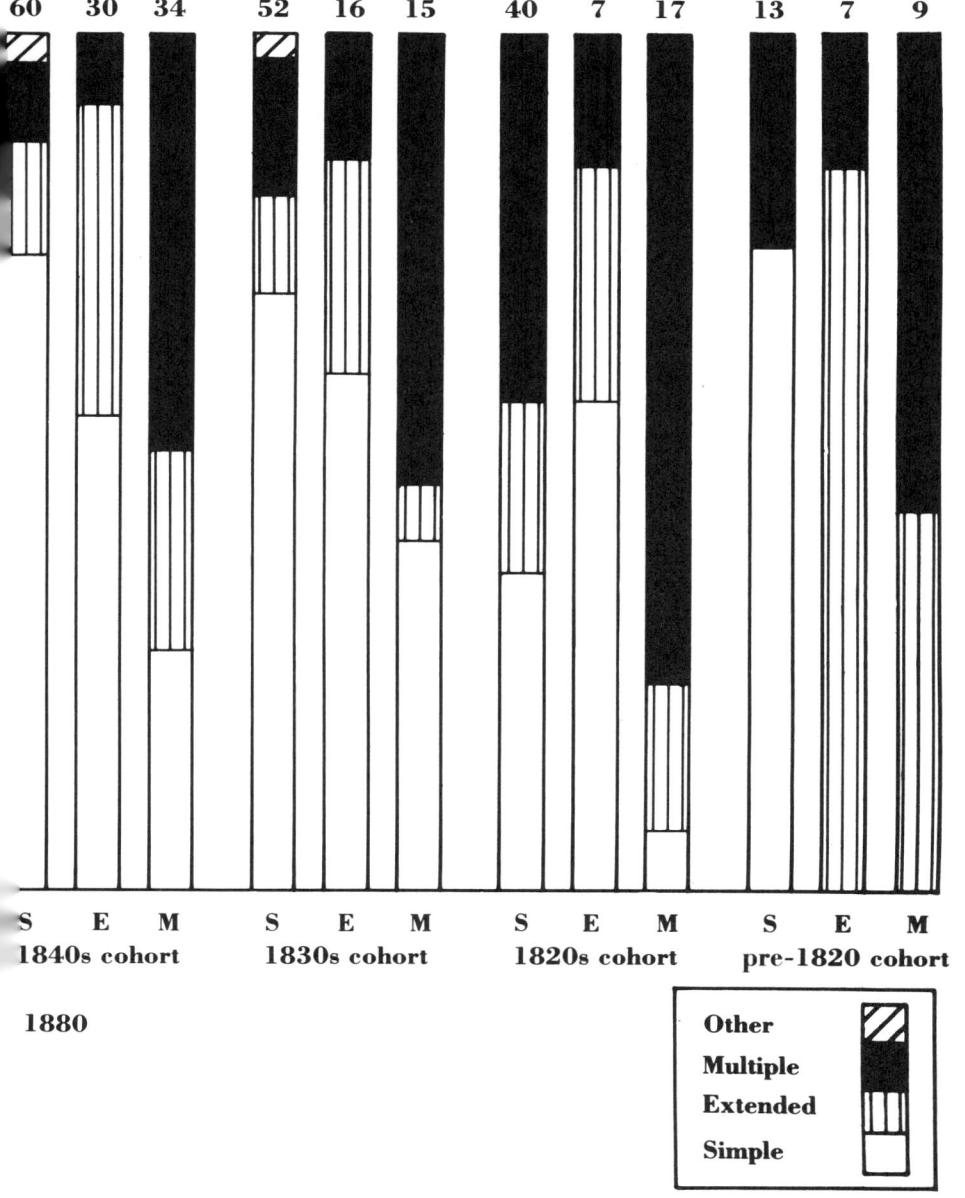

1880

Figure 6.2. *Individuals' Coresidential Situation in 1880 as a Function of Their Coresidential Situation in 1890, by Ten-Year Birth Cohorts*

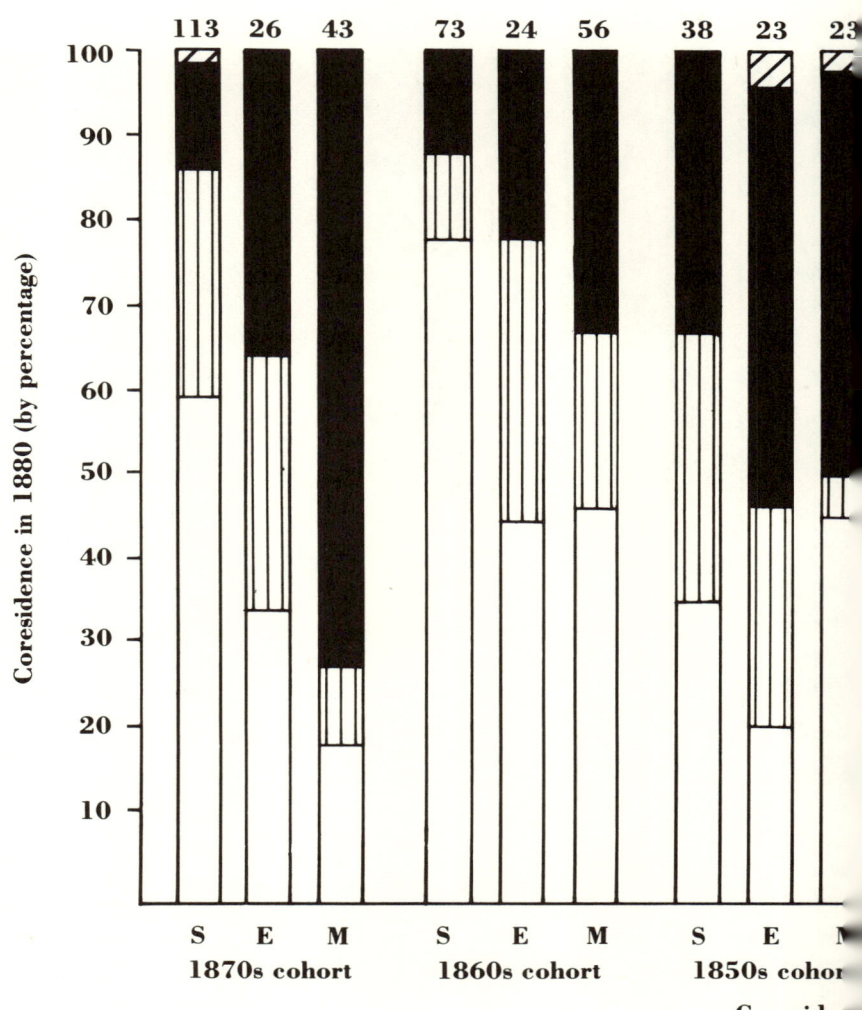

S = simple family household
E = extended family household
M = multiple family household

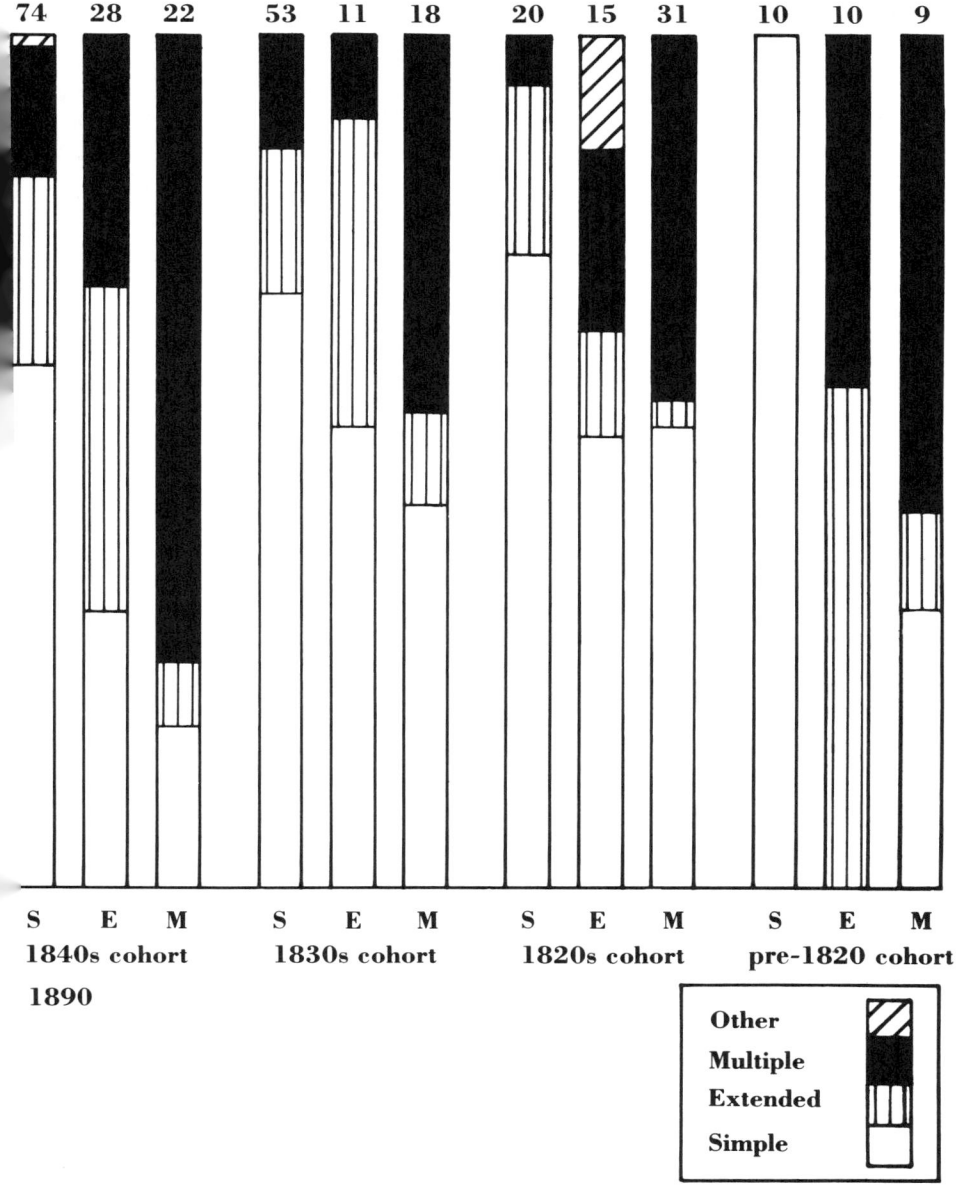

thirds (64.7 percent), reflecting a much greater propensity of those who began the decade in a simple family household to be found in one at the end of the decade.

To get at the social processes underlying this pattern we need to divide the population by age to see what sorts of changes are characteristic of which stages of life. We begin this examination by looking first at the 1880 residentially stable population, divided by household type and by ten-year age categories. In figure 6.1, each bar represents the population of 1880 residents from the indicated ten-year birth cohort living in a particular kind of household (i.e., simple, extended, or multiple). At the top of the bar is the number of individuals found in such households. Each bar is divided into three major segments, indicating the composition of the households these indivduals lived in at the end of the ten-year period. Thus, to illustrate, the first bar of figure 6.1 represents the individuals aged nine and under in 1880 (i.e., the 1870s birth cohort) who lived in a simple family households in 1880. Of these eighty-five children, 79 percent remained in a simple family household ten years later; 11 percent were found in extended family households; and 9 percent lived in multiple family households.

Given life course factors, we would generally expect to find a movement in this earliest age range toward a greater frequency of simple family households through this ten-year period. Hence, it is not surprising that over three-quarters of those individuals who began the period living in simple family households were still living in simple family households at the end of the decade. The situation of those living in extended family households in 1880 is in line with this expectation, as 70 percent had switched to coresidence in simple family households by 1890, and just 19 percent remained in extended family households. The situation of multiple family households, however, is rather different. A majority (57 percent) of children in this cohort who began the decade in multiple family households remained in multiple family households in 1890. This tends to support the notion that simple family households went through an extended family phase in order to take care of the elderly, whereas the multiple family household reflects a strategy adopted to meet certain long-range economic problems.

The instability of the extended family household is amply documented by a glance at each of the cohorts shown. Only in the oldest cohort, of individuals over age sixty at the beginning of the decade, are a majority of individuals living in extended family households still living in extended family households ten years later. In contrast, in five of the seven cohorts, a majority of individuals living in multiple family households at the beginning of the decade are found living in multiple family households at the decade's end. Moreover, even in the two cohorts—the 1850s and the 1840s—in which only a minority remains in multiple family households at the end of the decade, the minority is over 40 percent.

How are life course factors reflected in these data? If we look at those living in simple households in 1880, we see that those most likely to leave such coresidential arrangements are found in the birth cohorts of the 1860s, 1850s, and 1820s. These represent both those getting married during the period (or whose coresident siblings were being married) and those whose eldest children were getting married.

A different vantage point on these shifts can be obtained by looking at household composition from the perspective of the characteristics of the person's coresidential situation at the end of the decade (see figure 6.2). This format permits us to ask what kinds of household individuals are coming from to make up the simple, extended, and multiple family households in 1890. For example, if we look again at the first bar on the left, we see that of the 113 individuals in the 1870s birth cohort living in simple family households in 1890, 59 percent had been living in simple family households ten years earlier, whereas 27 percent had been living in extended and 12 percent in multiple family households.

Looking only at the people living in simple family households in 1890, we can see where the major shifts to simple family households occur by locating the bars having the largest segments representing individuals who at the beginning of the period were living in extended and multiple family households. These we find for the 1870s, 1850s, and 1840s cohorts. In the case of the 1870s, these coresidential shifts reflect the death of one or more coresident grandparents. In the case of the 1850s and 1840s cohorts, the shifts reflect the death of coresident parents, deaths not yet offset by the marriage, and postmarital coresidence of any of the individual's own children.

Were these patterns of life course coresidential experiences themselves changing over time? Were they similar in the more urbanized 1900s to the more agrarian, rural 1880s? We can find some help in answering these questions by comparing figures 6.1 and 6.2 with figures 6.3 and 6.4, which represent the experience of the residentially stable population of Bertalia twenty years later.

Starting again from the viewpoint of the household composition at the

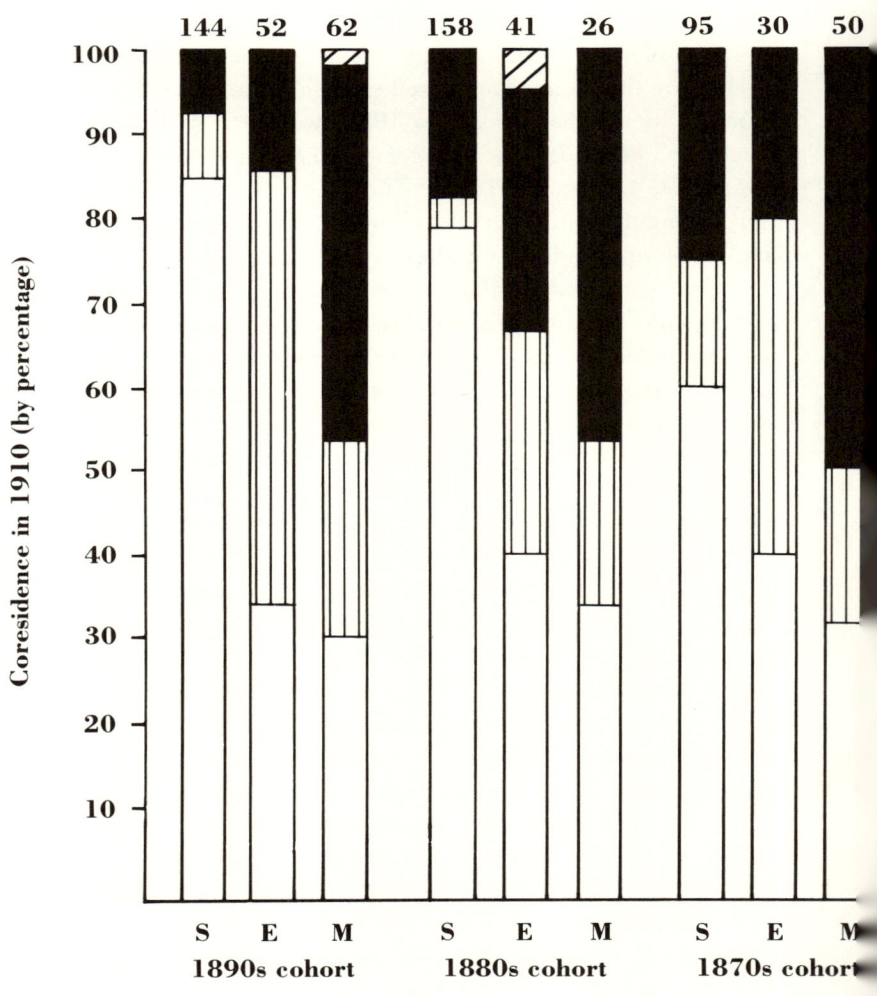

Figure 6.3. *Individuals' Coresidential Situation in 1910 as a Function of Their Coresidential Situation in 1900, by Ten-Year Birth Cohorts*

S = simple family household
E = extended family household
M = multiple family household

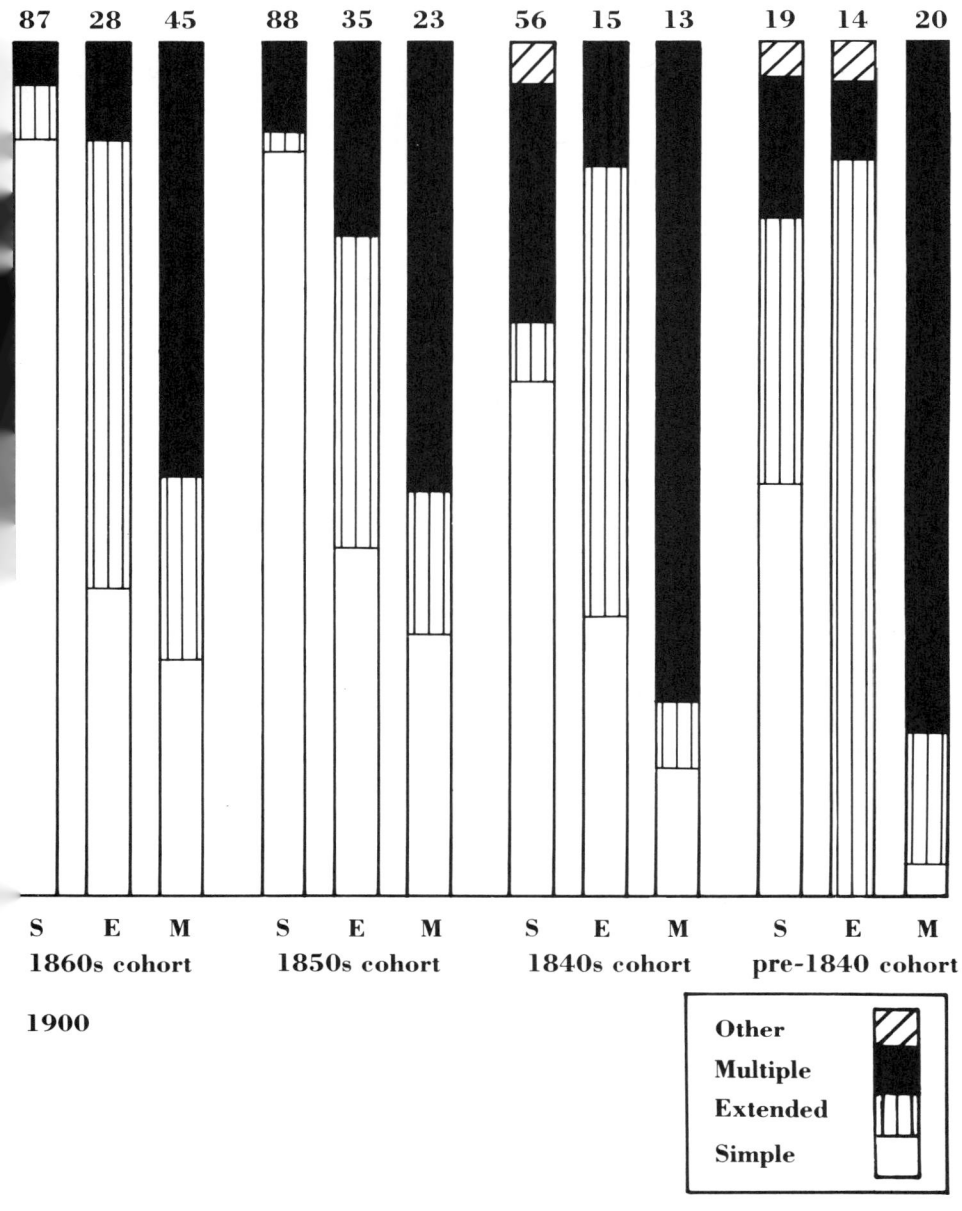

1900

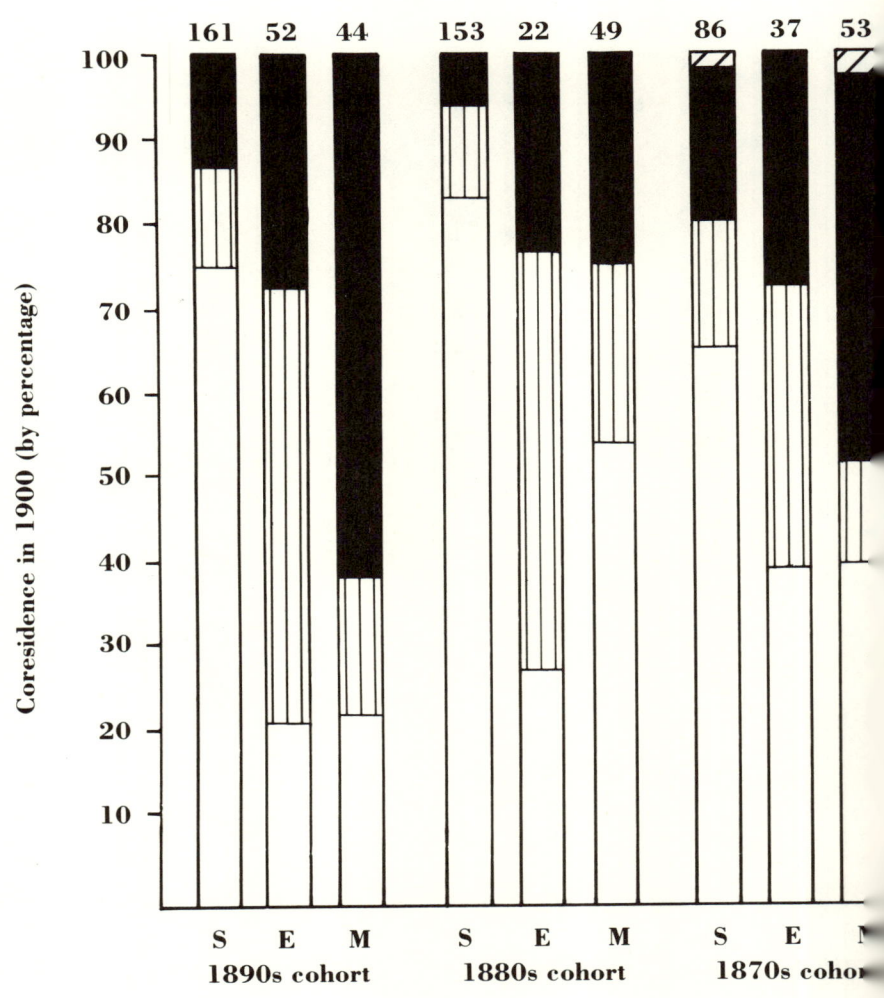

Figure 6.4. *Individuals' Coresidential Situation in 1900 as a Function of Their Coresidential Situation in 1910, by Ten-Year Birth Cohorts*

S = simple family household
E = extended family household
M = multiple family household

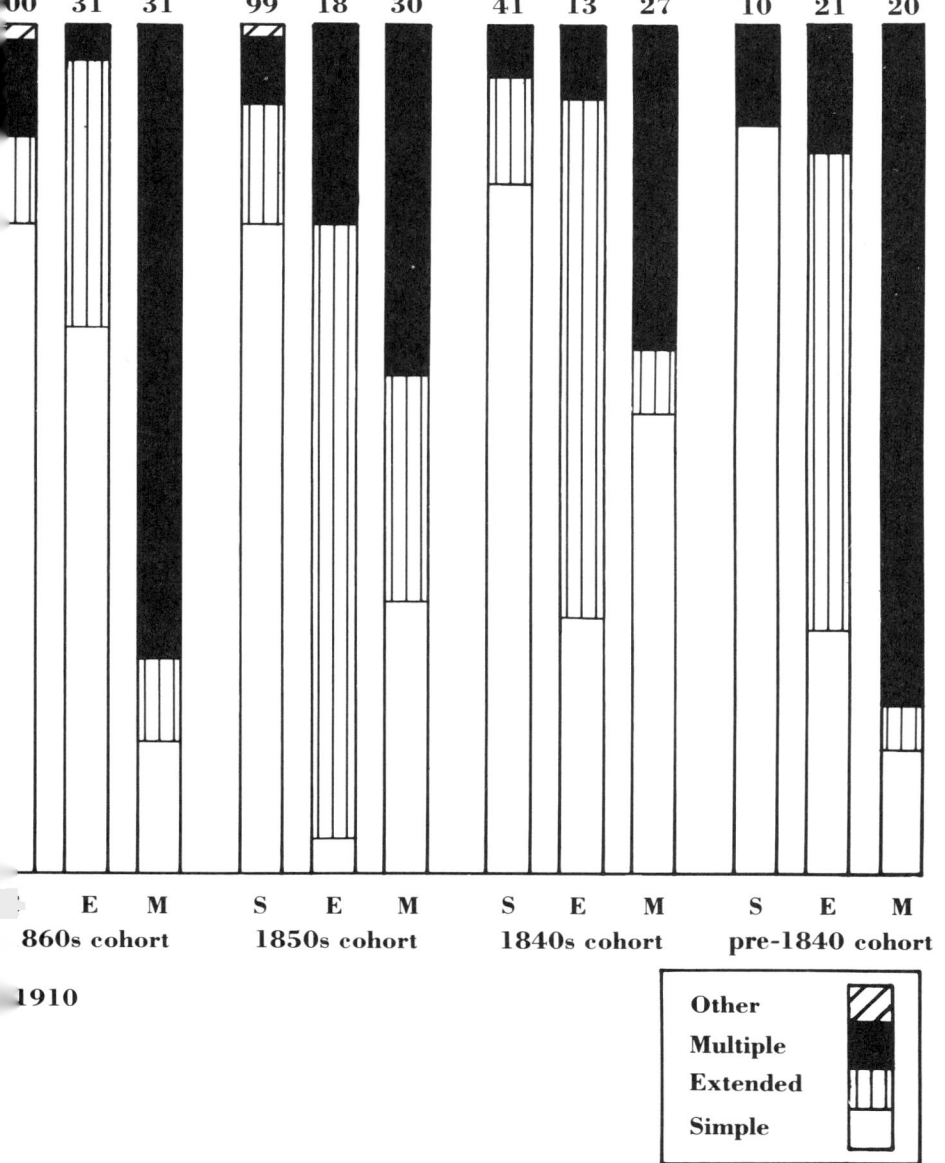

beginning of each of the decades under study (figures 6.1 and 6.3), the greatest similarity is found among individuals who began each period living in multiple family households. The pattern of households in which such individuals lived ten years later is remarkably similar for the comparable cohorts. In contrast, the situation for individuals living in simple family households at the initial year differs considerably for the 1880s and the first decade of the 1900s. In all cohorts but the eldest, individuals living in simple family households in 1900 were more likely to remain in simple family households at the end of the decade than were individuals living in simple family households in 1880.

The situation of individuals living in extended family households in the initial year of each decade is quite different. In fact, except in the cohort of individuals aged 10–19 in the initial year, people living in extended family households in 1880 were more likely to be found in simple family households ten years later than were individuals living in extended family households in 1900. Thus, the tendency for people living in extended family households to end up in simple family households after a decade, which characterized the 1880 population, is considerably weaker for the Bertalia population of 1900. There was a much higher rate of persistence among people living in the extended family household category in 1900–1910 that in 1880–1890.

It is also worth comparing coresidential flux in these two periods from the vantage point of people's household composition at the end of each decade. We do this by comparing the 1880–1890 population shown in figure 6.2 with the 1900–1910 population shown in figure 6.4. Again, we find that there is little difference between the two decades in the household origin of individuals living in multiple family households at the end of each decade. The differences are more striking, however, in the case of people living in simple and extended family households.

In the youngest age cohort, for example, 26 percent of the individuals living in extended family households in 1890 had lived in extended family households ten years earlier, whereas the comparable figure for individuals living in extended family households in 1910 was just 12 percent. In fact, all cohorts but one show a greater proportion of simple family household residents coming from extended family households in 1890 than in 1910. Hence, for reasons yet to be determined, there was less tendency for individuals living in extended family households to shift to simple family coresidence in the 1900s than in the 1880s. Seen from a different point of view, people living in extended family households at the end of each decade were, for most cohorts, more likely to have come from extended family households in 1910 than in 1880.

We can now sum up the pattern of coresidential change evident in the lives of the Bertalia residents who remained in the parish through each of these two decades. Overall, there was greater stability of coresidence in the latter decade than in the earlier, but in both periods a large minority of the population lived at the end of the decade in a household of a different type than the one in which they had been living at the beginning. In all, 54 percent of the 1880 Bertalia residents lived in a household having the same composition ten years later, whereas for the period 1900–1910 this figure rises to 64 percent (for the intermediate period of 1890–1900 the proportion is 61 percent). In the decade before the full effects of urbanization were being felt in the parish (1880–1890), when the great majority of the population was involved in agriculturally related work, one-third of the population lived in simple family households at both ends of the decade. Two decades later this proportion would rise to 45 percent.

Simple family household residence was the most stable in both decades under study, in the sense that a higher proportion remained in a simple family household at the end of each decade than remained in households of any other type. Extended family household residence was the least stable, with multiple family household residence moderately stable (generally around 50 percent). Both simple and extended family residence were more stable in 1900–1910 than they were in 1880–1890. There is virtually no overall difference in multiple family household stability between the two decades.

Life Course Coresidence of Sharecroppers and *Braccianti*

Although information on the coresidential situation of individuals at two different times provides some insight into how people's coresidential situations change through time, much of the process underlying coresidential stability and change is missed. The only way to understand satisfactorily these processes is by following people continuously. In this section we do just this, following a selected sample of Bertalia residents from their arrival in Bertalia to their departure, concentrating on the 1880–1910 period.[7]

We were especially interested in discovering the differences between *braccianti* and sharecroppers in their coresidential life course experience during this period of economic upheaval. This determined our choice of sample. The two populations from which the sample was drawn—*braccianti* and sharecroppers—constituted the largest occupational categories in Bertalia at the beginning of the period. The samples were drawn on the basis of occupation of household head, yielding a pool of 40 sharecropper households and 138 *bracciante*-headed households. Within these, the sample was not random but selected to provide a range of household composition and household size in the initial year, linked to a desire to select household heads of various ages and to select households still represented in Bertalia at least ten years later. Eleven sharecropper and ten *braccianti* households were selected. This number was augmented by following households that had split off from the original twenty-one households under study, leading to the inclusion of nine more sharecropper households and three more *braccianti* households.

Of this total of twenty sharecropping and thirteen *braccianti* households, three sharecropper and four *braccianti* households are presented in detail here to illustrate the processes of coresidence through time in Bertalia. In addition, to show the flux in residence, we follow three sharecropper residences through the 1880–1910 period, looking at the succession of different families living there. These sketches have the disadvantage of being relatively lengthy presentations of data regarding a small number of people. However, they allow us to flesh out the coresidential experience of the people of Bertalia in a way not possible through more aggregated data. By reading through the sketches that follow, the reader is likely to gain a kind of understanding of the lives of these people that cannot be acquired by reading a table.

Bracciante Case 1: Fiorini

Luigi Fiorini and his wife had been living in Bertalia since the 1860s, though they moved from one part of the parish to another at various times. In 1880 they were living with their daughter (age 11) and their son (4). Luigi died in the cholera epidemic of 1886. His daughter had died in 1883. Thus, after Luigi's death, just his widow and son remained in Bertalia. In 1890, at the age of fourteen, the son became a daily laborer (*giornaliero*). Four years later they left Bertalia.

Bracciante Case 2: Gualandi

For the first five years of their marriage, beginning in 1868, Serafino Gualandi and his wife lived in Bertalia. They then moved to the neighboring agricultural zone of Arcoveggio. In 1879 they returned to Bertalia and lived in four different places in the parish before moving out again in 1895. In 1880 their household consisted of Serafino (age 39), his wife (37), one daughter (12), and two sons (10 and 6). A second daughter was born to them in 1882, but she died at the age of 13 months. In 1890, their eldest daughter (22) married and left the household, leaving Serfino, his wife, and two unmarried sons. These four left for the city of Bologna in 1895, where both sons found work as pasta vendors.

Bracciante Case 3: Cane

A more complex household situation is illustrated by the case of Raffaele Cane (52), who lived in Bertalia in 1880 together with his wife (52) and two daughters, Florinda (25) and Enrica (15). Enrica had been born in Bertalia; her elder sister had been born in neighboring Corticella. In 1881 Florinda married and left home. Two years thereafter her sister, Enrica (18), bore a daughter, though she was still unmarried. In 1886 Enrica married and her husband briefly joined the household. However, the following year Enrica left Bertalia with her husband and daughter.

Raffaele and his wife then lived by themselves for five years, until his wife's death in 1892. In the wake of this death, Raffaele's elder daughter Florinda, who had left home at her marriage a decade before, rejoined the home of her father, bringing her husband and their one-year-old son with her. This arrangement, however, proved temporary, for when Raffaele (64) married a widow of the same age a year after his bereavement, Florinda and her family moved out.

Just a year after this remarriage, Raffaele's second wife died, again leaving him alone. But before the year (1894) was out, he married for the third time another sixty-four-year-old widow. At the time of this marriage he moved within Bertalia to take up residence next door to his brother, also a *bracciante*. There he lived with his third wife until her death in 1903. His brother had migrated out of Bertalia the previous year, and Raffaele followed suit.

Family Life in Central Italy

Bracciante Case 4: Grassilli

The family of Vincenzo Grassilli migrated to Bertalia in the 1870s from the agricultural commune of Medicina, about 30 kilometers to the east. In 1880 Vincenzo (age 53) was living with his second wife (47), two sons (14 and 12), and a daughter (10). The sixth member of the household was the daughter (13) of Vincenzo's deceased brother (it is unclear whether her mother was still alive). The following year this girl's twenty-year-old sister also joined the household.

Between 1886 and 1896 these girls, Vincenzo's nieces, married and left the household. In this period, too, his daughter married and moved in with her husband's family in Bertalia, and then his younger son married and, though remaining a *bracciante*, moved elsewhere in the parish. Thus, by 1896, Vincenzo's household was reduced to three members: Vincenzo, his wife, and his elder son. In 1900 his wife died, and Vincenzo and his son, both *braccianti*, left the parish.

Sharecropper Case 1: Brintazzoli

The Brintazzoli family moved to Bertalia in 1870 from a rural locality in the province of Bologna. At the time, the household contained Luigi (age forty), his wife and children, his unmarried older brother Gaetano, and Violante, the widow of Luigi's oldest brother, along with her children. Violante had lived with Luigi since her husband's death in 1865, when her youngest child was just four years old.

For fifteen years the composition of the household remained relatively stable. Luigi's youngest child was born in 1882, and the same year, Enrico, Violante's eldest child, was married, bringing his wife to live in the household. Thus, the household contained three nuclear family units spanning three generations. However, after his first child died in infancy, Enrico and his wife moved (1884) elsewhere in Bertalia, where he worked as a *boaro* (salaried livestock overseer).

Of Violante's four remaining sons in the household, one died (age 27) in 1886, and another (30) left for the city of Bologna in 1888. Two years after one of her remaining two sons (32) in the household married and brought his bride to live in the household (1893), Violante, her two sons, and her son's wife left to establish their own sharecropping household elsewhere in Bertalia.

This left Luigi, his wife and children, his unmarried brother, and his widowed sister, who had joined the household upon her husband's death in 1893. Over the next five years the household lost members through death (Liugi's sister and wife) and through the marriage of Luigi's daughters, all three of whom left at marriage (in 1897, 1899, and 1904). Yet this loss was offset by the successive marriages, in order of seniority, of his four sons, each of whom brought his wife into the household. As children were born to these sons, the household grew in size.

In 1910, one year after Luigi's death, the Brintazzoli family, approximating the ideal of sharecropper stability and postmarital patrilocality, continued to live on the same land they had been farming since 1870. The four married brothers and their wives and children coresided with their father's bachelor brother.

Sharecropper Case 2: Coltelli

The Coltelli household provides another example of a sharecropping family that remained on a Bertalia farm throughout the three decades under observation. Agostino Coltelli (age 75) moved to Bertalia in 1876 from a rural area eleven kilometers to the east. He brought with him his second wife and his two married sons—Giuseppe (age 56) and Angelo (44)—together with their wives and children. By 1880 there were fifteen resident family members plus a servant.

When Agostino died two years later, Giuseppe, his elder son, became household head. Over the next few years both of Giuseppe's daughters married (at ages 24 and 33) and moved away, leaving just his son. Angelo's elder son, Paolo (23), married in 1886, bringing his bride into the household. When Angelo died two years later, he left his wife, six children, a daughter-in-law, and two grandchildren in the household, together with his mother, his brother, and his brother's family.

In 1889, Paolo's eldest sister (age 24) married another Bertalia sharecropper and moved into his household. The following year, three members of the household died—Giuseppe's wife (68), and Paolo's wife (27) and second child (2). At this point three simple family nuclei coresided: that of Giuseppe, that of Angelo's widow, and that of Angelo's son Paolo. In addition, Giuseppe's stepmother was still living with them.

In the following years the household grew further through marriages of the sons of Giuseppe and Angelo and through the children born to them. Paolo, meanwhile, remarried a widow the year after his first wife died, and he had more children. By 1897, nine children had been born of these new marriages, while the last female of the third generation, Angelo's twenty-two-year-old daughter, married and left the household.

Although Giuseppe, as the male of the senior generation, remained household head in this period, his position was undermined by the four sons his now deceased brother Angelo had produced. Giuseppe had just one son, Raffaele; all four of Angelo's sons were in the household and two of them were already married. Apparently as a result, in 1898 Giuseppe's branch of the family moved out to the neighboring agricultural area of Arcoveggio, leaving the farm under the tutelage of Angelo's elder son, Paolo. Remaining on the farm, then, were Angelo's stepmother, his widow, his two married sons and their wives and children, and his two unmarried sons.

Over the next half dozen years the Coltelli household was enlarged by the marriage of the remaining two brothers, who brought their wives to join them. With the marriage of the last brother in 1904, four married brothers coresided with their wives, children, and widowed mother. But this arrangement, too, was transient, for five years after the death of his wife (at age forty) in 1903, the second brother, Ferdinando, remarried the widow of a Bertalia *bracciante* and moved with her and his four children to neighboring Castelmaggiore.

In 1910, then, there remained three married brothers, their wives, the ten surviving children, and their mother. The younger generation was beginning to come of age as Paolo's eldest child, a twenty-three-year-old daughter, married and moved away.

Sharecropper Case 3: Nerozzi

Our final example of a sharecropping family that remained in Bertalia throughout the 1880–1910 period is the Nerozzi family. Unlike our first two cases, the Nerozzi family changed residence in both 1890 and 1905, living on three successive Bertalia farms. They had come to the parish in the 1870s, moving from a farm fifteen kilometers away. Shortly after their arrival, the family patriarch died, leaving his widow and two married sons, Alfonso and Adolfo (ages 45 and 40), with their wives and children. Alfonso, the elder, was the household head. In 1887 they were joined by the 26-year-old blind daughter of Alfonso's deceased sister. This woman, whose father was also dead, remained with her mother's brother's household through 1910.

In the 1890s a series of important household changes took place. Alfonso's mother died in 1894, and Adolfo's eldest son married the following year, bringing his wife into the household. At this point Alfonso, the titular household head and elder, found himself outnumbered by the family of his brother. Alfonso's only son had died of cholera in 1886, whereas Adolfo had two sons, one of whom had already married. Thus, Alfonso and his wife left the household and took up work as *braccianti* elsewhere in the parish.

Over the years 1896–1905 Adolfo's three daughters married and moved out of the household. By 1910 Adolfo's younger son (age 32) still had not married. The household consisted of Adolfo (70), his wife, his married son and his wife and three children, and his unmarried son, along with Adolfo's blind niece. As throughout the period, a servant lived with them.

By selecting only the sharecropper families that remained in Bertalia throughout the decades under study, the previous sketches may give a misleading picture of what family life and household experience were like for the sharecroppers in this time of geographical and occupational mobility. As we have seen in chapter 5, there was considerable turnover of sharecropper families in these years. To capture some of this flux, and hence to complement our sketches of the more stable sharecropper households, three sharecropper *residences* were followed for the 1880–1910 period, that is, farms having a succession of families move in and out.

Sharecropper Residence 1

Six different households successively occupied the sharecropper residence in which the family of Raffaele Fiorini was living in 1880. This demographic flux was matched by occupational shifts as well, as the relationship between the household and the landowner changed over time. Although families 1, 3, and 6 were listed as sharecroppers, family 4 was headed by an *affituario* (farm renter), and families 2 and 5 were identified as *boari*, animal caretakers, who were paid an annual salary.

Raffaele Fiorini (age 55) arrived in 1878 from a rural area twenty kilometers to the north with his wife and daughter. But Raffaele remained on the farm for just three years, presumably losing his contract, for when he moved he became a *bracciante* and left Bertalia. At the same time, his daughter (age 15) became a servant, a position she held until her marriage eight years later.

There then entered the family of Michele Rubini, a *boaro*, who came to Bertalia from Longara, just four kilometers to the north. Michele (age 57) brought with him his wife, his unmarried son (25), and his unmarried daughter (19). When, four years later, the son married a woman from Longara, where he had been born, he brought her into the household. In 1888, Michele's daughter married and moved out of the household. Three years later the Rubini family—composed of Michele, his wife, his son, and his son's wife and two-year-old daughter—left Bertalia and moved into a neighboring agricultural area.

The Rubinis were replaced in 1892 by Giovanni Cesari (age 39), a bachelor, his married brother (37), with wife and child, and his two unmarried sisters. They came to Bertalia from Borgo Panigale, which borders Bertalia on the west, to which they returned in 1900. The only change in their household composition that occurred in these eight years was the birth of a second child to Giovanni's younger brother.

Following them was the bachelor Pietro Aldrovandi (age 39), who is listed as a farm renter (*affittuario*). He brought with him his three adult unmarried brothers, who were described as *giornalieri*, day laborers, and his two unmarried sisters (ages 22 and 19). Their widowed mother moved there with them but died the same year. Also living in the house, besides a servant, was the seven-year-old daughter of one of Pietro's brothers. Whether this brother was still alive is not known. In 1904, the elder sister married and left Bertalia, and in 1906, five years after their arrival, the entire family left the parish.

Family 5 then arrived, headed by Aniceto Venturi (age 39), a *boaro* who brought with him his mother, his wife and child, and his younger brother and his wife and children. They had come from a nearby agricultural area. This multiple family remained just two years, after which they moved elsewhere in the city of Bologna, taking assorted jobs—as *braccianti* and *carretieri* (carters)—to survive.

Finally, in 1909, the family of Cesare Guermandi (age 68) entered from Borgo Panigale. With him were his wife, his married son with his wife and child, and an unmarried son (18). They remained just three years before emigrating to Saragozza, another agricultural zone of the periphery of the city of Bologna.

Coresidence in Life Course Perspective

Sharecropper Residence 2

In the second sharecropper residence followed for these three decades, five families were successively resident, though the fifth remained there from 1893 until the end of observation in 1910. All are described as sharecroppers.

From 1874 to 1880, the family of Filippo Montanari lived on the farm. They had previously lived in Bertalia from 1866 to 1869 but in the intervening five years had lived in another rural part of the province. The Montanari family, at the time of their departure in 1880, consisted of (in addition to two servants) the widowed Filippo (age 76) and the families of his two married sons: Raffaele (age 32), Giuseppe (age 36), their wives, and Raffaele's two small children.

Geremia Tarozzi (age 52) then moved in with his wife, two sons (ages 25 and 15), and four daughters (ages 20, 18, 14, and 12) from a farm a dozen kilometers to the east. When, in 1882, Geremia's younger son married, he brought his bride into the household. Within four years of their arrival, though, the entire family migrated to Malalbergo, thirty kilometers north of Bertalia.

The Tarozzis were immediately replaced by the family of Angelo Marchesini (age 51), who came from nearby Castelmaggiore. With Angelo were his wife, his three unmarried sons (24, 23, and 19), and his married eldest son (26) with his wife and child. When Angelo's second son married three years later, he brought his wife into the household. But the following year, in 1889, the family of twelve, consisting of three married couples and four grandchildren, left the parish.

The fourth family to take up residence was that of Vincenzo Badini, moving from a farm eight kilometers to the north of Bertalia. Vincenzo, a sixty-nine-year-old widower, was accompanied by his married son (age 45), and his son's wife and their seven children (ages ranging from 5 to 23). Vincenzo died the year after their arrival, and the remaining conjugal family headed by his son remained just two more years, emigrating to Castelmaggiore in 1892.

The fifth and final family, that of Paolo Bonfiglioli, came from Zola Predosa, just a few kilometers to the west of Bertalia. With Paolo (age 66) were his wife, his spinster sister (47), his son Cesare (39), Cesare's wife and their four children: three daughters (12, 10, and 8) and one son (6). Paolo's wife died in 1895, just two years after their arrival, and Paolo remained a widower until his own death thirteen years later. In

1907, Cesare's eldest daughter (age 26) married and left the house. When last under observation, in 1910, the household consisted of Cesare, his wife, their two unmarried daugthers, and their unmarried son.

Sharecropper Residence 3

The final sharecropper residence followed showed greater stability than the previous two examples. Just two successive households were residents over the thirty-year period, and these were kin related.

Since 1877 Gaetano Turini (age 41) and his wife lived on the farm with their eight children. By 1880 two more children had been born, giving them three daughters and seven sons. Another boy, the eight-year-old son of Gaetano's deceased brother, lived with them. Interestingly, this boy was the child of the marriage of Gaetano's brother to Gaetano's wife's sister. In other words, Gaetano and his brother married two sisters. This boy left the household in 1887. Whether his mother was alive is unclear.

The second and third eldest daughters married in 1886 and 1894, leaving the household. The following year, in 1895, the eldest son (age 30) married and brought his wife into the household. When, the following year, the third son (27) married, he left the household to become a sharecropper on another Bertalia farm. The year after that, in 1897, the second son (30) married and brought his wife into the household.

In 1889, when the Turini family left Bertalia for a farm elsewhere in the periphery of Bologna, there were thirteen family members plus a servant. Gaetano, the sixty-five-year-old household head, lived with his wife, two married sons and their wives and children, one unmarried daughter (38), and four unmarried sons (28, 24, 21, and 20).

Replacing them on the farm was the family of Gaetano's eldest married daughter, Virginia, who had left her parents' household thirteen years earlier at her marriage, moving to San Paolo di Ravone, her own birthplace, with the family of her new husband, Giovanni Zocca (45), which contained ten family members plus two servants. In addition to Giovanni, Virginia (38), and their two small children, were Giovanni's unmarried sister (32), his married younger brother Enrico (40), and Enrico's wife and three children. Over the next decade just two changes took place, as Giovanni's brother had a fourth child, and Giovanni's sister, still unmarried at age 38, left the household. Thus, in 1910, the

Zocca household consisted of two married brothers, and their wives and children.

What do these individual household portraits tell us of coresidential processes through time in Bertalia? Examined in conjunction with the cross-sectional and panel data already examined, they reveal a pattern of coresidential flux, a flux that is the product of a number of interacting demographic, economic, and social principles.

Following the sharecropper households through time clearly shows the force of the rule of patrilocal postmarital residence. In our total sample of sharecropper households followed through time, there were 25 males and 26 females who were married for the first time while under observation. Of the 25 men, 22 brought their brides to live in their premarital household. Of the 26 women who married, every one departed from the parental home at marriage. Of the 22 men who brought their brides into their homes, 18 remained with their brides in that household throughout the entire period of observation; 4 remained in the household for a period of two to five years before leaving with their wives (and children).

The sample of *braccianti* households followed through time yields only 5 males marrying for the first time and 10 females. Even with such a limited sample, however, the data are suggestive. Of the 10 women marrying, just 1 remained in her parental household at marriage with her new husband, and they remained there for just one year before moving out. Of the 5 men marrying for the first time, 3 brought their wives into their premarital households; 1 of these left with his wife within a year, 1 only after twenty years.

More subjectively, in following the various sharecropper households through time one is struck by the number of individuals whose life course proceeds neither according to the ideal nor to the statistical norm. We find young children, for example, who do not live with their own parents but in the households of one of their uncles or aunts; in many of these cases the child's own parents are dead and there appears to be a moral obligation for the sibling of a deceased parent to take in the young niece or nephew. Also striking as a deviation from the normative view of the life course is the sizeable number of life-long bachelors and spinsters. These individuals are apt to remain in the household of their parents, coresiding with the remaining married sibling(s) after the parents' deaths. This phenomenon among the sharecroppers raises the obvious, yet important question of disincentives to marriage. Should a woman living in her parents' sharecropping household not find a match with another sharecropper, might she (or her family) prefer that she remain unmarried and aid in the parental (or fraternal) household rather than marry "down" to a *bracciante*? In the case of the bachelor, are there conditions (e.g., limited size of the farm or large number of already married brothers) that may force a man to leave his parental or fraternal sharecropping household if he marries? These questions require further study.

Another node of potential tension that has an important influence on the coresidential processes of sharecroppers is the relationship between married brothers. As in any agricultural society in which access to land is passed on from father to son, problems are created when more than one son survives and marries. Although two sons, in such a situation, may find it possible to coreside with their families after the death of the patriarch, when their own sons begin to marry the situation becomes untenable. Other farms must be found for some of the sons or the sharecroppers face downward mobility and economic hardship for their own children. When there is not sufficient access to additional sharecropping farms, or where remaining on the already occupied farm is seen as particularly desirable, tension within the household can become acute.

The actual nature of such struggles can only be partially ascertained through longitudinal data on coresidence. It does seem that where two married brothers coreside after the death of their father, and one brother has sons and the other does not, the position of the latter is weakened, sometimes to the point of being forced to leave the farm. Where both brothers have children, the brother having more sons has an advantage over the other and, by extension, the sons of the former have an advantage over the sons of the latter. In this model, then, should one brother have just one son and the other have three, and all marry and bring their wives into the household, there is a tendency for the single son of the first brother to be forced out.

A corollary of this is the greater importance of sons than daughters in sharecropper households. Sons represent the hope of the future for sharecroppers, and the sharecropper without any sons is in a vulnerable position. Daughters, on the other hand, are of less value, for they are expected to leave the household at marriage. Doubtlessly, through the marriage of daughters to other sharecroppers various mutual benefits accrue to the kin-linked households, but the importance of these links could hardly match the importance of having sons who, with their wives and children, permanently add to the adult labor pool of the household.

A final point concerns remarriage. Upon death of a spouse, men are much more likely than women to marry again. In 1880, for example, of men under age sixty-one who had lost their first spouse, 61 percent (30 of 49) had remarried compared to 32 percent (14 of 44) of widowed women of the same age. Overall, 45 percent of men who had lost their first wife had remarried, whereas only 22 percent of the widowed women had remarried. Thus, for a woman, the loss of a husband typically meant spending the rest of her life as a widow, generally living with one or more of her children. Men, particularly those under age sixty, were more free to choose remarriage. Indeed, judging from cases such as we have seen in which a man remarries within a few months of the death of his wife, some men found life without a wife very difficult. Although we cannot prove it, we would expect that this would be more true of *braccianti* than sharecroppers, for the *bracciante*, living more commonly in a simple family household, was in a more vulnerable position with the loss of his wife. The economic and, perhaps, also the social loss suffered through the death of a wife in a complex family household could be partially offset by the labor of the other women in the household and by the future addition of young wives brought in by one's sons. A man living alone with his wife, or with his wife and unmarried children, faced a more uncertain future.

7

Kinsmen beyond the Household

Although our primary focus in this book has been on the nature of coresidential groups and on the economic processes affecting coresidence, an exclusive focus on coresidence obscures the full role of kinship in social organization. People's everyday experiences are strongly influenced by the nature of the people with whom they reside. However, people do not need to coreside with kinsmen in order to have important social ties with them. Our examination of the coresidential patterns of kinsmen, then, provides only one element of an understanding of the nature and importance of kinship relations in this part of Italy. Or, to use Michael Anderson's expression, "Kinship does not stop at the front door" (1971: 56).

Anthropologists have long been interested in examining patterns of kinship relations in different societies, and studies of domestic groups are usually placed in a broad kinship framework (cf. Goody 1972). Historians and other scholars have increasingly recognized the importance of this broader perspective in dealing with the social life and coresidential characteristics of European peoples of the past. Indeed, some have lashed out at what they see as a one-sided preoccupation with household composition. Anderson, for example, argues that "it is totally inadequate to confine one's attention simply to the study of patterns of residence" (1972a: 50). As he notes, "There are few functions which can be performed by a coresiding kinsman which he cannot perform equally well if he instead lives next door, or even up the street" (1971: 56–57). Similar exhortations have been expressed by other scholars (Wheaton 1975: 601, 608; Plakans 1977; Anderson 1978: 4; Hareven 1978: 152; Hareven and Vinovskis 1978: 17–18; B. Laslett 1978: 478; Yanagisako 1979: 178). Although these calls have often been critical of Peter Laslett's approach, Laslett has recently stressed the importance of learning more about kin ties beyond the household in order to understand the historical social organization of Europe. He laments the fact that English population listings are such poor sources for the extraction of such information (1977a: 93).

Yet despite the growing chorus of calls for research into extrahousehold kinship ties in European historical study, few empirical studies of this kind have been conducted. The reasons for this are not difficult to find. Compared to the wealth of data found in various sorts of population enumerations and other documents detailing the characteristics of households, there are few simple sources of information on kin links between households. Once the problem of tracing kin ties beyond the immediate locality is raised, the research task becomes formidable indeed.

In this chapter we make a first attempt at tracing kinship links by determining what kin ties were found among the people of Bertalia. In doing this, our sources permit us only to trace out the kin relations. Hence, though we may state that, for example, a man's two married brothers live in other households in the parish, we are not in a position to state whether he had anything to do with them. In the case of distantly related kinsmen, as for example that of households linked by an affine of an affine (e.g. the brother-in-law of one's sister-in-law), we cannot even definitely say whether the people themselves recognized any bond of kinship between them. What we can do is show the extent to which people had kinsmen living in the same parish, characterize the nature of these kin links, and relate them to a series of factors such as age, migration characteristics, and occupation. What we present here, then, represents but one step toward the development of urgently needed historical research into kin ties beyond the household.

We are able to trace kin ties among the households of Bertalia by linking the names of people in each census, correlated with the names of their parents (provided for each individual). The fact that all women are identified by their maiden names greatly facilitated this effort. The linking was done by a combination of electronic and manual procedures.

An alphabetized list providing for the separate listing of an individual's name every time he or she appears as either a member of a household or as a father or a mother of an individual in the census was programmed by computer. Hence individuals could appear several times in the same year's alphabetized list, once for their own personal entry, and once as part of the entry of every child they had living in the parish. Each such listing provided an indication of the kind of entry involved (as the censused individual or as a parent) and the identification number of the individual whose entry was being listed. Hence Luigi Albertini might be listed five times, once giving his own entry in the census, and once for each of his four children. Two of these children might have the same household number as he, indicating coresidence, and two others might have household numbers indicating two other separate households. From this entry, after appropriate checking (to determine whether all entries for Luigi Albertini referred to the same person), three households could be linked. Following this procedure, we were ultimately in a position to draw kinship diagrams representing all households having at least one kin link to another Bertalia household. Hence, for each of the four parish censuses, we ended up with a series of diagrams representing clusters of from two to twenty-one kin-linked households.

The next step was to indicate, for each household having at least one kin tie with another Bertalia household, the number of other households to which kin links could be traced and, for each, the nature of its kin relationship with the household in question. A computer file was then created for each household head in which the following information was entered: total number of kin-linked households; the identification number of each household to which it is linked; for each of these, a three-digit code indicating the nature of the kin tie between the two households. In characterizing the kin link between two households, the closest kin relation was used, using the household head as point of orientation when his or her link with the other household was as direct as that of any other member of his household. In addition, for purposes of simplicity, in cases where one household is linked to another by a number of kinsmen, all from the nuclear family, an order of priority was established: father, mother, brother, sister. Thus, the fact that one household head is linked to another household by the residence of his or her father in that other household does not preclude the residence in the second household of his or her mother, brother, or sister.

Kinsmen beyond the Household

Kinds of Kin Links between Households

In each of the four years examined, just over 40 percent of all households had a kinsman living in at least one other household of the parish. This proportion crept up slightly (from 40 percent in 1880 to 43 percent in 1910) throughout this period as the population size of the parish increased substantially. As already mentioned, clusters of related kinsmen ranged from two to twenty-one households, but the great majority of households with any kin links had such links to no more than four other households. Thus, in 1880, 34 percent of all households having any kin links had just one, and an additional 43 percent had two to four kin-linked households. A similar pattern was found throughout the period. Moreover, where kin links were traced among many households, no one household was linked to more than four others by direct kin ties (i.e., father, mother, brother, sister, son, daughter). It is in the large clusters that the networks of affines of affines become prominent.

If we take as our point of orientation the male household heads (excluding for the moment cases where women were household heads), we can begin to portray the constellation of kinsmen surrounding the people of Bertalia. Sibling ties dominate this category (see table 7.1). In each of the four years under study, a male household head is more likely to have a sibling living in another parish household than he is to have a child in another household, and he is more likely to have a child than a parent living in one of the other households of Bertalia.

This pattern is explicable largely in terms of life course variables, for many household heads are of an age at which their parents are already deceased, and others have yet to reach the age at which their own children had moved out of the parental home. Note that the larger number of father links than links traced through mothers is a product of our method of simplification of ties between households, so that a household containing both a man's father and his mother is coded as an example of a tie with the household head's father. The slightly greater number of ties with brothers than with sisters in each of the four years might also be accounted for in these terms. However, one clear difference is found between frequency of links with other households through the household head's sons and his daughters. In each of the years such links are much more frequently found through daughters than through sons. This can be explained largely through the patrilocal residence patterns, for though

Table 7.1. *Nature and Frequency of Kin Links between Bertalia Households*

Kin relationship	1880 N	1880 %	1890 N	1890 %	1900 N	1900 %	1910 N	1910 %
Kin of male household head								
Father	9	1.6	9	1.5	15	2.4	25	2.1
Mother	5	0.9	3	0.5	7	1.1	5	0.4
Brother	43	7.5	48	7.2	64	10.4	64	5.3
Sister	34	5.9	46	7.7	53	8.6	56	4.7
Son	10	1.7	9	1.5	15	2.4	26	2.2
Daughter	23	4.0	26	4.3	33	5.3	52	4.3
Affines of offspring and siblings	145	25.2	142	23.7	144	23.3	396	33.0
Kin of wife of household head or female household head								
Father	15	2.6	18	3.0	27	4.4	30	2.5
Mother	13	2.3	6	1.0	5	0.8	25	2.1
Brother	23	4.0	33	5.5	35	5.7	32	2.7
Sister	22	3.8	38	6.3	34	5.5	50	4.2
Affines of brother, sister	114	19.8	65	10.8	77	12.5	130	10.8
Kin of household head's coresident daughter-in-law	16	2.8	34	5.6	26	4.2	133	11.1
Other kin links	103	17.9	123	20.5	82	13.3	176	14.7
Total	575	100.0	600	100.0	617	100.0	1,200	100.0

many sons take their brides into their parental home at marriage and thus do not add to the extrahousehold kin network of their parental household directly, women leave home at marriage, and quite a few remain in the parish, bolstering the local network of kin-related households.

Turning to households that are linked through the wife of the household head or through a female household head, we find, in comparison to links through the male household heads, more ties with parents living in other households and fewer ties with siblings. The fact that there should be relatively more ties with parents living in other households is again to be expected given patrilocality, for fewer women would have their parents coresiding in their households with them. As for the greater frequency of siblings of the male household head than siblings of his wife living in other households of the parish, this, too, is related to patrilocality. Given the tendency for women to move to the parish of their husband's parental family, we would expect more dispersion of the sib-

Table 7.2. *Nature and Frequency of Indirect Affinal Kin Ties Linking together Bertalia Households*

	Households having at least one kin link of indicated kind							
	1880		1890		1900		1910	
Kin relationship	N	%	N	%	N	%	N	%
Kin of male household head								
Brother's direct affines	11	3.2	17	4.0	18	3.6	21	3.5
Brother's indirect affines	8	2.3	6	1.4	8	1.6	22	3.7
Sister's direct affines	11	3.2	9	2.1	12	2.4	13	2.2
Sister's indirect affines	8	2.3	12	2.8	10	2.0	9	1.5
Son's direct affines	5	1.4	2	0.5	9	1.8	12	2.0
Son's indirect affines	3	0.9	1	0.2	4	0.8	4	0.7
Daughter's direct affines	9	2.6	10	2.3	13	2.6	21	3.5
Daughter's indirect affines	4	1.2	2	0.5	7	1.4	18	3.0
Kin of wife of household head or female household head								
Brother's direct affines	12	3.5	12	2.8	10	2.0	17	2.8
Brother's indirect affines	5	1.4	4	0.9	6	1.2	12	2.0
Sister's direct affines	9	2.6	12	2.8	15	3.0	9	1.5
Sister's indirect affines	6	1.7	6	1.4	7	1.4	8	1.3
Total number of households in parish	347	100.0	430	100.0	502	100.0	601	100.0

lings of the wife than the siblings of the husband. Although a man's sisters also tend to move into or near the parental household of their husband, the residential dispersion of their marital partners would tend to be centered near their own home. A woman would be less likely to live at the geographical center of the cluster of her siblings' residences.

There are three primary categories of kin links among households in addition to those discussed above: affinal relations of the direct kinsmen of the male household head; affinal relations of the direct kinsmen of the wife of the household head (or female household head); and the kinsmen of the coresident daughter-in-law of the household head.

More distant kin ties link households through kin intermediaries (see table 7.2). For example, to take the case of a direct affinal tie traced through the household head's brother, we find a household related by the fact that one of the parents or siblings of the household head's brother's wife lives there. To make this more concrete, we can visualize the situation of three households, that of Luigi, that of his brother Paolo, and that of Paolo's father-in-law Giuseppe. Giuseppe represents a direct affinal tie to Luigi's brother, and hence the household of Luigi and that of

Giuseppe have a kin tie. More distant, but still traceable and potentially of social significance is an indirect affinal tie through the brother of a household head (the second-listed category in table 7.2). Here let us suppose that Giuseppe's wife's brother, Filippo, lived in a fourth household. We could trace the maze of kinship between the household of Luigi and Filippo. Filippo is considered to be the indirect affinal relation of Luigi's brother Paolo.

Looking briefly at the frequencies of these indirect affinal ties, we find that no single type is very common but that, taken together, a significant proportion of all Bertalia households in each of the four years has such kin-linked households residing in the parish. It must be one of the goals of future historical research to determine just what social significance such distant kinsmen had, if any. Were there particular circumstances in which the idiom of kinship could be used among such people in order to enlist material aid or moral support? Was a person who was enmeshed in a complex kin network, including many indirectly kin-linked households, at some advantage economically, socially, or politically in the parish? These questions are prompted by the discovery of the web of kin ties linking the households of Bertalia but as yet they remain unanswered.

Kin Links and Coresidence

Having argued that both the nature of domestic groups and the nature of extrahousehold kinship ties are important, an obvious next step is to see just what relationship exists between these two aspects of a kinship system. Does the kinship organization of a household have anything to do with the kinds of kin ties the household has with other local households? To our knowledge, this question has never before been addressed empirically in European social history.

Which households have the most kin ties with other local households and how much difference is there among the various household types in these kin links? Multiple family households have such kin links more frequently than simple and extended family households (see table 7.3). As would be expected, people living as solitaries and in no family units are least likely to have kinsmen living elsewhere in the parish. The fact that it was so uncommon for people to live by themselves suggests that only an individual having no living kinsmen was likely to live alone. The

Table 7.3. *Proportion of Households Having Kin Links to Other Bertalia Households, by Household Composition*

Household composition	1880 Percentage having kin links	Total N	1910 Percentage having kin links	Total N
Solitary	14	7	12	17
No family	0	2	0	9
Simple family	39	222	42	381
Extended family	41	56	36	90
Multiple family	50	58	57	101
Unrelated families	50	2	100	1

greater frequency of kin links involving multiple family households is largely a result of the presence of more than one married woman in such households. This provides one more path of kin relatedness to other households than is found in nonmultiple family households.

Having noted the relationships between household composition and extrahousehold kin ties, we can address the question of what relationship exists between the composition of the household and the exact nature of its kin links to other local households (see table 7.4) Note that when a particular household is linked by the same kind of kin tie to more than one other household, it is entered as only one case in the table.

Looking first at the kin ties to other households traced through the male household head, we find that, though relatively few household heads have parents living in another household of the parish, such links are most commonly found among simple family households; they are rarely found in the case of complex family households. Again, this is related to the fact that multiple family households are overwhelmingly extended patrilaterally, and hence an elder man and his son(s) would be expected to be living together. This pattern is also heavily influenced by the greater tendency of multiple family household heads to be old. Thus, few of them have living parents compared to simple family household heads.

Looking at households linked through siblingship with the household head, no clear pattern of differences on the basis of household composition emerges. Almost one-fifth of all households are linked to other households in Bertalia in this way and, though there are changes in this

Table 7.4. *Frequency of Kin Links of Specified Kind, by Household Composition*[a]

	Simple family			
Kin relationship	1880	1890	1900	1910
Kin of male household head				
Father	3	2	5	6
Mother	2	1	1	1
Brother	11	10	13	9
Sister	9	7	11	8
Son	0	1	2	4
Daughter	3	5	5	8
Kin of wife of household head or female household head				
Father	5	5	7	6
Mother	4	2	1	6
Brother	6	8	7	5
Sister	8	8	9	9
Son[b]	1	—	0	1
Daughter[b]	3	2	1	1
Total number of households in parish	222	258	326	380

[a] No household is counted more than once for a particular kin-linked category.

[b] Only children of wives by a previous marriage are counted here.

pattern over time, the frequency distribution of such ties in 1910 is not much different from that of 1880.

Intriguingly, the frequency of kin links through the children of the household head is related to the composition of the household. Multiple family households have much higher proportions of such links to other households than do either simple or extended family households in all four years. The contrast is most dramatic in 1880, when 9 percent of multiple family households had sons of the household head living in another Bertalia household, whereas only 1 of 222 simple family households had a son living in another household of the parish. In that year, 19 percent of the multiple family household heads compared to just 3 percent of the simple family household heads had daughters living in

	Extended family				Multiple family			
	1880	1890	1900	1910	1880	1890	1900	1910
	2	3	—	1	—	—	—	1
	—	—	1	—	—	—	1	—
	7	14	10	8	12	13	9	7
	12	15	5	12	3	9	9	7
	4	4	5	1	7	4	3	9
	7	5	1	3	19	9	14	12
	4	5	5	6	2	—	1	1
	4	1	3	3	2	—	—	—
	4	5	9	7	9	4	1	1
	2	9	4	7	5	3	3	4
	2	—	—	—	—	—	—	—
	—	—	1	2	—	—	—	5
	56	74	77	90	58	79	76	101

other Bertalia households. In general, the extended family households fall near the simple family end of the frequency distribution.

It is also noteworthy that in both the simple family and the multiple family households (the extended family household pattern differs through time in this respect) daughters of the household head are more commonly found in other households than are sons. In the case of the simple family households, it can be argued, this is a result of the fact that families having sons who marry are more likely to have the son bring his bride into the household and thus move out of the simple family category. A family having only married daughters (and not sons) is more likely to remain in the simple family household category. The reason for the predominance of the daughter link in the case of multiple family households is related. Here we would expect that sons who marry remain in the household (indeed, their having remained in the household leads to the multiple family categorization of their household).

Turning briefly to the ties to other households traced through the wife of the household head, we note that in general simple family households have a greater frequency of such ties than do multiple family households. This is to be expected in the case of the woman's parents for the same reasons discussed for the parents of the household head, namely the greater average age of multiple family household heads and their wives compared to that of simple family household heads and spouses. These data also suggest that women living in simple family households are less likely to have married outside their home parish than are women living in multiple family households. However, the relationship between household composition and parish endogamy requires further research before it can be confirmed.

Changes through the Life Course

Given the dearth of empirical studies of the ties of kinship that link households in a community, we know little about the relationship of these ties to life course factors. We should expect that the nature of kin ties linking members of a given household to members of other households in a locality would change through the individual's life course. As a corollary, we should expect that the extent to which any household has kin links with other local households is influenced by life course factors as well. We have already considered the influence of such life course elements on the internal kinship combinations found within households; we now turn to the external kin links to put them in a similar perspective.

As discussed in the Appendix, the household is in many respects ill suited as a unit for longitudinal study. What exist through time are individual people, not households and not household heads. However, in seeking to study the relationship between life course variables and kin links between households, it is convenient and, if the proper cautions are observed, fruitful, to characterize each household by a single life course variable, namely, age of household head. At the same time, it must be remembered that, depending on the composition of the household, the age of its head may have different implications for the nature and existence of kin links with other local households.

Taking the most common case, that of the household headed by a male (almost always married or widowed) of the senior generation, we can consider how the kin links with other households might correlate with his age. In considering the availability of kinsmen to provide such kin links with other households, we will focus on three kin categories: parents, siblings, and children. As should be obvious, the availability of each of these kin types is dependent on the person's age and, moreover, the nature of this relationship between age and availability differs for each of the three categories.

A simplified schematic matrix of this relationship, using relevant demographic parameters from Bertalia, is provided in table 7.5. Taking first the case of the availability of parents living in other local households, we may assume for illustrative purposes an average generational distance of thirty-five years for men and thirty for women, and an average age at death of 60 for people who have lived into their reproductive years. Thus, a household headed by a person from twenty-five to thirty-four years old would have a *relatively* good chance of having a parent of either the household head or, more likely, of his wife (if the household head is male, as is almost always the case in this age range) still alive. The wife of the household head is more likely to have a parent living in another household not only because of her younger average age than her husband but also because of the heavily patrilateral bias of coresidence.

As we pass beyond age thirty-four, the likelihood of a surviving parent of the household head or wife of household head grows increasingly remote, so that by the time that the household head is in his mid-forties, even if he has a wife several years younger than himself, the survival of a parent is unlikely.

In contrast, for a number of years following marriage the probability increases that children of the head live in the household. In the case of Bertalia, children who left the parental home and moved into other local households did so in most cases on the occasion of their marriage. There was a significant number of young adolescent and sometimes preadolescent children who left the parental home to become servants or *garzoni* in the homes of their employers. However, the great majority of these left the parish, finding employment elsewhere. Similarly, some older adolescents and young unmarried adults left the parental home to find employment elsewhere, but, again, these people also generally left the parish.

Table 7.5. *Relationship between Age of Household Head and Frequency of Kinsmen Living in Other Households*

Age	Likelihood of residence in another household of head's		
	Parents	Siblings	Children
25–29	+ +	−	=
30–34	+ +	+	=
35–39	+	+	=
40–44	−	+ +	=
45–49	=	+ +	=
50–54	=	+ +	=
55–59	=	+	−
60–64	=	+	+
65–69	=	−	+ +
70⁺	=	−	+ +

KEY
+ +   maximum likelihood of having kin who are residents in an other household
+   moderate likelihood of having kin who are residents in another household
−   low likelihood of having kin who are residents in another household
=   minimal likelihood of having kin who are residents in another household

Thus the availability of children of a household head or his wife to be living in another household of Bertalia is largely a function of the likelihood of the head being old enough to have married children. As first children in Bertalia during this period were born to fathers in their late twenties and mothers in their mid-twenties, and as first marriage came at about the same time in the life course, we would not expect a household head to have a married child until age fifty-five, with the probability of having one or more married children increasing with time beyond this point. To the extent that sons live with their parents for the first years of their marriage, we would expect the likelihood of having a married child living in another household to be even lower in the first parental years beyond age fifty-five.

The probability of a household head or his wife being linked to another parish household through a sibling (not including siblings still living with their parents, which would constitute links redundant with those between household heads and their parents) is dependent on two factors: probability of having living siblings and probability of their living in households other than that of the household head or his parents. A third factor, that of probability of a sibling living in a different community, will be dealt with in our discussion of migration below.

The greatest likelihood of a household head or his wife having a sibling living in another household (not that of their parents) is in the middle years of adulthood. A very young household head is likely to have a higher proportion of unmarried siblings who are thus not in independent households. An elderly household head is likely to have fewer siblings still alive than a middle-aged household head (assuming for the purposes of this discussion constant fertility and mortality rates pertaining through the life course of all cohorts).

With these considerations behind us, we can now turn to the actual experience of the people of Bertalia in the 1880–1910 period. By plotting the frequency of households having *no* kin ties with other Bertalia households as a function of age of household head (see figure 7.1), we can readily see that each of the years shows a somewhat different relationship between the variables; there is no clear historical movement from one kind of relationship to another. However, we can identify a common general movement through the life course (as shown by our synthetic cohorts each based on cross-sectional data).[1]

The lowest frequency of households having kin ties with other Bertalia households is found among those with middle-age heads (particularly ages 50 to 54), while the highest frequency of households having kin ties is found among those having heads age 30–39 and 60–64. Examination of the graph shows that this relationship corresponds generally with that predicted by our schematic matrix.

Our concern here is to stimulate more thinking and research on the relationship between life course factors and kin ties linking households rather than to reach any substantive conclusions based on such limited data. In this spirit, it is worth pondering just how this relationship might change through time as a result of changing historical forces. There are four especially important factors of interest here: fertility, mortality, migration, and household composition. A change in any one of them may produce a change in the relationship between age and extrahousehold kin ties.

Changes in fertility and mortality through time influence the relative proportion of siblings to children. To illustrate this, let us hold mortality constant and lower fertility by 50 percent over the period of a generation. In such a situation, through time there would be a tendency for siblings

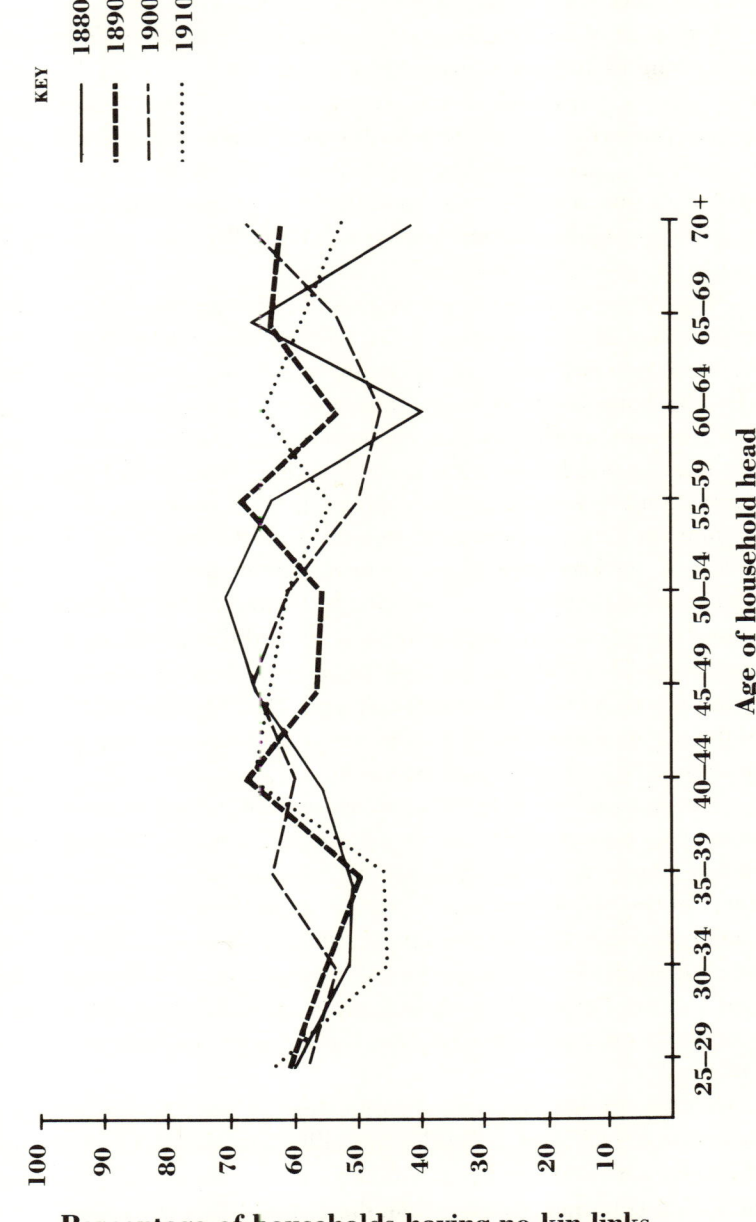

Figure 7.1. *Percentage of Households Having No Kin Links to Other Bertalia Households, by Age of Household Head—1880, 1890, 1900, 1910*

to become relatively more numerous bases for interhousehold ties than links between parents and their married children, until the point was reached where the household heads themselves were products of the era of lowered fertility. If, on the other hand, fertility remained constant but life expectancy for adults were significantly raised, the cohorts benefitting from increased longevity would enjoy a higher proportion of siblings living in other households than would earlier cohorts, altering the relative proportion of siblings to married children as sources of kin ties with other households.

Changes in migration flows may have an even more dramatic effect, for one cohort may experience no migration, another cohort 100 percent migration. Where different cohorts have different migration experiences as a result of changing historical circumstances, the relative weight of the presence of parents, married siblings, and married children in the community may be greatly altered. Where, for example, changing economic circumstances result in a high degree of emigration of the young population, siblings become relatively more frequent bases of interhousehold kin ties than married children.

Finally, even with no changes in fertility, mortality, or migration, life course effects on the nature and frequency of interhousehold kin ties can result from changes in processes of coresidence. For example, a shift from patrilocality to neolocality, that is, from the newlyweds moving in with the groom's family to the formation of an independent household for the newlyweds, would result in a higher proportion of married children living in other households for older household heads, compared to earlier cohorts.

The study of the ways in which kin ties outside of the household change through the individual's life course has scarcely begun. Given the frequency with which scholars have cited the social, economic, and psychological importance of kinsmen beyond the household, and given the potential impact of life course variables on the availability of such kin ties, we hope our observations here help to clear the conceptual groundwork and encourage other, more ambitious studies.

Occupation and Kin Ties

In examining the pattern of kin relationship among households, we are interested in the nature of people's employment. We would first like to

Table 7.6. *Kin Ties with Other Bertalia Households, by Occupation of Household Head, 1880 and 1910*

Occupation of household head	Percentage of households having indicated number of kin ties						Number of household heads	
	0		1		2 or more			
	1880	1910	1880	1910	1880	1910	1880	1910
Bracciante	57	47	17	17	26	36	136	141
Sharecropper	52	54	10	5	38	41	42	39
Boaro	72	75	6	12	22	13	18	24
Other agricultural	71	50	—	—	29	50	7	2
Railroad	54	71	15	9	31	20	26	66
Factory	50	56	—	19	50	25	2	52
Service	31	74	23	13	46	13	13	23
Artisan	64	49	11	27	25	24	28	41
Construction	64	55	7	16	29	29	14	56
Merchant	100	48	—	12	—	40	8	33
Elite	69	76	31	8	—	16	13	25
Housewife	72	58	11	13	17	29	18	69
Other	64	77	14	17	22	6	22	30
Total	60	58	14	15	26	27	347	601

know whether people in certain occupations tended to be enmeshed in more locally centered networks of kinsmen than people in other occupations. This obviously relates to the link between occupation and geographical stability. Presumably people in those occupations that foster the least mobility would find themselves surrounded by more kinsmen in the locality than people having occupations involving greater geographical mobility.

A second aspect of the link between occupation and kin ties beyond the household concerns occupational homogeneity of kinsmen. To what extent do congeries of kinsmen share the same occupation? Here we have a question of major importance in social history, for it reflects two crucial processes: intergenerational transmission of occupation (i.e. the extent to which sons enter the same occupation as their father), and occupational endogamy in marriage (people choosing their spouses from families having the same occupational characteristics as their own).

In order to see what relationship exists between occupation of a household head and the frequency of kin ties with other Bertalia households, we look first at the data from 1880 (see table 7.6): among the major occupational groupings sharecropper households had the greatest frequency of kin ties with other parish households, with almost half of the sharecropper households having direct kin ties to another Bertalia household and 38 percent tied to two or more households. The predominance of the sharecroppers in this regard is hardly surprising, given their relatively greater geographical stability than people in other occupations at the time. What is surprising, from this point of view, is the fact that the households headed by artisans had a lower frequency of kin ties with other Bertalia households than did the parish population as a whole. This is surprising insofar as the artisans, along with the sharecroppers, were among the most geographically stable of the parish population. The *braccianti*, more migratory than the parish mean, exhibited a slightly greater frequency of kin ties with other parish households than did the population as a whole in 1880. Similarly, the relatively transient railroad workers were more likely to have kin ties with other parish households than was the Bertalia population as a whole.

But before we try to make sense of this pattern, let us pause to contrast the 1880 results with those of thirty years later. For the sharecroppers, the 1910 situation was almost identical to that of 1880, but in the case of the *braccianti* people were significantly more likely to be tied by kinship bonds to another Bertalia household than they were thirty years before. Indeed, in 1910, 36 percent of the *braccianti* households were linked to two or more other local households by direct kinship ties.

When we turn from the agricultural to the urban sector, we see that the railroad workers of 1910 were much less likely to have kinsmen living in the parish than were the railroad workers of 1880. The other two categories of urban workers that had grown so dramatically with the urbanization of Bertalia—the factory and construction workers—show patterns of kin ties with other local households very much near the parishwide norm. The merchants, another category that grew rapidly with urbanization, showed more frequent links with kinsmen in other Bertalia households than was true of the parish as a whole, with 40 percent of merchant-headed households having kin links with two or more other Bertalia households. Members of the elite, the most highly transient occupational category of Bertalia residents, fulfilled expectations in showing considerably fewer kin ties with local households than was true of the parish as a whole.

What does this all add up to? It is striking, first of all, that despite the great economic and, hence, occupational shifts that took place in this thirty-year period, so little overall change in the frequency of kin ties

Table 7.7. *Occupational Characteristics of the Household Heads of Kin-Linked Households, 1880*

Occupation of household head	Percentage of kin ties to other households in which household head has occupation indicated			
	Bracciante	*Sharecropper*	Boaro	*Railroad*
Bracciante	41	17	3	9
Sharecropper	43	29	11	3
Boaro	33	44	—	—
Railroad	44	6	—	11
Construction	36	—	—	9
Artisan	38	—	—	14
Service	21	7	—	7
Housewife	43	29	—	—
Percentage of all Bertalia household heads having occupation indicated	39	12	5	7

among local households occurred. Yet this is less surprising in light of our discovery that population flux was not a product of late nineteenth century urbanization, that high rates of geographical transiency had characterized the agricultural population of the nineteenth century as well. The expectation that rural communities have a high frequency of kin-linked households is clearly tied to the image of such rural communities as composed of geographically stable populations. The expectation that an urban locality having the same population size as a rural community would have fewer kin ties among its households is based on the assumption that population turnover would be significantly higher in the urban context.

Comparing the various occupations in Bertalia, what is perhaps most striking is how little difference there is between household heads employed in the rural sector and those employed in the urban sector in terms of the frequency of their kin ties to other local households. We clearly do not find the dichotomy of a rural population bound together by ties of kinship and an urban population living in a kin-free environment in the social organization of Bertalia. It is also worth highlighting the

Construction	Artisan	Service	Housewife	Other	Total N
5	9	3	3	10	86
—	—	3	6	6	35
—	—	—	—	22	9
6	17	6	—	11	18
18	18	—	9	9	11
10	24	14	—	—	21
—	21	29	7	7	14
14	—	14	—	—	7
4	8	4	5	12	347

impressive proportion of *braccianti* in 1910 who had kinsmen living in other households. In fact, of all the occupational categories, the *braccianti* had the highest proportion having such kin links. This is made more dramatic by the fact that the *braccianti* in 1910 were among the most migratory of the parish population. These data raise the question of whether a more migratory population may make up for the lack of kin ties with other local households based on generational processes and marital endogamy by showing a strong preference for moving into localities where they already have resident kinsmen.

Did the households that were kin linked share common occupational characteristics? Did *braccianti* tend to be linked to other *braccianti* by kinship ties and sharecroppers to sharecroppers? Did people with jobs in the more urban sector tend to be linked to others having urban employment? An attempt to address this issue was made by examining the direct kin links between households in Bertalia. For each household, characterized by the occupation of the household head, we looked at the households in which one of the household residents had a primary kinsman (i.e. father, mother, brother, sister, son, daughter). Each such

Table 7.8. *Occupational Characteristics of the Household Heads of Kin-Linked Households, 1910*

Occupation of household head	Percentage of kin ties to other households in which household head has occupation indicated				
	Bracciante	Sharecropper	Railroad	Factory	Service
Bracciante	32	9	8	9	2
Sharecropper	26	33	—	2	2
Railroad	31	—	12	6	3
Factory	27	2	5	29	—
Service	25	8	8	—	—
Artisan	19	6	6	6	3
Construction	17	11	15	11	4
Merchant	21	—			9
Housewife	37	10			
Percentage of all Bertalia household heads having occupation indicated	23	6	11	9	4

household was itself characterized by the occupation of its head. This enables us to provide, for all households headed by *braccianti*, for example, the proportion of all direct kin links that were with households headed by *braccianti*, by sharecroppers, by railroad workers, and so on.[2]

Tables 7.7 and 7.8 present these data in matrix form. The manner of presentation of the data can be illustrated by looking at table 7.7. If we glance at the top row, labeled *bracciante*, we discover that 41 percent of all ties between *bracciante*-headed households and other households were with households headed by *braccianti*. Seventeen percent of all households with kin ties to *bracciante*-headed households were headed by sharecroppers, and so on. In all, as we see in the last column, there were eighty-six kin ties linking *bracciante*-headed households to other households in 1880. At the bottom of the table, data are provided on the proportion of all households in Bertalia in 1880 that were headed by *braccianti*, by sharecroppers, and so on. These data are given in order to provide a measure of the extent to which chance alone would account for

Artisan	Construction	Merchant	Housewife	Other	Total N
6	6	6	17	17	126
5	12	—	14	7	43
6	22	3	9	6	32
5	12	7	7	5	41
8	17	25	8	—	12
19	8	14	17	3	36
6	9	6	13	9	47
15	9	18	12	6	34
10	10	7	7	7	59
7	9	5	11	13	(601)

the occupational pattern of kin links among households. For example, to judge whether the fact that 29 percent of the sharecropper household kin ties are with other sharecropper-headed households represents a preference for occupational endogamy, we need to know the proportion of sharecropper-headed households in the parish. Knowing that the proportion is 12 percent, we conclude that there was a tendency for sharecroppers to have ties with other sharecropper-headed households.

These kin-linked occupational matrices show that kinsmen living in different households of the parish did exhibit some tendency to have the same occupation. Individuals having certain occupations were especially likely to have kinsmen with the same occupation heading other local households. However, for no occupational category of heads were as many as half of their kin-linked households headed by an individual falling in that same occupational category. In short, kinship ties linking households commonly bound together individuals employed in different occupations.

This occupational heterogeneity of kinsmen is perhaps most strikingly illustrated by the case of the *braccianti*. In 1880, of the eighty-six kin ties linking *bracciante*-headed households to other Bertalia households, just 41 percent involved pairs of households both headed by *braccianti*, virtually identical to the proportion that would be expected if there was no tendency toward occupational homogeneity of kin (since 39 percent of all parish households were headed by *braccianti*). Ties between these households and households headed by people employed in the various other occupations were found in roughly the same proportion as these other occupations were represented in the population.

For the other occupations, the tendency toward kin links with households headed by individuals having the same occupation is evident, though not predominant. In both 1880 and 1910 about a third of households linked to sharecropper-headed households were themselves headed by sharecroppers, a higher proportion than would be expected if there were a random distribution of kin links by occupation. In the more urban sector of employment, the railroad workers showed little tendency to have occupationally homogeneous webs of kinship, and the factory workers of 1910 showed a strong tendency toward such homogeneity. Artisans, who in a traditional model of peasant society might have been thought to show a strong tendency toward occupationally homogeneous kin networks, in fact, show such a tendency only slightly.

Migration

Our discussion (in chapter 5) of the relationship between migration and complex family coresidence remains incomplete without consideration of the relationship between migration and extradomestic kin ties. This relationship has rarely been studied by family historians and again, in this section, we hope to suggest a potentially fruitful approach and a useful perspective on the problem, while employing our limited data to ground the discussion in the social world of late nineteenth-century Bologna.

The relationship between in-migration and extrahousehold kin in the receiving community is implicit in our discussion of immigration and household composition. Insofar as rural migrants to urban areas move to areas in which their kinsmen have already established residence, we would expect immigrants to have local kinsmen. Even where such immigrants move into the household of their kinsmen on arrival, this is often merely a transitional stage until they can find jobs and housing. In such cases, then, we would expect relatively recent immigrants to have kinsmen often living in other local households. This expectation runs counter to the more traditional thesis of "modernization" and the progressive demise of extended family relations in which geographical mobility is portrayed as leading to the geographical isolation of nuclear families from their kin network.

When we compare immigrants to persisters, we are posing the problem of the extent of extrahousehold kin links in relative terms. Should we expect recent immigrants to have kin ties with other local households as often as do people who have lived in that community for a longer period of time? Clearly, even if we accept the thesis that migrants tend to select destinations at which they have kinsmen, this does not imply that recent migrants will have a higher frequency of extrahousehold kin links in a community than do nonmigrants.

Looking at the data from 1890, 1900, and 1910—those years for which we have a ten-year retrospective record on which to judge migration status—we find that the persisters are considerably more likely to have kinsmen living in other Bertalia households than are the immigrants. In 1890, 51 percent of the persister-headed households had kinsmen elsewhere in the parish compared to just 33 percent of the immigrant-headed households. In 1900 this disparity was 50 percent against 35 percent, and in 1910 it was 53 percent as opposed to 33 percent. In short, households headed by persisters were from 15 to 20 percent more likely to have kinsmen living elsewhere in Bertalia than were the immigrant-headed households.

This is a sizeable difference. But it could be hypothesized that the difference in frequency of kin ties between households among immigrants and persisters may be less a function of the migration experience per se than a function of differences in the ages of the two. We know that immigrants were disproportionately drawn from the younger age range. It is possible that immigrants show a lower proportion of kin ties with other households simply because of this life course phenomenon.

To test this, we can disaggregate our two migration categories by age (see table 7.9). In virtually every one of the ten-year age ranges for each of the three years, persisters have a higher frequency of kin links with other households than do immigrants, proving that there is no support for this explanation. Taking the four age categories for which we have large enough numbers to make comparison meaningful (i.e. excluding the age

Table 7.9. *Relationship between Age of Household Head and Absence of Kin Ties with Other Bertalia Households: Persisters versus Immigrants*[a]

Age of household head	1890				1900			
	Immigrants		Persisters		Immigrants		Persisters	
	N	Percentage	N	Percentage	N	Percentage	N	Percentage
20–29	24	71	10	40	23	65	12	42
30–39	71	68	31	42	83	57	41	42
40–49	57	72	56	55	76	71	65	51
50–59	39	59	43	54	45	76	64	61
60+	43	65	52	46	35	54	53	43

[a] Expressed in terms of percentages with no kin links to other households.

range 20–29), we find the difference in frequency of extrahousehold kin ties between persisters and immigrants ranging from a low of 5 percent to a high of 38 percent in the years under study. The years 1890 and 1910 show a similar pattern, with the greatest difference between persisters and immigrants found among households with young (30- to 39-year-old) heads.

Two conclusions can be reached from these data. The first is that a substantial number of immigrants (approximately one-third) to the parish had kin links with other households. Thus the notion of new immigrants as isolated from extrahousehold kin is inaccurate for Bertalia in this period and, by extension, should be viewed with caution when applied elsewhere as well. Second, persisters have kin ties with other local households more frequently than do immigrants; this difference is not simply related to differences in age between immigrants and nonimmigrants.

Before concluding our discussion of the relationship between kin ties beyond the household and migration, a few words should be said about the possibility that the propensity to emigrate is affected by such extrahousehold kin ties. It has been argued, though rarely demonstrated, that people who are most enmeshed in a localized kinship network are the least likely to migrate (Bieder 1973). According to this logic, those having no local kinsmen outside the household are more likely to emigrate.

We can test this proposition for Bertalia by dividing the population of 1880, 1890, and 1900 into three categories: those who remained in the

	1910			
	Immigrants		Persisters	
N	Percentage		N	Percentage
33	16		7	57
80	58		39	20
80	74		67	54
67	66		85	51
48	71		80	50

parish ten years later, those who had emigrated during the decade, and those who died in the parish during the decade. Leaving aside this latter category, we can ask whether and to what extent household heads whose households had no local kin ties were more likely to emigrate than those who had such ties. What we find is that there is the expected difference, but it is not great. In the three years examined, 54 to 58 percent of the persister household heads had no kin ties locally, and 60 to 64 percent of the emigrant household heads were without local kinsmen. In short, having kinsmen living outside one's household in the parish may have acted as a weak basis for preventing emigration, but at least in the Bertalia case it was not a major force of residential stability.

8

Conclusions

We have ranged widely in these pages, from analyzing the coresidential system of an entire region of Italy to describing individual lives, from testing broad theoretical formulations regarding coresidence and industrialization to tracing kin ties among households in one community. In these closing pages we take a step back and, rather than repeat our conclusions from earlier chapters, ask what we have learned about domestic life in European history and what role anthropology can play in the interdisciplinary mix that makes European social history such an exciting field today.

The Role of Anthropology

It is hoped that some of the contributions that anthropologists can make in historical European household research are evident in these pages. But there are other potential contributions that have yet to be explored and that bear mentioning.[1] Anthropologists are interested in documenting the variations in coresidential patterns found throughout the world. In looking at coresidential processes in any particular society, such as in Western Europe, anthropologists draw on their global pool of ethnographic and cross-cultural studies to determine the attributes of the

Conclusions

coresidential system being observed. Although the tendency among most scholars is to examine a coresidential system by seeing to what extent it differs from their own, the anthropologist is trained to transcend these cultural blinders.

To argue this case in less abstract terms an illustration is useful. Anthropologists studying domestic groups have long recognized the central importance of rules of postmarital residence. In some societies the newlywed couple is supposed to join the household of the parents of the groom; in others they are supposed to join the parents of the bride; in some societies the couple should move in with one set of their parents, but they are free to choose between the parents of the bride and those of the groom, while in other societies newlywed couples are supposed to establish a completely independent household.[2] The existence of such rules and their interaction with a variety of social, economic, and demographic factors in practice play a large role in determining who resides with whom and how this constellation of coresidents changes through a person's life course and through historical time. Yet though postmarital residence rules have been subject to much anthropological inquiry—both ethnographic and theoretical—they have received little attention from European historians, sociologists, economists, and demographers.[3] Scholars in these fields have referred to the importance of understanding household composition in terms of underlying diachronic principles but have not fully recognized the role of postmarital residence rules in this dynamic.

This question relates to another matter traditionally addressed by anthropologists (but, of course, not only by anthropologists): the relationship between cultural norms and social practice. In coming to terms with this crucial issue, demographers and survey-oriented sociologists have often adopted opposing approaches, with anthropologists struggling (not always successfully) for a middle ground. Insofar as social scientists rely on people's own view of their activity, they confront the danger of formulating a description of society that diverges from actual social behavior. This is a risk run by sociologists who rely on interviews and questionnaires, by oral historians, and by those using first-person written accounts from the past. On the other hand, the demographer, insofar as he or she must rely on quantitative forms of demographic data, has no direct insight into the norms propelling the social machinery but only sees the product of the interaction of those norms with social, economic, and biological factors.

Ideally we would like to analyze both the guiding norms and the actual behavior and plot the relationship between the two. Certainly anthropologists cannot claim to be the only ones interested or expert in such inquiry, but the discipline has placed a great emphasis on just this relationship, on combining normative study with systematic observation of behavior. In the multidisciplinary mix anthropology can continue to caution us against studies that either portray the world in overly normative or in flat statistical terms.[4]

Finally, anthropology can contribute to European family history through the study of kinship systems. As we have discussed in previous chapters, there has been widespread recognition among European family historians that family life, and social life more generally, cannot be satisfactorily understood without knowledge of the kin network in which people were enmeshed. Coresidential processes are closely linked to larger kinship dynamics and cannot be fully understood without them. In addition, the extent to which people sought and received help from their kinsmen, the nature of this help, and how it varied from place to place and through time are central questions for European social history. As we begin to plot this historical territory, anthropologists, as practitioners of a discipline that has specialized in kinship study, can make important contributions.

Coresidence in Italy

Richard Smith has recently written of a household and kinship system that typified pretransitional southern Europe. The elements of this system include emphasis on kin ties through the male line, frequent coresidence of married sons with their parents, family labor units, and, in contrast with early modern England, "no notions of socially approved minimum living standards for marriage" (1981: 618). Like any such geographically sweeping generalizations, this one is open to criticism on the grounds that it lumps together quite different societies that have different kinship practices. However, if we consider it in terms of the sharecropping area of Italy, where it fits best, the generalization has some merit. There was an emphasis on kinship through the male line, sons did routinely bring their wives to live with them in the parental home, and the family was the basic labor unit. However, with a growing number of agricultural wage laborers in pretransitional central Italy, these patterns

Conclusions

weakened. Smith's contention that there was no cultural norm dictating a minimal living standard for getting married is more open to question. Certainly there was less need to accumulate capital than found in some northern European societies, but Italians did not marry early, and the comparison he makes to Bangladesh, where women marry much earlier than they did in pretransitional Italy, is not appropriate. There are reports of early age of female marriage in central Italy, but these refer to a much earlier period.[5]

Bologna falls on the northern fringes of the central Italian sharecropping economy, an economy that evolved for hundreds of years before beginning to disintegrate in the latter part of the nineteenth century. Historians of Western European family life recognize the importance of the central Italian case and see it as a notable exception to the family household pattern found in much of the rest of the western part of the continent. This makes the central Italian case of great theoretical interest both for the study of factors influencing preindustrial household organization and for the study of the impact of industrialization and urbanization on this system. It would indeed be surprising if, given the diversity of economic and political systems under which the peoples of Western Europe lived, coresidential processes everywhere exhibited the same forms. In this sense, any attempt to speak of *the* Western European peasant household is misdirected. It is the economic diversity of the area that makes Western Europe theoretically interesting for the study of household composition, for only by understanding its diversity can we properly identify the factors that lie behind coresidential processes.

Although we have demonstrated that multiple family coresidence was the cultural norm, fostered by a particular set of economic relations, among the sharecroppers of central Italy, we must be wary of some of the more enthusiastic statements regarding the size and kin extension of these households. There was a tendency for observers to be so struck by the example of very large households that these came to be the ones most often described in the historical literature. Typical is Priore's (1906) description of an exemplary sharecropping family in Umbria, having twenty-one members, including three married couples, one widower, one widow, and some unmarried adults as well. Similarly, in books and museums dedicated to chronicling the life of Italian sharecroppers, the classic photographs are those of three-generation multiple family households composed of the patriarch, matriarch, and two or three married sons and their families. In response to Silverman's description of this ideal (1968: 8–9), Saporiti asked to what extent such ideals could survive demographic and social constraints to become the statistical norm (1978: 33). The evidence we have presented, including data from a number of previously unpublished studies, shows that the ideal was manifest in a surprisingly large proportion of cases. However, the mean size of a sharecropper household in central Italy was eight to eleven and not twenty to thirty, as some authors of the past have suggested.

The fact that sharecropper families commonly incorporated two or more male-linked conjugal families did not mean that people were geographically fixed on the family farm. Other scholars' statements that "it is usual for a farm to be occupied by the same family of cultivators for decades, sometimes even for generations" (Silverman 1968: 7) should be read with some skepticism. The bulk of the evidence indicates that mobility was common well before the nineteenth century (Todd 1975) and that, indeed, the whole sharecropping system was based on the ability of landowners to move sharecroppers among farms to match family size with farm size, and to deprive the workers of any claim to the land.

In explaining the peculiarities of Italian sharecropping households in the European context, we have largely relied on economic determinants. However, at the same time we have recognized the force of cultural norms, norms that influence all individuals in the society regardless of their specific occupational pursuits. Peter Laslett (1981) has recently addressed these issues, citing, in fact, the Italian sharecropping case to make this point. Laslett argues against simple economic determinism and maintains that the penchant of Italian sharecroppers for multiple family coresidence cannot be explained by economic factors alone. The basis for his judgment is the observation that nonsharecroppers in this area showed higher frequencies of multiple family coresidence than is found in most of the rest of Western Europe. Laslett's point is that a "normative system" existed that was part of the social structure of the society and not a function of the demands of a domestic unit of production.

This emphasis on the importance of culture and on the way culture works to homogenize people involved in different economic pursuits is certainly well taken. Indeed, we have argued that the high proportion of multiple family households among the wage laborers in central Italy can only be understood in terms of this cultural heritage. However, this argues only against the crudest form of economic determinism, one that does not take into account the dialectic between economic forces and forms of social organization and culture. We do not explain social behav-

Conclusions

ior by attributing it to culture; we are left with the necessity of explaining culture and explaining why cultures differ. The explanation for the cultural norms of multiple family coresidence in central Italy must be sought through historical study of the relationship between an evolving system of production (sharecropping) and preexisting norms of coresidence and forms of social organization.

Italy was not unified politically until little more than a century ago, and it should not be surprising that the country shows as much cultural diversity as it does. Thus, we must be wary of generalizations about "the southern European family system" or even the "Italian family system." For example, in the southern portion of Italy multiple family households were generally rare, and the coresidential processes found in the sharecropping areas of the center and north were largely absent. With few exceptions, simple family households were the norm, both on the peninsula and in Sicily. There were, though, significant differences in kin relations in various parts of southern Italy, differences related in part to different economic systems. In some areas cultivators owned their own land, whereas in other areas they owned small scattered parcels that they supplemented with wage work. In some areas sharecropping or tenant farming was common; in others large plantations employed wage laborers. Unlike central Italy, though, the southern Italians did not typically live on the land they farmed but instead in the protected urban centers, commuting daily to their plots.[6]

Yet the multiple family household was far from absent in the south of Italy. In some areas, not yet fully charted, complex family coresidence was the cultural norm. The best studied such case is that of Agnone, in the region of Molise. Douglass (1980) found that of all conjugal units there in 1753, over 50 percent coresided with other conjugal units. Strikingly, almost a quarter of all conjugal units (23 percent) lived in joint family households, containing two or more married brothers, usually with one or both of their parents. Households followed the patrilocal principle found in central Italy, with various economic benefits accruing to cultivators, artisans, and landowners who lived in such complex households. It remains to be seen whether similar household dynamics are found anywhere in the deep south or Sicily, but again the example suggests we be wary about simple divisions of Italy into a north and a south, or between sharecropping Italy with its complex households and the rest of Italy with its presumably simple family households.

We have been able to show that the multiple family household is more than merely a myth of the European past. Complex family coresidence was not limited to Eastern Europe, where high frequencies of multiple family households have been reported for the eighteenth and nineteenth centuries (Laslett 1977b: 22–23; Czap 1982; Plakans 1982). It was found both in parts of France and in a good portion of Italy for a number of centuries.

Toward a Life Course Perspective

One of our major themes has been the importance of examining household composition in individual life course perspective. This is not an original postion, but few scholars have gone much past statements of the necessity for life course longitudinal studies; few have worked with data that provide a direct glimpse into diachronic processes at the individual level. A life course perspective involves simultaneous study of processes of individual aging and study of how historical forces affect the individual's aging experience (Riley, Johnson, and Foner 1972; Elder 1975, 1978). The norms themselves (whether statistical or ideological) for what is appropriate behavior and what are the appropriate roles for an individual of a given age change over time. These changes are closely associated with changes in the structure of the economy but also reflect such political factors as the imposition of military conscription or, more drastically, the advent of war. Historical changes also include more direct demographic alterations such as those that are caused by an epidemic. If we are interested in the nature of family life and, in particular, coresidential processes in the past, we need to incorporate into our inquiry both these elements of the individual's passage through the life course and the changing environment in which such passage takes place.

Note that the life course approach is different from the family-cycle approach, for the former focuses on the individual rather than a larger unit. In the Appendix we discuss some of the reasons why the family (or the household) is an inappropriate unit for longitudinal analysis. The individual sketches of people through time provided in chapter 6 point up another problem, namely, the fact that a significant number of people do not follow the "ideal" family-cycle pattern. For example, a substantial proportion of the population (and this is a general characteristic of the European experience until recent times) never married. Many children lost both parents at an early age and many of them went to live with othe'

Conclusions

kinsmen. For central Italy in the eighteenth and nineteenth centuries there is also the formidable mass of newborns, many born to married mothers, who were left at the "wheel' of the orphanage, some of whom were later reclaimed by their parents (Corsini 1976). Thus, constructing ideal types of family cycles may obscure more of the processes of coresidence than it illuminates.

Despite our implied criticism of all those who have called for longitudinal study of coresidential processes without undertaking such work themselves, it must be admitted that in this book we have only begun to deal with the complex conceptual and methodological problems involved in the longitudinal study of coresidence. We are still in the position of knowing more about what is wrong with the field than knowing just how these defects can be overcome. If the flaws linked to cross-sectional approaches to coresidence are to be superseded, the Italian case holds much promise of contributing to the solution, for it offers some of the most complete sources of longitudinal data found in Europe.

It is well here to recall the limitations of the data examined in this book for the development of a life course perspective on coresidence. Except for a small sample described in chapter 6, we did not follow individuals continuously through time but, at best, observed them at ten-year intervals. One of the implications of this, aside from the tremendous amount of coresidential flux that was lost as a result of having ten-year blind spots, was our inability to link household processes directly to such phenomena as migration. We could determine which individuals moved out of the parish in a given decade, but we could not know what their coresidential circumstances were at the time of the move. We were able to characterize new immigrants by their househld characteristics, but these were not necessarily the characteristics of their coresidential situation at the time they first entered the parish. None of these matters can be satisfactorily addressed without complete longitudinal records and, hence, a massive amount of data.

There is an additional problem, a problem that would affect us even if we had been able to use continuous longitudinal data for the parish: geographical transiency. Even using our ten-year intervals, we only followed geographically stable individuals through time. There is no good reason to believe that such individuals were identical (or even similar) in their coresidential processes to the large number of more transient individuals. By focusing on the stable population for longitudinal analysis, we introduce an unspecifiable bias into our portrayal of coresidential experience. This is a flaw that can only be addressed by tracing individuals across communal boundaries, throughout their lives. Yet, given the awesome methodological and practical problems posed by such a task it is not surprising that few have even attempted it (cf. Rozat 1977). Without such cross-communal studies, we are particularly handicapped in our understanding of such mobile occupational groups as servants. One of the most striking impressions left by reading through the parish censuses of the latter part of the nineteenth century in Bertalia is the tremendous flux in servants. It was not uncommon for a household to change servants at least once a year. Tracing the life course of young servants involves following the young people from household to household, in movements that appear to show little respect for the convenient administrative boundaries so dear to the church, the state, and the historical demographer.

Lessons from Bertalia

Despite all these limitations we have been able to draw a number of conclusions concerning processes of coresidence in the changing late nineteenth-century parish of Bertalia and to formulate, as a result, hypotheses requiring testing in a much wider geographical and temporal range of social contexts. We will not review each of these conclusions again here, but it is worth briefly noting some of them. We found in Bertalia and elsewhere in central Italy that sharecroppers lived in complex family households much more commonly than agricultural day laborers. This was not surprising and we expect that a similar relationship pertains throughout Western Europe and beyond. But in this part of Italy we found that almost all occupational categories, including the daily laborers, showed significantly higher proportions of complex family households than are found in much of Western Europe. This pattern needs to be charted more systematically throughout Italy in order to see its boundaries and its socioeconomic correlates. Once this is done, we will be further along in our understanding of the nature and the determinants of household arrangements in preindustrial Europe.

Analysis of the Bertalia case has also pointed out the complexity of the relationship between urbanization and household composition. Although most of our data were limited to a single parish, our conclusion is that the most commonly held theories of the impact of urbanization on house-

Conclusions

hold composition are simplistic. As Mendels (1978: 782) has argued, monocausal models of the determinants of household composition are inadequate and must be replaced by multicausal models.

In understanding the impact of urbanization and/or industrialization on rural, agricultural people, we cannot take for granted an idealized view of what the life of the agricultural population was like, nor is it justified to assume that this life had been unchanging until the advent of industry and the expansion of the cities. In Italy, as in many other countries, the years preceding the boom of industrialization and urbanization were years of crisis, dislocation, and change for the rural population. In the case of Emilia-Romagna, these changes entailed the erosion of the once predominant sharecropping system and the rise of a more capitalistic mode of farm operation, complete with wage labor. Along with these economic changes, demographic pressures were fueling the creation of a large, economically precarious population in the countryside. Thus, in examining the impact of urbanization on the family life of the rural people, the preexisting rural social and economic system must be studied as carefully as the new forces of transformation.

It is hardly surprising that these processes of economic transformation affect elements of the population differently. This is true not only in terms of social class or specific way of making a living but also in terms of age. In Bertalia the early urbanization of what had been an overwhelmingly agricultural community affected the young differently than it did the elderly. This phenomenon has long been recognized in research on occupational change but has not yet been fully studied insofar as it bears on changing patterns of coresidence. For example, by the end of the nineteenth century there developed in Bertalia and elsewhere in this part of Italy the practice of youngsters finding work in textile factories, work that they performed for a limited number of years. In the past, some of these youths might have found work as servants in other people's homes. Insofar as this occurred, early industrialization kept more youngsters in their natal home. At the same time, though, what was happening to the middle-aged people who were losing their sharecropping contracts and forced to take work as *braccianti* affected the coresidential situation of the youngsters, who became less likely to coreside with their uncles, aunts, and cousins. In short, the forces of economic change had a differential impact on peoples of different ages (and sexes), but the impact on people of one age had ramifications for the coresidential situations of people of all ages.

Family Life in Central Italy

Bertalia in 1880 to 1910 was a community facing the early blasts of urbanization, a community much like hundreds of others lying outside the urban centers of central and northern Italy. Unlike some of these other communities, which were completely devoured by the advancing steamroller of urban envelopment, Bertalia held on to its rural roots well past the middle of the twentieth century. On the northern fringe of the city of Bologna, partially isolated by multitudinous railroad crossings and by the canal and the river, as late as the 1970s there was still some land being farmed and other expanses of green guarded, ironically, by urban land speculators. Today, ties with kinsmen outside the nuclear family are strong and tend to be geographically localized. People can often be heard lamenting the fact that their brother or sister lives so far away, meaning by this that they live on the other side of the city. Various factors have discouraged multiple family residence, but it is not uncommon to see related nuclear families occupying two separate floors of the same building. In addition, the widowed elderly are still today taken into their married children's homes. To leave one's old parent to live by him- or herself is still seen as cruel, and to put the parent in an old folks home is regarded by many as sinful. Young people still normally live at home until they marry, and the unmarried young man or woman (but particularly the latter) who, at the age of twenty-five, asks to move into an apartment of his or her own is regarded with anger and chagrin by her shocked parents.

In the past century Bertalia has changed from a parish of cultivators to a parish of proletarians, from an expanse of fields to an ever-expanding number of high-rise apartment buildings. People try to hang on to their piece of the rural past—renting a grape press once a year to make wine, or visiting their kinsmen in the nearby countryside—as fewer and fewer signs of the agricultural era survive in the parish. Their families, the people with whom they share their homes, though, remain a central focus of their lives. The household today is rarely the basic unit of production, but the people who live together continue to shape one another's view of the world, and they continue to pool resources to confront life together.

Appendix
Methods of Household Study

The Importance of Methodology

Moving from consideration of some of the large historical and theoretical questions regarding the family in European history to a discussion of methodology, we run the risk of frustrating the reader. What could be less interesting than scholars' continual pedantry in their arguments over terminology and typologies?

Although I sympathize with this sentiment and often wish that more effort could be expended in empirical historical research and less in methodological quibbles, the fact is that there is no history without methodology; the history we read is filtered through the methodological lens of the scholar who has produced it. We are consequently unable to evaluate any historical generalization without knowing what methods were used. These concerns are magnified in research such as ours, where the aim is ultimately comparative, for we cannot compare such social phenomena as coresidence patterns without being sure that we are using the same methods in all the different areas we want to include in our comparison or, at least, making appropriate corrections where dissimilar methods are used. Here, then, we briefly review the most prominent methods used in the historical study of households, indicate the strengths and weaknesses of each, and weigh the methods that we have employed and their advantages over alternate approaches.

The Study of Households

The burst of scholarly activity in the demographic study of European family history has had two primary centers of inspiration: a French group associated with the work of Louis Henry, and a British group, centered around Peter Laslett, and having its institutional base in the Cambridge Group for the History of Population and Social Structure. Although the approaches represented by each of these have been the subjects of vigorous methodological and substantive criticism, together they have provided many new insights into family life in Europe's past. Temporal priority goes to the French group, which pioneered the technique of family reconstitution in order to study the behavior of people of the past. As France lacks good regular listings of the population before the past century, Henry and his associates devised means of utilizing vital statistics records (births, marriages, and deaths) to follow individuals through time (Fleury and Henry 1965).

But for those interested in coresidential behavior, with whom people shared their homes, and how this changed through the person's life course and through time, the French reconstitution approach is of little aid. Although it permits us to follow an individual's life from birth through successive marriages, childbirths, and death, it provides no direct evidence of who lived with whom. We know that a certain child was born to a particular mother and father, but we do not know if the child ever lived with his or her parents after birth, nor even if the parents lived with each other. For the limited issue of historical fertility patterns, the method is instructive, though not without some problems.[1] But to find out more about the lives of people in the families of the past, other methods had to be employed. It is in this context that the work of Laslett and the Cambridge group must be seen.

The Cambridge group had a great advantage over their French colleagues, for they had local enumerations of the British population going back a number of centuries. Through the use of these records, they devised methods enabling them to study historically changing patterns of household composition, as well as to analyze marital patterns and a variety of other family-related matters.

Laslett's typology for studying household composition has become the most widely employed framework for comparative household research.[2] The scheme consists of five major categories and a number of subcategories. The major categories are solitaries, no family, simple family, extended family, and multiple family households (Laslett 1972a; also found in Hammel and Laslett 1974). The cornerstone of this system is the concept of the conjugal family unit (CFU), which consists of a husband and wife with or without offspring, or a lone parent living with offspring. Neither the solitary nor the no family household has any CFU. The simple family household incorporates one such CFU without any other kin. The extended family household consists of a CFU with a coresident kinsman from outside the CFU. The multiple family household contains two or more kin-related CFUs.

Extended family households are further categorized by Laslett according to the generational direction of their extension: *upwards* if the additional relative (outside the CFU) is of an earlier generation, *downwards* if the relative is of a later generation, and laterally if of the same generation. Multiple family households are subcategorized as having secondary units up, down, or all on the same level, depending on whether the CFU not containing the household head con-

Appendix: Methods of Household Study

tains a conjugal link that is at an earlier, later, or the same generational level as that of the household head.

The reasons for the popularity of Laslett's scheme are not hard to find. Just as scholars were beginning to make use of demographic records for studying family life in the past, Laslett offered a scheme that allowed them to categorize their cases easily and to compare their own results with that of other scholars working in other areas. This latter benefit derived less from the analytical merits of Lastlett's typology than from the influential position Laslett occupied at the center of the Cambridge group. The chaotic situation found in much of the rest of the literature confirms the merits of a common approach. A plethora of different household typologies have been employed, with categories that cross-cut one another, and with distinctions deemed vital in one being totally ignored in another. Comparison of results in such situations is difficult at best.

There are, though, reasons for this lack of typological consensus. Some scholars are working with richer data sources than others, allowing them to make finer distinctions. In addition, different languages provide different kinship terminologies and, hence, different ways of grouping kinship ties (Hammel and Laslett 1974: 80).

Some have questioned whether creation of a common scheme for classifying households is even desirable. They reject the idea of cross-culturally applicable household typology on the grounds that forcing data into such a framework violates the integrity of the historical and cultural context. In this vein, for example, Medick (1976: 295) has charged that "in the interest of too rigorous a claim for quantification, Laslett the methodologist sacrifices *a priori* and categorically the historical 'meaning' of the phenomena to be measured and compared in favour of a universal scale of comparison and measurement." Among some historians, as among anthropologists, there are deep reservations about the comparative approach. Berkner (1975) charges Laslett with simply taking an English model of what constitutes the household and elevating it to the status of a cross-culturally applicable analytical tool. Berkner grants the importance of constructing a cross-culturally valid typology of household composition, yet it is not clear that any typology could meet his criteria of flexibility in coping with cultural variability in folk definitions of the household.[3]

Berkner and others have raised a similarly important point regarding the cross-cutural validity of the concept of the household itself. Practically speaking, the way Laslett and other analysts of European census data have defined the household has been to use the distinctions made by the census takers. Berkner warns of the perils of this approach for comparative study: "One may not be comparing households at all, but the way in which census enumerators made divisions. . . . To find out what these divisions mean is difficult and must be based on the work of social historians at the local or regional level" (1975:

727). Yet such particularistic study can only benefit comparative research if explicit cross-culturally applicable guidelines for what constitutes a household have previously been articulated. This task should not be confused with trying to find out what the folk conception of the household is, for that only leads away from comparative goals.

A related, but more radical criticism of household study holds that the unit being studied, the household, is not a particularly important entity (Stone 1981). More commonly found is a modified version of this position, which maintains that by focusing on household composition, there is an indefensible yet ineluctable tendency to ignore family and kin relations not circumscribed by household limits. Thus Anderson (1972a: 50) writes:

> . . . it is now becoming clear that it is totally inadequate to confine one's attention simply to the study of patterns of residence. The sharing of a home and of obligations incurred by commensality is only a sphere of family activity, and its significance can only be assessed in the context of a much wider review of all the functions provided by the family, and of the extent to which individuals see themselves overall as being dependent on family relationships.

Anderson's own work on nineteenth-century Lancashire offers good evidence of the virtues of just such a broader focus and the insights that it can provide. Yet what implications do these observations have for comparative household studies? Berkner, in attacking Laslett, maintains that sociologists and anthropologists have established "that the composition of the predominant residential family unit does not describe the family structure and is not the important thing upon which to focus. Laslett concentrates only on this group and at the end of his essay even tries to make the composition of the coresident domestic group equivalent to the institution of the family" (1976: 732). But to recognize that family and kin relations cannot be adequately understood by synchronic household study alone does not mean that household analysis is unimportant. Problems of cross-culturally applicable definition of the household, earlier lamented by Berkner, pale in comparison to the problem of defining the family, a concept having no necessary behavioral referent.[4]

It is true that there has been much confusion between the family as a basic kinship unit and the household as a basic coresidential unit. But in understanding people's lives in the past, the questions of with whom they lived, how this constellation of coresidents changed through an individual's life course, and the relation of these experiences to economic and other exogenous factors are crucial. The different impact of coresiding with a variety of kinsmen outside the nuclear family as opposed to residing only with nuclear family members cannot be assumed, but identifying such patterns of coresidence is necessary to further historical understanding of people's lives. Likewise, discovering that many couples go to live with the groom's parents upon their marriage cannot in itself tell us the full meaning of this arrangement to the people involved, yet identifying the frequency and the social, demographic, and economic correlates of this behavior is of no small importance.

Patterns of coresidence also provide important information on the relationships among kinsmen and on the kind of social environment in which people lived. It is true, however, as Wheaton (1975: 601) has pointed out, that "recent historical attention has focused on the family household while relatively little attention has been given to the ties of kinship as they extend beyond it" (see also Bender 1967; Hareven 1974: 323). This is a serious deficiency in European historical demography and one that can be rectified, in part, by devising better methods for linking households by kin ties. We discuss this matter in detail in chapter 7. It must be admitted, though, that identifying kin links between households in a community tells us little about the nature of the social ties existing between such households. Studies of contemporary family life and kinship in the West have demonstrated the importance of these interhousehold ties (e.g., Young and Willmott 1962), yet methods that are utilized in these studies to calculate frequency of social contact and to determine the content of relationships are not easily adapted for use with historical sources.

Categorizing Households

Although Laslett's approach to historical household study has had tremendous influence, it has also generated a large critical literature.[5] The primary criticism of Laslett's approach is that it fosters a static view of what is a dynamic process. It has been pointed out by several scholars that a "snapshot" view of household composition at any one point in time cannot tell us what underlying processes are at work to produce such households (Berkner 1972, 1975; Wheaton 1975: 606; Bradley and Mendels 1978: 381–382; Carter 1981: 16). For example, if we find an elderly woman living with her married son and his wife and children, this could be the result of the son bringing his wife into his parental home at the time of his marriage (patrilocal residence), or it could be a case of a widow finding shelter in the home of a married child at the time of her widowhood.

Along similar lines, Laslett's approach has been criticized for failing to recognize the role that demographic constraints play in determining household composition. The fact that a small minority of households are of a complex composition at any one time may not reflect any preference for simple family households but, rather, may be the product of fertility, marriage, and mortality rates that determine how many adult married couples actually had living parents. We must be careful not to leap too quickly from synchronic observations of household composition to statements of what the underlying structure of household processes is.

Laslett has also been criticized for paying too little attention to the economic forces that people had to contend with in deciding where to live (Medick 1976). This, however, may be less attributed to the typology that Laslett employs than the fact that the English historical demographers were working with parish population listings that had little occupational data.

Lutz Berkner, a European historian, has been the preeminent critic of Laslett's approach, and it is worth pausing a moment to consider his position. Berkner has argued in a series of publications that the picture of household composition derived from cross-sectional analyses of census listings is misleading, for it fails to identify the underlying developmental processes that determine what kind of household individuals live in at any particular moment. Through the study of a 1763 population listing for a group of villages in Austria (Berkner 1972), and later in similar studies elsewhere (1976, 1977), Berkner reconstructs the life cycle of individual peasants and their households. This he does by determining at what stage in its developmental cycle each household is at the date of the census, and by using a variety of legal documents regarding inheritance practices. At the basis of his method is the concept of households as following a developmental cycle tied to the passing on of the peasant landholding from one generation to the next.[6] Berkner maintains that this approach is superior to Laslett's in incorporating the developmental nature of household processes and relating these to local economic circumstances.

Although in recent years many scholars have cited Berkner as discrediting the "typological" approach to household study, Berkner's developmental cycle alternative has itself been the subject of attack. Laslett (1978) himself has launched a counterattack, pointing out that though Berkner calls for a processual view of households, his own analysis is based on cross-sectional population listings rather than on the tracing of individuals through time. Moreover, by using a developmental cycle model and focusing on household units and retirement contracts governing inheritance, we tend to ignore those individuals who did not stand to inherit the parental farm and who often moved to other communities (Mitterauer and Sieder 1979: 259–260, 277). Insofar as just a single son inherited the farm, the proportion of the population that is not analyzed is considerable.

Further flaws with the developmental or family-cycle approach to historical household study have been identified by Elder (1977) and Vinovskis (1977), both of whom call for adoption of a life course approach in its place. They fault the family-cycle approach for failing to cope adequately with variation, or with the timing and duration of family events. Moreover, there has been little attempt to articulate family stages with historical changes that brought about changes in coresidential practices. What is needed, Elder and Vinovskis argue, are studies

Appendix: Methods of Household Study

that focus on individuals over time, investigating the ways their lives are affected by changing historical circumstances, and determining the degree and nature of variability among individuals in family-related behavior.

Where does all this leave us? Laslett's approach has been heavily criticized as static; basic flaws have been found in the once glamorous family-cycle approach of Berkner and others; and the life course approach has yet to be fully employed in historical research on coresidence, in part because its data requirements—fully longitudinal data on individuals for their entire lives—are enormous. In the remaining pages of this chapter I would like to suggest a way in which some progress can be made in historical household study while relying primarily on population listings, an approach that we have employed in our Italian case study.

The primary goals of historical household research are to determine people's coresidential experiences in the past and to explain similarities and differences in these experiences within and among populations. The aim must always be better understanding of process and choice: how people came to live in the kinds of households they did and what choices affected their subsequent changes in coresidential arrangements. Obviously, these questions require a time dimension, which involves both historical time and life time or age. Historical time refers to the prevailing economic, social, cultural, and political arrangements in the world in which the individual lives, and the changes in these through the years of the individual's life. Life time refers to the age or stage of development of the individual at any point in time. Different cohorts—people born at the same time (e.g., in the same year)—are characterized by the fact that their intercept of historical time and life time is identical. They all live their early childhoods in one historical period, live their adolescences in another, and their elderly years in still another. Their life experiences can be seen as the joint product of certain age-linked processes (linked to such phenomena as birth, having children, growing old, and dying) and certain historical processes (e.g., a war calling all men to arms in their early adulthood, or an epidemic hitting the cohort in their early childhood years).

Once coresidence is cast in this light, it is clear that the most satisfactory materials for analysis are longitudinal life course data that follow all individuals in a variety of cohorts through the historical period of interest to us. However, such research involves tremendous resources of time, personnel, and money. Although such studies are desperately needed, it must be admitted that scholars will for the most part have to settle for less costly approaches to the historical study of coresidence. If this is so, what are the best alternatives?

The approach used here represents something of a compromise between the efficiency of using population listings for household analysis and the necessity of breaking away from static, ahistorical studies (cf. Watkins 1980). In order to determine the interaction of historical change with coresidential behavior, we examine in detail four censuses, each ten years apart, over the period of early urbanization in Bertalia, 1880–1910. Examining these censuses not only allows us to consider the changing relationship of age to coresidence through these years but also us to determine just how much movement there is in the population, taking us from a static view of the population to a view of the population in flux.

Yet by tracing the population from decade to decade we lose much of the coresidential processes that are most important to study, processes percolating throughout the ten-year intercensal periods. To provide us with some insight into this more continuous coresidential flux, in chapter 7 we followed a limited sample of Bertalia residents continuously from year to year throughout the historical period under study. This was done through use of the annual parish census and the Bologna population register, which allowed us to follow these sample members as they migrated to other parts of the city of Bologna. This procedure provides a further benefit, for there are dangers in limiting our study only to people who remain through long stretches of their lives in a single locality. Since the more migratory population may well differ in coresidential characteristics from the less migratory population, any generalizations about coresidence based on the study of the persisters remain suspect.

We utilize Laslett's general typology, in part because so much of the published historical household research has utilized it and it thus greatly facilitates historical and cross-cultural comparison. Although granting that this household typology approach can lead to a slighting of the underlying coresidential processes in any society, we hope to overcome these limitations by fully considering the changing historical context—including economic factors affecting coresidence—and by making use of our sequence of censuses, and by our limited use of full life course data.

Laslett's typology of household composition must, however, be somewhat altered for it to be used by anyone interested in the kinship structure underlying coresidence systems. His manner of dealing with households more complex than simple nuclear families makes little sense if we are interested in the kinship rules of household formation, and consequently we propose an alternative.

Complex family households fall into two primary categories in Laslett's scheme: extended family households and multiple family households. It will be recalled that the extended family household consists of a simple family plus one or more other kinsmen who themselves do not constitute any additional conjugal family unit. A multiple family household, on the other hand, consists of two or more conjugal family units. But once we take a developmental perspective, the distinction between these two forms may become murky or misleading. Consider, for example, the case of the Italian sharecropper who lives with his wife, his son, and his son's wife and children (see figure A.1(a)). When the man's wife dies, in Laslett's scheme, the household is transformed from one major category

Appendix: Methods of Household Study

Figure A.1. *Complex Family Household Categorization*

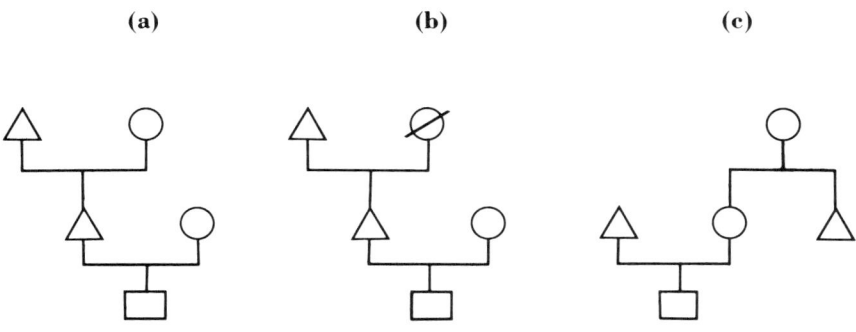

to another (multiple to extended) (figure A.1(b)). If, instead, the old man and his wife had both left, and the son's wife's brother and widowed mother joined them, there would be no change noted in major household category (figure A.1(c)). For most purposes, though, we would conceive of households (a) and (b) as quite similar, expressing the same structure and norms but reflecting the vagaries of mortality. Likewise, from most viewpoints, households (a) and (c) are dissimilar. Is a typology that groups together (a) and (c) and separates (a) and (b) satisfactory?

In defense of Laslett, the extended/multiple distinction does touch on a potentially important difference in household composition. Households containing a conjugal family unit plus a widowed parent are usefully distinguished from households having two or more conjugal family units. We would generally expect authority relations and social experiences to differ between such households. Moreover, if we found a high proportion of extended family households but a low proportion of multiple family households in a community, we would be able to infer certain coresidential norms (e.g., the obligation of married children to take in their widowed parents).

Recognizing that any categories we create will inevitably do violence to the actual social processes they depict, it is preferable to ask how we can get the most from a typology rather than to despair over finding a typology that divides the world up into unassailable categories. Looked at from this perspective, Laslett's basic framework can be utilized for comparative historical purposes but only with some alteration.

The alterations required are those that must be obvious to the anthropologist

Figure A.2. *The Household as Longitudinal Unit*

(a)

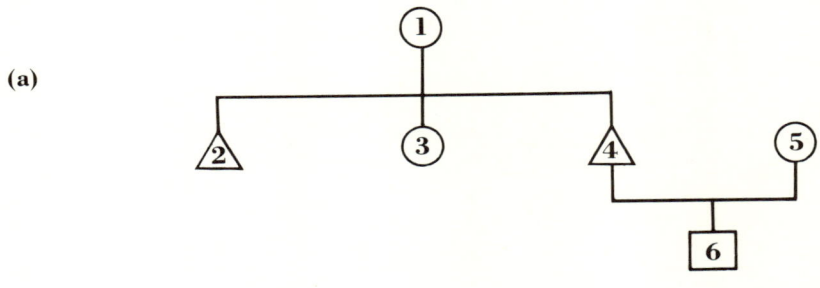

(b)

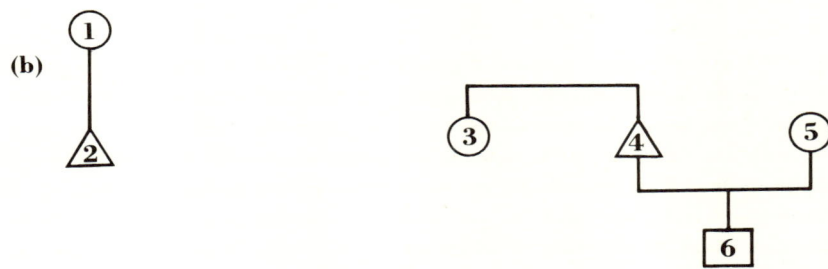

examining Laslett's scheme. We need to incorporate more data on kinship composition into the typology to better reflect the social processes at work. Laslett has created types of complex family households based largely on the household's generational characteristics. At the same time, little kinship information is considered. According to Laslett, a change in who is listed first in the household depicted in figure A.2(a) (from the man of the first generation to the man of the second) alters the composition of the household even though there has been no change in personnel.[7] Yet, as noted before, a drastic change of both personnel and kinship structure may not be reflected at all in the Laslett typology.

Our modification of Laslett's typology, reflected in some of the detailed tables on coresidence found in this book, largely entails dividing complex family households by the direction of their kinship extension, expressed in kinship terms. Rather than being primarily concerned with whether the household head belongs to a senior or junior generation, we are concerned with the nature of the kinship relationship tying the coresidents together. Thus, both extended and multiple family households are divided into three major categories: patrilateral,

Appendix: Methods of Household Study

matrilateral, and other. In patrilateral households the bond of kinship runs through the male line; in matrilateral households the kin are bound through the female line. The importance of this distinction is well illustrated in the case of Bertalia, where the overwhelming majority of complex family households results from patrilateral extension. It is, of course, always possible to introduce greater complexity and detail by subcategorizing these by number of generations present in the household.

One other modification of the Laslett typology that we have added concerns the category of no family households. Here it is desirable to distinguish between those households that represent corporate non-kin-based groupings from those founded by their coresidents more spontaneously. In other words, the structure of a coresidential unit consisting of a convent or an orphanage is considerably different from that of a household formed by two friends. This difference should be reflected in the categorization scheme.

Even if it be granted that this variant represents an improvement in the use of Laslett's typology, it may be asked whether any household typology is suitable for use with longitudinal data. Indeed, if we were to survey the attempts that have been made to date to study households in developmental terms, we would have to be pessimistic. It is striking that, despite the many pleas for longitudinal study of coresidence, little progress has been made in developing analytical tools appropriate for such analysis.

There is an important distinction to be made here, and that is between households as longitudinal units and individuals as longitudinal units. Attempts to study coresidence over time have almost all used the household as the unit to be followed, yet they have not dealt with the problem of defining just what constitutes the same household at two points in time.

The futility of following households can be illustrated by reference to the standard method of identifying a household through time by its head or, if the head has died, by the head's successor. Let us take the case of the household shown in figure A.2, pictured before (a) and after (b) a split has taken place. If we are following the developmental cycle of the household, what can we say about the household's composition at the latter point in time? Which of the two households is to be considered the continuation of our original household? Is this question to be decided simply on the basis of which people remain in the same physical dwelling? What justification could be given for this procedure? Are both households to be considered as representative of a later point in the developmental cycle of the original household? If so, a host of methodological difficulties is created.

We dealt with the question of tracing households through time in chapter 6, where an attempt is made to analyze coresidential developmental processes during the period under study. But let me suggest here that we may need to reconceptualize the entire question of developmental cycles of household formation. Following Schiaffino (1977, 1981), I question whether the household can ever be a suitable unit for processual analysis, despite such well-known pleas for such study as have been advanced by Hareven (1974). The household, in fact, can only be seen cross-sectionally, unless it be seen as a property-holding corporation. The only stable unit for study through time is the individual. As individuals combine and recombine with others through time in various coresidential living arrangements, focusing on the progress of preexisting multiperson units (i.e., households) leads to conceptual confusion. Ideally, then, what we need are studies that follow individuals through their life course and that elucidate the determinants of their coresidential behavior with whom they coreside and when (Kertzer and Schiaffino 1983; Schiaffino and Kertzer n.d.). In this view, household typologies may be employed as an aid in examining the coresidential situations in which individuals find themselves.

It is appropriate to conclude this discussion of the role of typology in household study by making a point about the relationship between typology and theory. Why, after all, should we pay so much attention to the admittedly uninspiring details of categorization? Our answer can most conveniently be formulated in reaction to the view of Hammel and Laslett (1974: 103):

> We have suggested ways in which the historian can code and draw his data in order to handle a substantial corpus of information that might be otherwise unmanageable, and so that some generalizations will naturally emerge simply through the procedures employed. But it must be recognized that in all these suggestions for distillation of the original we have intended to force no theory, although we prefer some over others. Alternatives have been presented, and these should be employed wherever appropriate.

The notion that in constructing a typology for the analysis of data we are simply allowing the data to speak for themselves is hardly defensible. We cannot construct a typology without a guiding theory, for what provides the basis for categorization if not criteria that are nonarbitrary, linked to a theory of what is important? Moreover, insofar as the task is defined in terms of the cross-sectional analysis of household composition, we are not merely allowing generalizations to emerge from the data but rather we are dealing with data in such a way that only certain interpretations are possible.[8]

Notes

Chapter 1: Introduction

1. The literature has been critically reviewed by Berkner (1973), Dupâquier (1975), Sharlin (1977), and Vinovskis (1977).

2. Not all interesting historical family questions, of course, can be answered directly from such records. Yanagisako (1979: 180) rightly questions the "proclivity of some social historians to infer changes in sentiments and cultural conceptions from alterations in demographic patterns." Demographic sources must be used in conjunction with other sources if any satisfactory answer to such questions is to be forthcoming.

3. See also Coale (1965) and Goode (1963: 371).

4. Most notable of these studies is the long-term investigation of family life in fifteenth-century Tuscany conducted by Herlihy (1969, 1977) and Klapisch (1972; Klapisch and Demonet 1972), reported most fully in their book *Les Toscans et Leurs Familles* (1978).

5. However, others have excluded southern France but not Italy from such generalizations, as is the case with Michael Anderson (1978: 3).

6. A similar equation of farm ownership with the possibility of complex family household formation is made by Goody (1972: 118) using the comparative perspective afforded by African materials.

7. Occupational data are obviously critical in relating household characteristics to economic factors. Lacking such data, as Levine (1977: 149) has pointed out, scholars using English parish registers have been "susceptible to the so-called 'ecological fallacy' which occurs when one generalizes from aggregated evidence to the behavior of one of the groups which composed the aggregation."

Chapter 2: Economy and Social Organization

1. The 1901 census provides some indication of the frequency of sharecropping in the various regions of Italy. The four regions having the highest fre-

Notes to Pages 25–56

quency, measured in number of sharecroppers per 1,000 males employed in agriculture, are the Marches (606), Tuscany, (532), Umbria (437), and Romagna (421). The latter includes the provinces of Bologna, Ferrara, and Ravenna but excludes the eastern provinces of Emilia (Livi 1915: 34).

2. The single best source of this landowners' perspective is provided by the *Annali della Società Agraria della Provincia di Bologna*, published annually beginning in 1862.

3. Anselmi's comments regarding the importance of livestock to the sharecropping of the Marches come to mind here:

> We can thus explain the terrible saying attributed to the peasants: "a misfortune in the barn is worse than a misfortune in the family [*una disgrazia nella stalla è più grave di una disgrazia in famiglia*]. The death of an ox, in fact, almost always means an economic disaster, since the beast of burden and of meat is shared with the *padrone*, and the peasant does not have the financial means to replace it, while a "misfortune in the family," however sad it may be, is part of a vision of life in which men, from the time they are children, are brought up to realize the precariousness of life and the necessity to become familiar with the fact of death. A lost child can be replaced, but a cow no. (1978: 17–18)

4. Writing of Tuscany in the mid-nineteenth century, Toscanelli (1861: 258–259) maintains that in extended family households in which there are more than one couple of the senior generation, the *reggitore* and the *reggitrice* are drawn from two different branches of the family. It is questionable if this was ever the common practice in Tuscany or the other regions of the sharecropping zone, but this does give an indication of the importance of managing tensions among the different married couples of the household.

5. Landlords were not only concerned about the number of adults in the household but also about the ratio between the able-bodied adults and the dependents. It is in this light that we can understand the reported practice by sharecroppers of hiding their infants in the cupboards when the *padrone* came to visit (Poni 1978: 227).

6. The extent to which kinship ties were involved in the sharecropper labor exchange is not known.

7. For examinations of the course of early industrialization in Italy as a whole, see Gerschenkron (1955) and Cafagna (1976).

8. A similar point, regarding the region of the Marches in the nineteenth century, has been made by Anselmi (1978: 93).

9. Pasolini (1892a: 327–328) makes the interesting point that the discontent and readiness to revolt of the *braccianti* may be in part a result of the presence of former sharecroppers in their ranks. Those falling from sharecropper to *bracciante* status, according to Pasolini, are likely to be the most rebellious sons

of sharecroppers. Of the *braccianti*, these former sharecroppers are also likely to be the most unsatisfied with their peasant lot, contrasting it with their earlier life expectations and experiences. Whether these individuals were in fact the most active in revolt is not known. Note should also be made of the role intellectuals played in spreading socialist ideas in the countryside. Indeed, Scarselli (1890: 34), voicing a viewpoint common among the *padroni*, singled out the rural elementary schoolteachers as taking advantage of the "ignorance" of the peasants to spread their socialist ideals and to foment revolt among the poor.

The economic organization of central Italy and the associated militant class-based political movements may also help to account for the low level of transoceanic migration from this area in comparison with southern Italy. In an interesting article, Macdonald (1963) has argued that labor militancy may be seen as an alternative to out-migration, with the rise of labor militancy being a function of the clarity of class distinctions and the efficiency of governmental repression.

Chapter 3: Sharecropping and Coresidence

1. Another of the significant expenses connected with sharecropper marriages in Emilia-Romagna in the nineteenth century was the necessity to sponsor a large feast as part of the wedding festivities. For a description, see INEA (1931: 22).

2. A similar tendency to endogamy among the sharecroppers and the agricultural wage laborers in an area of nineteenth-century France has been noted by Segalen (1976: 1166).

3. Illegitimate births are, unfortunately, difficult to measure in this period of Italian history due to the state's refusal to recognize church weddings and the church's refusal to recognize the validity of civil marriages. The result is that a child born to a woman married only in church was registered by the state as illegitimate. Since the church recognized only church weddings, the converse was also true. Illegitimacy was probably not particularly high in this region in this period, though it was probably higher among the *braccianti* than among the sharecroppers (Preti 1955: 59; Livi-Bacci 1977: 60–77). On foundlings and orphanages in central Italy, see Corsini (1976, 1977, 1981).

4. We can only estimate the rate of infant mortality in Bertalia because we do not have parish data available on all births during the decade. Our estimate is based on the prevalent provincial birthrate for the 1880s (34 per 1,000) and a figure of 2,000 for the mean size of the parish population in these years (Livi-Bacci 1977: 62–63).

5. Each individual entry includes first and last name, sex, father's and mother's names (all women are listed by maiden name), age, birthplace, marital status (including name of deceased spouse for widows and widowers), and occu-

pation. See Bellettini (1974) and Corsini (1974) for more detail on the scholarly use of the Italian *status animarum*.

6. Joel Halpern (1972) has used this distinction between counting households and counting people to good effect in analyzing household size in Serbia.

7. This point has been made by numerous scholars, including Berkner (1972). For a fuller discussion of this issue, see the Appendix.

8. For fuller discussion of the methodological issues involved in life course analysis of cross-sectional data, see Riley, Johnson, and Foner (1972: chap. 2) and Riley (1973).

9. See Wachter, Hammel, and Laslett (1978) for a comprehensive discussion of these demographic effects.

10. In summary, the composition of sharecropper-headed households in Bertalia in 1821 was as follows: 38 percent of the households with 26 percent of the coresidents were simple; 19 percent of the households with 17 percent of the coresidents were extended; and 42 percent of the households with 57 percent of the coresidents were multiple.

11. Of households in Bertalia in 1880 headed by sharecroppers, 5 percent had one generation, 55 percent had two generations, and 38 percent had three generations. Corresponding figures for the *bracciante*-headed households are 17 percent one generation, 67 percent two generations, and 14 percent three generations. For all 347 households in the parish the breakdown is 11 percent one generation, 67 percent two generations, and 20 percent three generations.

12. The 1,052 sharecropper households in the suburbs of Bologna studied by Angeli and Bellettini (1979: 158) had a mean size of 8.8 in 1847. The 1,249 *bracciante*-headed households had a mean size of 4.4.

13. The size difference between sharecropper and wage laborer households is undoubtedly of long standing. In a Tuscan community in 1684, for example, mean sharecropper household size was 9.3, whereas that for *braccianti* was 3.4 (McArdle 1978: 131).

14. Silverman has put this matter simply, "the *mezzadria* system is feasible only if a general balance is maintained between the size of the peasant family and the size of the farm." She provides data for a rural community in Umbria for 1960 showing just such a relationship (1975: 51).

15. These data, reported by Poni (1977: 102), regard the communes of Borgo Panigale and Zola Predosa and are based on a study of 380 sharecropper households. Households on farms under 4 *corbe* (the *corba* was a Bolognese measurement equal to approximately 80 meters square) had a mean size of 4.8, those on farms of 4–7 *corbe* numbered 7.6, on farms of 8–11 *corbe* 10.0, on farms of 12–15 *corbe* 13.4, and on farms of 16 or more *corbe* 18.7.

16. Sardi (1973), writing a thesis for her *laurea* at the University of Florence, did not employ Laslett's categories. However, her distinction between households that are *nucleari* and those that are *aggregati* closely corresponds to

the Laslettian distinction between simple family households and solitaries on the one hand, and extended and multiple family households on the other.

17. The full 1858 household data for the parish of Corniglio are as follows: 7.0 percent solitary; 5.6 percent no family; 47.6 percent simple family; 19.6 percent extended family; and 20.2 percent multiple family. The total number of households is 143.

18. Silverman (1975) employs a non-Lastettian household typology but one that permits reaggregation in Laslett's categories.

19. There was a total of 405 sharecropper households in Sesto Fiorentino in 1861 and 256 households headed by *braccianti*. A large proportion of the population was in fact nonagricultural (1,446 of the 2,107 household heads), for Sesto had a flourishing series of small industries and was especially known for its ceramics and its straw hats. The data on patrilateral extension of multiple family households, then, reflect not only a preference among the sharecroppers but also a norm among artisans who had multiple family households. However, just 12 percent of the nonagricultural households were multiple in composition (Pesciullesi 1978).

Another Tuscan case of interest is that of the small rural commune of Altopascio, which was newly settled at the beginning of the seventeenth century. From 1618 to 1767, the period of McArdle's (1978) study, complex family households became increasingly frequent, reaching 36 percent of all households by the end of the period. In all, about half of the population lived with kinsmen outside the nuclear family. McArdle attributes this movement toward greater household complexity to the "passage of the settlement from youthful colonization to mature operation and, along with that development, the disappearance of available land" (1978: 134–135). This community was only partially composed of sharecroppers, however, having a relatively large number of farm renters, artisans, and day laborers.

20. Of the 7,263 sharecropper households living in rural Tuscany in 1427 that were examined by Herlihy and Klapisch (1978: 486), 1.5 percent were categorized as solitaries or no family, 55.0 percent as simple family, 12.3 percent as extended family, and 31.2 percent as multiple family.

21. In the city of Florence itself, three-generation households were less than half as common as they were in the countryside (Herlihy 1977: 148n).

22. Much of the discussion regarding departmental differences in households and in demographic behavior in France has concerned legal issues regarding partibility of inheritance and the change brought on by Napoleonic reforms. See, for example, Hermalin and Van de Walle (1977).

23. It is notable that one of the only accounts of complex households in any frequency in northern France involves sharecroppers and specifically excludes farm laborers. This is reported by Segalen (1976: 1151–1152; 1977: 225–226) for a community in Bréton in the west of France.

24. Within each of the French regions there is, of course, considerable diversity in both patterns of household composition and in economic characteristics. For example, also in southeastern France is the village of Marlhes, in the department of Loire, where Lehning (1980) argues that the nuclear family household was dominant. This, however, is not a sharecropping area but, rather, a mixture of farm laborers, farm renters, small farm proprietors, and protoindustrial workers. It is significant that, of those households with landholdings of over five hectares in the nineteenth century, about one-third were of complex family composition (1980: 105). Were these people's lives looked at longitudinally, with a focus on individuals, a much higher proportion would be found to experience complex family coresidence.

It is worth noting that a similar pattern has been uncovered in rural Peru for the 1970s, where a majority of the households of the "middle and rich peasant strata" were found to be complex in composition (Deere 1978: 436).

25. Peyronnet's data are based on 627 individuals living in households headed by sharecroppers and 302 individuals living in households headed by day laborers. He found the following pattern of household composition among the sharecroppers: 23.0 percent living in simple families, 17.6 percent in extended families, and 59.4 percent in multiple families. In contrast, the day laborer-headed households consisted of 2.0 percent solitaries, 1.4 percent no family, 82.6 percent simple families, 11.6 percent extended families, and 1.4 percent multiple families.

26. Berkner and Shaffer (1978) make a similar argument in accounting for patterns of household composition in central France. They find a high correlation between sharecropping and complex family households in the eighteenth and early nineteenth centuries. Peasants who owned their own land were much more likely to live in simple family households. They concluded:

> These differences indicate that while peasants with land were dividing their holdings and creating new households, the farms worked by sharecroppers remained intact because they did not control the disposition of the land which they farmed. It was because the domaines remained intact that joint households continued to flourish among sharecroppers well into the nineteenth century. (1978: 158)

Chapter 4: Urbanization and Coresidence

1. Demographic changes accompanying nineteenth-century industrialization and urbanization have been mentioned by Flandrin (1979: 72) as explaining any increase in complex family households occurring in that period. He argues that increased longevity and decreased age difference between mothers and children

provided conditions more favorable to complex family household formation. In other words, there was greater possibility for three-generational households under the new demographic conditions than under the old. Of course, before this can be accepted as an explanation, it must be established that these demographic conditions in fact existed and that they distinguished places with higher proportions of complex family households from those with lower frequencies.

2. Charles Tilly provides us with a convenient definition of what we mean by the proletariat in this context: "all people whose survival depended on the sale of their labor power" (1979: 29).

3. In recent years the diverse effects on family life of different kinds of industrialization are becoming more clear. Textile industries, with their characteristic use of female and child labor, have quite a different impact on family life from heavy metal industries. For more on the textile industry and its effects on family life, see Smelser (1974), Reddy (1975), Dublin (1979), and L. Tilly (1979a, 1979b, 1979c).

4. Labor force data are confined almost exclusively to males as the parish census generally listed women as working at home (*lavoro a domicilio*), even when they were economically active in the outside world.

5. As previously discussed, inferring life course effects from cross-sectional data such as these is problematic. However, the similarity of the life course curve for both 1880 and 1910 increases our confidence in a life course interpretation of the data.

6. For more on the impact of industrialization on age at marriage, see Wrigley (1961: 145–146) and Levine (1977).

7. Louise Tilly (1979a: 148) makes a similar point regarding adolescent and young adult children in Roubaix, France, in 1872.

8. The great extent to which the elderly lived with their married and unmarried children in nineteenth-century urban communities is also supported by the evidence presented by Chudacoff and Hareven (1979) for Providence, Rhode Island.

9. Seward (1978), in a comparison of nineteenth-century regions of the United States based on census data, found no significant relationship between urbanization, industrialization, and complex family frequency.

Chapter 5: Migration

1. The larger issue of the importance of extended kin relations to migrants was discussed by Litwak (1960) quite a few years ago. See also Hareven (1974, 1975). Recent studies of rural-urban networks in Mexico (Lomnitz 1977) and among black Americans (Stack 1974; Aschenbrenner 1975) also lend support to this position.

2. This is similar to Katz's (1975) distinction between "persisters" and "transients."

3. In chapter 6 we analyze individuals from a prospective migratory view. In such a way we can examine factors that distinguish individuals likely to migrate from those likely not to migrate.

4. For a discussion of high female migration rates see Weber (1968: 276–278).

5. In a similar study of occupation and persistence based in Hamilton, Ontario, Katz and colleagues found no clear relationship existing between persistence and occupational status (1977: 166).

In some cases, it appears that people with the greatest resources may be the most likely to leave the rural hinterland and make the move to the city, though often retaining an interest in the home town. Such is the case of the Greek village of Vasilika described by Friedl (1976: 381).

6. Italy may have been unusual in Western Europe in this regard, for elsewhere the rural-urban movement of large numbers of single young men and women has been noted. Moch (1981a, 1981b), for example, in studying the French city of Nîmes, at the turn of the twentieth century, concluded that "most young migrants . . . did not arrive with their families. Rather, the migration of single young people predominated over family migration" (1981b: 36). Although many of the single migrants were servants and thus comparable to those found in Bertalia, many were workers who lived in rented rooms, something not found in Bertalia at all.

Chapter 6: Coresidence in Life Course Perspective

1. They are also constrained by the fact of in- and out-migration that results in a population biased in favor of nonmigratory individuals. However, this is a factor that affects almost all fully longitudinal historical life course studies as well.

2. For fuller discussion of the analytical virtues of a life course approach to family study, see Elder (1975, 1977) and Vinovskis (1977). On the application of the life course approach to European family history, see Kertzer and Schiaffino (1983).

3. As mentioned in chapter 1, Schiaffino and Kertzer are currently in the midst of just such a longitudinal study of coresidence for the period 1865–1921 in Casalecchio (in the province of Bologna), in which an attempt is being made to overcome these hurdles.

4. Further discussion of the La Hulpe population register data can be found in Van de Walle and Blanc (1975), Gutmann and Van de Walle (1978), and Watkins and McCarthy (1980).

5. I would like to thank Marco Melega who was responsible for dealing with these *anagrafe* records.

6. Clearly we are dealing with a biased sample in analyzing occupational mobility only for the residentially stable population. Whether, for example, *braccianti* who moved out of the parish were more likely to enter a new occupation and, if so, to what extent, are questions we cannot answer with single parish data. It is also apparent that by taking just two points in time we are missing occupational mobility that took place between those two points, as with the *bracciante* in 1880 who became a construction worker in 1882 and then returned to *bracciante* employment in 1888.

7. This approach, using the Italian population register, has been previously employed by Schiaffino (1977). Annual parish censuses have been used by Monti (1978) to follow sharecropper families continuously in a commune of Ravenna for the period 1766–1797. Monti's study focuses on the sharecroppers' debts over time, relating these to the ratio of workers to consumers in the family.

Chapter 7: Kinsmen beyond the Household

1. See earlier discussion of cautions in the use of this procedure in chapter 3 and in the Appendix.

2. Where a single household had direct kin ties with more than one other household, each of these links was counted. Hence in the computations based on these data, some households were counted more than once.

Chapter 8: Conclusions

1. The interest of historians in the application of anthropological perspectives to the study of European social history has been often expressed in recent years. Stone, for example, has written:

> In America, and to a lesser extent in England, anthropology has had a considerable impact on the historical profession. Anthropologists have always been intensely concerned with such matters as kinship structures, incest taboos, and endogamy and exogamy in marriage, and it is from them that the historians developed their interest in such matters as marriage customs and the roles of the patriarch, lineage, and kin. (1981: 53)

2. In fact, there are a number of other postmarital residence rules found in the world, including avunculocality and brideservice followed by virilocality.

3. The most thorough consideration of postmarital residence rules in this regard is provided by the anthropologist Eugene Hammel, working in collabora-

tion with Wachter and with Laslett (Hammel and Wachter 1977; Wachter, Hammel, and Laslett 1978).

4. An interesting discussion of the relationship of cultural norms to demographic and economic variables in European family history is provided by Richard Smith (1981). Smith stresses the importance of ideology in explaining what he calls the "northwest European household formation system." Rather than portraying the economy as determining the culture, Smith opts for a different causal emphasis, maintaining that "in this system the family, demographic, economic, and political systems were linked in a *culturally determined moral economy*" (1981: 618).

5. The most comprehensive account of family life in fifteenth-century Tuscany is found in Herlihy and Klapisch (1978). Also see Herlihy (1972), Klapisch (1972), Klapisch and Demonet (1972), and Herlihy (1977). A collection of studies of family and kinship in medieval Italy has been edited by Duby and Le Goff (1981). It primarily deals with the nobility but contains some material on serfs and peasants as well.

6. For anthropological descriptions of coresidence and kinship in a variety of southern Italian communities, see Pitkin (1959–60), Moss and Cappannari (1960), Maraspini (1968), Cronin (1970), Brogger (1971), Chapman (1971), Davis (1973), Schneider and Schneider (1976), and Tentori (1976). For an anthropologically informed historical view, see Bell's (1979) study of four rural Italian communities, three of which are found in the south.

Appendix: Methods of Household Study

1. For a discussion of the limitations of the French reconstitution approach, see Livi-Bacci (1975: 35–37) and Schiaffino (1975, 1976). A good summary of the results of reconstitution studies may be found in Flinn (1981).

2. Examples include Katz (1975), Van de Walle (1976), Netting (1979), and Ring (1979).

3. Laslett (1978: 96) has recently made a similar criticism of Berkner's position.

4. An example of the amorphousness of definitions of the family is provided by Wrigley (1977: 73).

5. This literature will not be fully reviewed in this book. A comprehensive review and critique is available in Kertzer and Schiaffino (1983).

6. Classic anthropological statements on the developmental cycle are found in Fortes (1958) and Goody (1958).

7. Laslett puts much more stock in the significance of the first-listed individual or household head than I think advisable for comparative historical purposes. Not only is there a question of on what basis the census enumerator

Notes to Page 208

chooses whom to list first; it must also be recognized that the social and jural roles of the household head differed greatly between societies and time periods and even between people of different occupations in the same community at the same point in time.

8. See related discussions in Berkner (1975) and Medick (1976). Eugene Hammel in a private communication, has voiced his agreement with the point I make in this paragraph, stating that the passage quoted is open to an interpretation other than that which he intended.

Bibliography

The publication *Annali della Società Agraria Provinciale di Bologna* is abbreviated as *Annali* in this bibliography.

Anderson, Michael. 1971. *Family structure in nineteenth century Lancashire.* Cambridge: Cambridge University Press.
———. 1972a. The study of family structure. In *Nineteenth-century society: Essays in the use of quantitative methods for the study of social data,* ed. E. A. Wrigley, 47–81. Cambridge: Cambridge University Press.
———. 1972b. Household structure and the industrial revolution: Mid-nineteenth century Preston in comparative perspective. In *Household and family in past time,* ed. Peter Laslett, 215–235. Cambridge: Cambridge University Press.
———. 1976. Sociological history and the working-class family: Smelser revisited. *Social History* 3: 317–334.
———. 1978. *The family and industrialization in Western Europe.* The Forum Series. St. Louis: Forum Press.
———. 1979a. Some problems in the use of census type material for the study of family and kinship systems. In *Time, space and man,* ed. Jan Sundin and Erik Soderlund, 69–80. Atlantic Highlands, N. J.: Humanities.
———. 1979b. The relevance of family history. In *The sociology of the family: New directions for Britain,* ed. Chris C. Harris, 49–73. Sociological Review Monograph 28. Keele: University of Keele.
Anelli, Aldo, Enzo Siri, and Lamberto Soliani. 1979. Analisi della fecondità per strutture familiari. *Genus* 35: 173–187.
Angeli, Aurora, and Athos Bellettini. 1979. Strutture familiari nella campagna bolognese a metà dell'ottocento. *Genus* 35: 155–172.
Anselmi, Sergio. 1978. *Mezzadri e terre nelle Marche.* Bologna: Pàtron.
———. 1980. Città e campagna: Conflitti e controllo sociale. *Annali dell' Istituto Alcide Cervi* 2: 31–57. Bologna: Il Mulino.
Arbizzani, Luigi. 1961. *Sguardi sull'ultimo secolo: Bologna e la sua provincia, 1859–1961.* Bologna.

———. 1977. Ideali ed istituti nuovi nella cultura contadina post-unitaria (1859–1945). In *Cultura popolare nell'Emilia-Romagna*, ed. Giuseppe Adani and Gastone Tamagnini, 219–241. Milano: Silvana Editoriale d'Arte.

Armstrong, W. A. 1972. A note on the household structure of mid-nineteenth-century Preston in comparative perspective. In *Household and family in past time*, ed. Peter Laslett, 205–214. Cambridge: Cambridge University Press.

Aschenbrenner, Joyce. 1975. *Lifelines: Black families in Chicago*. New York: Holt, Rinehart.

Aymard, Maurice, and Gerard Delille. 1977. La démographie historique en Italie: Une discipline en mutation. In *Annales de Démographie historique 1977*, 447–461. Paris: Mouton.

Balugani, Angela, and Silvio Fronzoni. 1979. Poderi e mezzadri di una "impresa" bolognese, 1720–1770. *Quaderni Storici* 40: 105–129.

Bandera, Ulisse, et al. 1875. Rapporto della commissione incaricata dalla Società Agraria dal Comizio di proporre provvedimenti contro la illecita contrattazione delle canape e stoppe. *Annali* 13: 140–147.

Barnabè, Carla. 1977. *Struttura delle famiglie nelle campagne romagnole agli inizi dell'800*. Diploma thesis, Faculty of Economics and Commerce, University of Bologna under the direction of Andrea Schiaffino.

Bell, Rudolph M. 1979. *Fate and honor, family and village: Demographic and cultural change in rural Italy since 1800*. Chicago: University of Chicago Press.

Bellettini, Athos. 1961. *La popolazione di Bologna dal secolo XV all'Unificazione Italiana*. Bologna: Zanichelli.

———. 1971. *La popolazione delle campagne bolognesi alla metà del secolo XIX*. Bologna: Zanichelli.

———. 1974. Gli "status animarum": Caratteristiche e problemi di utilizzazione nelle ricerche di demografia storica. In *Le fonti della demografia storica in Italia*, ed. Comitato Italiano per lo Studio della Demografia Storica, 1: 3–42. Rome: CISP.

———. 1978. La popolazione di Bologna nel corso dell'ottocento. *Storia Urbana* 5: 3–23.

———, and Franco Tassinari. 1977. *Fonti per lo studio del suburbio di Bologna dal secolo XVI alla fine dell'ottocento*. Bologna: Istituto per la Storia di Bologna.

Bender, Donald R. 1967. A refinement of the concept of household: Families, coresidence and domestic functions. *American Anthropologist* 69: 493–504.

Berkner, Lutz K. 1972. The stem family and the developmental cycle of the peasant household: An eighteenth-century Austrian example. *American Historical Review* 77: 398–418.

———. 1973. Recent research on the history of the family in Western Europe. *Journal of Marriage and the Family* 35: 395–405.

Bibliography

———. 1975. The use and misuse of census data for the historical analysis of family structure. *Journal of Interdisciplinary History* 5: 721–738.

———. 1976. Inheritance, land tenure and peasant family structure: A German regional comparison. In *Family and inheritance: Rural society in Western Europe, 1200–1800*, ed. Jack Goody, Joan Thirsk, and E. P. Thompson, 71–95. Cambridge: Cambridge University Press.

———. 1977. Household arithmetic: A note. *Journal of Family History* 2: 159–163.

———, and John W. Shaffer. 1978. The joint family in the Nivernais. *Journal of Family History* 3: 150–162.

Bernardi, Bernardo, Carlo Poni, and Alessandro Triulzi, eds. 1977. *Fonti orali: Antropologia e storia*. Milan: Franco Angeli.

Biagi, Bruno. 1935. Norme consuetudinarie per la divisione delle famiglie coloniche nel bolognese. *Archivio 'Vittorio Scialoja'* 1: 42–50.

Bieder, Robert E. 1973. Kinship as a factor in migration. *Journal of Marriage and the Family* 35: 429–439.

Bissoli, Renzo. 1979. Lavoro e rendita in un'azienda agraria bolognese del XVIII secolo. *Quaderni storici* 40: 389–413.

Blayo, Yves. 1970. La mobilité dans un village de la Brie vers le milieu du XIXe siecle. *Population* 25: 573–605.

———. 1972. Size and structure of households in a northern French village between 1836 and 1961. In *Household and family in past time*, ed. Peter Laslett, 255–266. Cambridge: Cambridge University Press.

Bouchard, Gerard. 1977. Family structures and geographic mobility at Laterrière, 1851–1935. *Journal of Family History* 2: 350–369.

Bradley, Brian P., and Franklin F. Mendels. 1978. Can the hypothesis of a nuclear family organization be tested statistically? *Population Studies* 32: 381–394.

Broccoli, Armide. 1979. *Chiamavano pane il pane*. Bologna: Edagricole.

Brogger, Jan. 1971. *Montevarese: A study of peasant society and culture in southern Italy*. Bergen: Universitetsforlaget.

Bruno, Salvatore. 1923. *La mezzadria*. 2d ed. Turin: Biblioteca di Ragioneria Applicata.

Buffini, A. 1845. *Ragionamenti storici economici statistici e morali intorno all'ospizio dei trovatelli in Milano*. Milan.

Cafagna, Luciano. 1976. The industrial revolution in Italy, 1830–1914. In *The emergence of industrial societies*, ed. Carlo M. Cipolla, pt. 1, 279–328. Fontana Economic History of Europe, vol. 4. London: Harvester.

Camera di Commercio ed Arti di Bologna. 1888. *Notizie sulle condizioni industriali e commerciali della provincia di Bologna*. Bologna.

Carlos, Manuel L., and Lois Sellers. 1972. Family, kinship structure, and modernization in Latin America. *Latin American Research Review* 7: 95–124.

Carrara, Mario. 1896. Feudalismo rurale: Il patto colonico in Galizia e nell'Emilia. *La Critica Sociale* 6: 123–127.

Carter, Anthony T. 1981. Household histories. Paper presented at the Wenner-Gren Conference, Households: Changing Form and Function, Mt. Kisco, N.Y.

Cazzola, Franco. 1980a. La formazione del bracciantato agricolo di massa in Emilia Romagna. In *Il proletariato agricolo in Emilia Romagna nella fase di formazione*, ed. Franco Cazzola, 19–63. Bologna: CLUEB.

———. 1980b. La formazione di una popolazione marginale in agricoltura: Alcune ipotesi di lavoro. *Annali dell'Istituto Alcide Cervi* 2: 79–86. Bologna: Il Mulino.

Chapman, Charlotte Gower. 1971. *Milocca: A Sicilian village*. Cambridge, Mass.: Schenkman.

Chudacoff, Howard P., and Tamara K. Hareven. 1979. From the empty nest to family dissolution: Life course transitions into old age. *Journal of Family History* 4: 69–83.

Ciuffoletti, Zeffiro. 1980. L'introduzione delle macchine nell'agricoltura mezzadrile toscana dall'Unità al fascismo. *Annali dell'Istituto Alcide Cervi* 2: 101–120. Bologna: Il Mulino.

Clough, Shepard B. 1964. The economic history of modern Italy. New York: Columbia University Press.

Coale, Ansley J. 1965. Appendix: Estimates of average size of household. In *Aspects of the analysis of family structure*, ed. Marion J. Levy, Jr., 64–69. Princeton: Princeton University Press.

Collomp, Alain. 1972. Famille nucléaire et famille élargie en Haute Provence au XVIIIe siècle (1703–1734). *Annales: Economies, Sociétés, Civilisations* 27: 969–975.

———. 1974. Ménage et famille. *Annales: Economies, Sociétés, Civilisations* 29: 777–786.

Comizio Agrario di Bologna. 1881. *Monografia del podere bolognese*. Bologna.

———. 1905. *Capitolato generale per la conduzione a mezzadria dei fondi rustici nella provincia di Bologna*. Bologna.

Commissione Mista della Società del Comizio Agrario e dell'Accademia dei Ragionieri. 1874. Modulo di nuova scritta colonica e capitolato agrario. *Annali* 11: 22–37.

Commissione per lo Studio sulle Condizioni della Colonia nella Provincia di Bologna. 1883. Adunanza del 22 Gennato 1882. *Annali* 22: 87–97.

Commissione Sanitaria Municipale di Bologna. 1887. *L'epidemia di cholera-morbus nel comune di Bologna, L'anno 1886*. Bologna.

Comune di Bologna. 1971. *Annuario statistico 1970*. Bologna.

Conenna, Lucia Bonelli. 1980. Mezzadria senese: Dimore rurali e vita economica nel XVIII secolo. *Annali dell'Istituto Alcide Cervi* 2: 121–150. Bologna: Il Mulino.

Conklin, George H. 1974. The extended family as an independent factor in social change: A case from India. *Journal of Marriage and the Family* 36: 798–804.

Consiglio Provinciale di Bologna. 1932. *La provincia di Bologna nell'anno decimo.* Bologna.

Conti, Emilio. 1905. *La proprietà fondiaria nel passato e nel presente.* Milan.

Corsini, Carlo A. 1974. Gli "status animarum," fonte per le ricerche di demografia storica. In *Le fonti della demografia storica in Italia*, ed. Comitato Italiano per lo Studio della Demografia Storica, 1: 85–126. Rome: CISP.

———. 1976. Materiali per lo studio della famiglia in Toscana nei secoli XVII–XIX: Gli esposti. *Quaderni Storici* 33: 998–1052.

———. 1977. Self-regulation mechanisms of traditional populations before the demographic revolution: European civilizations. In the *Proceedings of the international population conference*, 3: 5–23. Liège: International Union for the Scientific Study of Population.

———. 1981. Structural changes in infant mortality in Tuscany between the 18th and the 19th century. *Quaderni del Dipartimento Statistico*, no. 16. University of Florence.

Crispolti, Tommaso. 1894. Della partecipazione del lavoro al prodotto della terra. *Annali* 34: 125–141.

Cronin, Constance. 1970. *The sting of change: Sicilians in Sicily and Australia.* Chicago: University of Chicago Press.

Czap, Peter, Jr. 1982. The perennial multiple family household, Mishino, Russia 1782–1858. *Journal of Family History* 7: 5–26.

Dal Pane, Luigi. 1969. *Economia e società a Bologna nell'età del Risorgimento.* Bologna: Zanichelli.

Darroch, A. Gordon. 1981. Migrants in the nineteenth century: Fugitives or families in motion? *Journal of Family History* 6: 257–277.

Davis, John. 1973. *Land and family in Pisticci.* London: Athlone.

Deere, Carmen D. 1978. The differentiation of the peasantry and family structure: A Peruvian case study. *Journal of Family History* 3: 422–438.

Diolaiti, Nino. 1973. *Sotto la polvere dei secoli.* Bologna.

Douglass, William A. 1980. The south Italian family: A critique. *Journal of Family History* 5: 338–359.

Dublin, Thomas. 1979. *Women at work: The transformation of work and community in Lowell, Massachusetts, 1826–1860.* New York: Columbia University Press.

Duby, Georges, and Jacques Le Goff, eds. 1981. *Famiglia e parentela nell'Italia medievale.* Bologna: Il Mulino.

Bibliography

Dupâquier, Jacques. 1975. La demografia storica in Francia: Studi recenti. In *Demografia storica*, ed. Ercole Sori, 43–60. Bologna: Il Mulino.

Elder, Glen H., Jr. 1975. Age differentiation and the life course. *Annual Review of Sociology* 1:165–190.

———. 1977. Family history and the life course. *Journal of Family History* 2: 279–304.

———. 1978. Approaches to social change and the family. *American Journal of Sociology* 84: S1–S38.

Evangelisti, Valerio. 1980. Forme di produzione agricola e carratteristiche generali del bracciantato emiliano-romagnolo (1880–1914). In *Il proletariato agricolo in Emilia Romagna nella fase di formazione*, ed. Franco Cazzola, 65–108. Bologna: CLUEB.

Faina, Eugenio. 1905. Dei guadagni e dei consumi dei contadini nei paesi di mezzadria. *Nuova Antologia* 40 (802): 263–292.

Fine-Souriac, Agnès. 1977. La famille-souche pyrénéenne au XIXe siècle: Quelques réflexions de méthode. *Annales: Economies, Sociétés, Civilisations* 32: 478–487.

Finzi, Roberto. 1980. Controllo sociale e organizzazione del lavoro in un' "impresa" del bolognese agli inizi del secolo XVII. *Annali dell'Istituto Alcide Cervi* 2: 87–100. Bologna: Il Mulino.

Firth, Raymond. 1964. Family and kinship in industrial society. In *Sociological Review Monograph*, ed. Paul Helmos, no. 8, 65–87. Keele: University of Keele.

Flandrin, Jean-Louis. 1979. *Families in former times: Kinship, household and sexuality*. Cambridge: Cambridge University Press.

Fleury, Michel, and Louis Henry. 1965. *Nouveau manuel de dépouillement et d'exploitation de l'état civil ancien*. Paris: Institut National d'Études Demographiques.

Flinn, Michael W. 1981. *The European demographic system, 1500–1820*. Baltimore: Johns Hopkins University Press.

Fortes, Meyer. 1958. Introduction. In *The developmental cycle in domestic groups*, ed. Jack Goody, 1–14. Cambridge: Cambridge University Press.

Freed, Stanley A., and Ruth S. Freed. 1982. Changing family types in India. *Ethnology* 21: 189–202.

Friedl, Ernestine. 1976. Kinship, class and selective migration. In *Mediterranean family structures*, ed. J. G. Peristiany, 363–388. Cambridge: Cambridge University Press.

Gambi, Lucio. 1977. La casa dei contadini. In *Cultura popolare nell'Emilia Romagna*, ed. Giuseppe Adani and Gastone Tamagnini, 161–189. Milan: Silvana Editoriale d'Arte.

Garbaglia, L. 1906. Intorno alla mezzeria piemontese e alla sua riforma. *La Riforma Sociale* 16: 688–698.

Bibliography

Gerschenkron, Alexander. 1955. Notes on the rate of industrial growth in Italy, 1881–1913. *Journal of Economic History* 15: 360–375.

Giorgetti, Giorgio. 1974. *Contadini e proprietari nell'Italia moderna.* Turin: Einaudi.

Giusberti, Fabio. 1982. Mobilité de la population et territoire urbain, un secteur de Bologne dans les années 1816 et 1820. *Annales de Démographie Historique*, 183–190.

Goode, William J. 1963. *World revolution and family patterns.* New York: Free Press.

Goody, Jack. 1972. The evolution of the family. In *Household and family in past time*, ed. Peter Laslett, 103–124. Cambridge: Cambridge University Press.

———, ed. 1958. *The developmental cycle in domestic groups.* Cambridge: Cambridge University Press.

Goretti, Cesare. 1882. Sunto della monografia della tenuta detta Minerbio. *Annali* 21: 129–195.

———. 1883. Sulle mutate condizioni agricole del territorio bolognese. *Annali* 22: 54–64.

Grabinski, Giuseppe. 1892. Lo sciopero e la questione sociale nelle campagne. *Annali* 32: 139–175.

Gutmann, Myron P., and Etienne Van de Walle. 1978. New sources for social and demographic history: The Belgian population registers. *Social Science History* 2: 121–143.

Hajnal, John. 1965. European marriage patterns in perspective. In *Population in history: Essays in historical demography*, ed. David V. Glass and David E. Eversley, 104–143. Chicago: Aldine.

Halpern, Joel M. 1972. Town and countryside in Serbia in the nineteenth century. In *Household and family in past time*, ed. Peter Laslett, 401–427. Cambridge: Cambridge University Press.

Hammel, Eugene A., and Peter Laslett. 1974. Comparing household structure over time and between cultures. *Comparative Studies in Society and History* 16: 73–109.

Hammel, Eugene A., and Kenneth W. Wachter. 1977. Primonuptiality and ultimonuptiality: Their effects on stem-family-household frequencies. In *Population patterns in the past*, ed. Ronald D. Lee, 113–134. New York: Academic.

Hareven, Tamara K. 1974. The family as process: The historical study of the family cycle. *Journal of Social History* 7: 322–327.

———. 1975. The labourers of Manchester, New Hampshire, 1912–1922: The role of the family and ethnicity in adjustment to industrial life. *Labour History* 16: 249–265.

———. 1977. Family time and industrial time: Family and work in a planned corporation town, 1900–1924. In *Family and kin in urban communities, 1700–1930*, ed. Tamara K. Hareven, 187–208. New York: New Viewpoints.

———. 1978. The dynamics of kin in an industrial community. *American Journal of Sociology* 84: S151–S182.

———, and Maris A. Vinovskis. 1978. Introduction. In *Family and population in nineteenth-century America*, ed. Tamara K. Hareven and Maris A. Vinovskis, 3–21. Princeton: Princeton University Press.

Harris, Chris C. 1977. Changing conceptions of the relation between family and societal form in Western society. In *Industrial society: Class, cleavage and control*, ed. Richard Scase, 74–89. New York: St. Martin's.

Herlihy, David. 1969. Veillir à Florence au quattrocento. *Annales: Economies, Sociétés, Civilisations* 24: 1338–1352.

———. 1972. Mapping households in medieval Italy. *Catholic Historical Review* 58: 1–24.

———. 1977. Deaths, marriages, births, and the Tuscan economy (ca. 1300–1550). In *Population patterns in the past*, ed. Ronald D. Lee, 135–164. New York: Academic.

———, and Christine Klapisch. 1978. *Les toscans et leurs familles*. Paris: Fondation Nationale des Sciences Politiques.

Hermalin, Albert I., and Etienne Van de Walle. 1977. The Civil Code and nuptiality: Empirical investigation of a hypothesis. In *Population patterns in the past*, ed. Ronald D. Lee, 71–111. New York: Academic.

Hollingsworth, Thomas H. 1970. Historical studies of migration. *Annales de Démographie Historique 1970*: 87–96. Paris: Mouton.

Istituto Nazionale di Economia Agraria (INEA). 1931. *Monografie di Famiglie Agricole. Contadini della Valle del Panaro (Emilia)*. Pt. 6. Studi e Monografie, no. 14. Milan.

Jacini, Stefano. 1860 (1976). La mezzadria e la famiglia patriarcale in Lombardia. In *Un'Italia sconosciuta*, ed. Massimo Guidetti and Paul H. Stahl, 75–78. Milan: Jaca Books.

———. 1882. *Atti della giunta per la inchiesta agraria e sulle condizioni della classe agricola. Vol. III. La toscana agricola*. Rome.

Jansen, Clifford J. 1970. Introduction. In *Readings in the sociology of migration*, 3–35. Oxford: Pergamon.

Katz, Michael B. 1975. *The people of Hamilton, Canada west: Family and class in a mid-nineteenth-century city*. Cambridge, Mass.: Harvard University Press.

———. 1978. *York social history project. Third report*. Toronto: York University.

Katz, Michael B., and Ian E. Davey. 1978. Youth and early industrialization in a Canadian city. *American Journal of Sociology* 84: S81–S119.

Katz, Michael B., Michael J. Doucet, and Mark Stern. 1977. Population per-

Bibliography

sistence in Hamilton, 1851–1861 and 1861–1871. Working paper 22, Social History Project, York University. Toronto: York University.

Kertzer, David I. 1978. The impact of urbanization on household composition: Implications from an Italian parish (1880–1910). *Urban Anthropology* 6: 1–23.

Kertzer, David I., and Andrea Schiaffino. 1983. Industrialization and coresidence: A life course approach. In *Life-span development and human behavior*, ed. Paul B. Baltes and Orville G. Brim, Jr., vol. 5, 359–391. New York: Academic.

Klapisch, Christine. 1972. Household and family in Tuscany in 1427. In *Household and family in past time*, ed. Peter Laslett, 267–282. Cambridge: Cambridge University Press.

―――, and Michel Demonet. 1972. A uno pane e uno vino: La famille rurale toscane au début de XVe siècle. *Annales: Economies, Sociétés, Civilisations* 27: 873–901.

Kussmaul, Ann. 1981. *Servants in husbandry in early modern England.* Cambridge: Cambridge University Press.

Landi, Fiorenzo. 1977. I contratti agrari. In *Cultura popolare nell'Emilia Romagna*, ed. Giuseppe Adani and Gastone Tamagnini, 139–145. Milan: Silvana Editoriale d'Arte.

Laslett, Barbara. 1978. Family membership, past and present. *Social Problems* 25: 476–490.

Laslett, Peter N. 1968. Le brassage de la population en France et en Angleterre au XVIIe et XVIIIe siècles. *Annales de Démographie Historique 1968*: 99–109. Paris: Mouton.

―――. 1972a. Introduction: The history of the family. In *Household and family in past time*, ed. Peter Laslett, 1–89. Cambridge: Cambridge University Press.

―――. 1972b. Mean household size in England since the sixteenth century. 125–158. In *Household and family in past time*, ed. Peter Laslett, 125–158. Cambridge: Cambridge University Press.

―――. 1973. The comparative history of household and family. In *American family in social-historical perspective*, ed. Michael Gordon, 19–33. New York: St. Martin's.

―――. 1977a. Characteristics of the Western family considered over time. *Journal of Family History* 2: 89–115.

―――. 1977b. *Family life and illicit love in earlier generations.* Cambridge: Cambridge University Press.

―――. 1978. The stem-family hypothesis and its privileged position. In *Statistical studies of historical social structure*, by Kenneth Wachter, Eugene A. Hammel, and Peter Laslett, 89–111. New York: Academic.

―――. 1981. Family and household as work group and kin group; areas of traditional Europe compared. Paper presented to the Istituto Internazionale di Storia Economica, Prato, Italy.

———, ed. 1972. *Household and family in past time*. Cambridge: Cambridge University Press.

———, and John Harrison. 1963. Clayworth and Cogenhoe. In *Historical essays, 1650–1750*, ed. H. E. Bell and R. L. Ollard, 157–184. London: Black.

Lee, William Robert. 1981. Past legacies and future prospects: Recent research on the history of the family in Germany. *Journal of Family History* 6: 156–176.

Lehning, James R. 1980. *The peasants of Marlhes: Economic development and family organization in nineteenth-century France*. Chapel Hill: University of North Carolina Press.

Lemaitre, Nicole. 1976. Familles complexes en Bas-Limousin: Ussel au début du XIXe siècle. *Annales du Midi* 88: 219–224.

LePlay, P. G. F. 1871. *L'organisation de la famille*. Paris: Tours.

Levine, David. 1977. *Family formation in an age of nascent capitalism*. New York: Academic.

Levy, Marion J., Jr. 1965. *Aspects of the analysis of family structure*. Princeton: Princeton University Press.

Litwak, Eugene. 1960. Occupational mobility and extended family cohesion. *American Sociological Review* 25: 385–394.

———. 1965. Extended kin relations in an industrial democratic society. In *Social structure and the family*, ed. Ethel Shanas and Gordon Streib, 290–323. Englewood Cliffs, N.J.: Prentice-Hall.

Livi, Livio. 1915. *La composizione delle famiglie*. Florence.

Livi-Bacci, Massimo. 1975. Una disciplina in rapido sviluppo: La demografia storica. In *Demografia storica*, ed. Ercole Sori, 29–42. Bologna: Il Mulino.

———. 1977. *A history of Italian fertility during the last two centuries*. Princeton: Princeton University Press.

Lomnitz, Larissa A. 1977. *Networks and marginality: Life in a Mexican shantytown*. New York: Academic.

Luzzatto, Gina. 1968. *L'economia italiana dal 1861 al 1894*. Turin: Einaudi.

McArdle, Frank. 1978. *Altopascio: A study in Tuscan rural society, 1587–1784*. Cambridge: Cambridge University Press.

Macdonald, J. S. 1963. Agricultural organization, migration and labor militancy in rural Italy. *Economic History Review*, 2d ser., 16: 61–75.

Macfarlane, Alan. 1978. *The origins of English individualism*. Oxford: Basil Blackwell.

Marangoni, G. 1948. *Divisione e stime coloniche nella mezzadria, affitto e proprietà-coltivatrice dei fondi rustici e degli orti con particolare riguardo alle consuetudini dell'Emilia-Romagna*. Ravenna.

Bibliography

Maraspini, A. L. 1968. *The study of an Italian village.* Paris: Mouton.

Martelli, Domenico. 1854. Considerazioni sul contratto di mezzadria generalmente addottato nell'agricoltura bolognese. In *Memorie lette nelle adunanze ordinarie della Società Agraria della provincia di Bologna*, vol. 7. Bologna.

Masulli, Ignazio. 1980. *Crisi e trasformazione: Strutture economiche, rapporti sociali e lotte politiche nel bolognese (1880–1914).* Bologna: Istituto per la Storia di Bologna.

Medick, Hans. 1976. The proto-industrial family economy: The structural function of household and family during the transition from peasant society to industrial capitalism. *Social History* 3: 291–315.

Mendels, Franklin F. 1972. Proto-industrialization: The first phase of the process of industrialization. *Journal of Economic History* 32: 241–261.

———. 1978. La composition du ménage paysan en France au XIXe siècle: Une analyse economique du mode de production domestique. *Annales: Economies, Sociétés, Civilisations* 33: 780–802.

Merriman, John M. 1979. Introduction. In *Consciousness and class experience in nineteenth-century Europe*, ed. John M. Merriman, 1–16. New York: Holmes and Meier.

Ministero di Agricoltura, Industria e Commercio. 1891. *I contratti agrari in Italia.* Rome.

———. 1915. *Censimento della popolazione del regno d'Italia al 10 giugno 1911.* Vol. 6. Rome.

Mitterauer, Michael, and Reinhard Sieder. 1979. The developmental process of domestic groups: Problems of reconstruction and possibilities of interpretation. *Journal of Family History* 4: 257–284.

Moch, Leslie Page. 1981a. Marriage, migration, and urban demographic structure: A case from France in the Belle Epoque. *Journal of Family History* 6: 70–88.

———. 1981b. Adolescence and migration: Nîmes, France, 1906. *Social Science History* 5: 25–51.

Monti, Lia. 1978. *Famiglia, podere e congiuntura: La tenuta Fenili e Rotonda (1766–1797).* Laurea thesis, Faculty of Political Sciences, University of Bologna, under the direction of Carlo Poni.

Moss, Leonard, and Stephen Cappannari. 1960. Patterns of kinship, comparaggio, and community in a south Italian village. *Anthropological Quarterly* 33: 24–32.

Nardi, Sergio. 1957. La famiglia mezzadrile nel comune di Ravenna. In *Le campagne emiliane nell'epoca moderna*, ed. Renato Zangheri, 267–282. Milan: Feltrinelli.

———. 1980. Il lavoro del bracciante nelle campagne ravennati di fine '800. In *Il proletariato agricolo in Emilia Romagna nella fase di formazione*, ed.

Franco Cazzola, 147–184. Bologna: CLUEB.

Netting, Robert M. 1979. Household dynamics in a nineteenth century Swiss village. *Journal of Family History* 4: 39–58.

Nimkoff, M. F., and Russell Middleton. 1960. Types of family and types of economy. *American Journal of Sociology* 66: 215–225.

Otterbein, Keith F., and Charlotte Swanson Otterbein. 1977. A stochastic process analysis of the developmental cycle of the Andros household. *Ethnology* 16: 415–425.

Owens, Raymond. 1971. Industrialization and the Indian joint family. *Ethnology* 10: 223–250.

Pagani, Aldo. 1930. *La distribuzione del lavoro umano nell'azienda agraria.* Bologna.

———. 1931. *Inchiesta sul bracciantato della valle padana.* Piacenza: Federazione Italiana Consorzi Agrari.

———. 1932. *I braccianti della valle padana.* Rome: Istituto Nazionale di Economia e Agraria.

Parish, William L., and Moshe Schwartz. 1972. Household complexity in nineteenth century France. *American Sociological Review* 37: 154–173.

Parsons, Talcott, and Robert F. Bales. 1955. *The family, socialization and interaction process.* New York: Free Press.

Pasolini, Maria. 1891. *Una famiglia di mezzadri romagnoli nel comune di Ravenna.* Bologna.

———. 1892a. Monografie di alcuni operai braccianti nel comune di Ravenna, pt. 1. *Giornale degli Economisti* 5: 311–343.

———. 1892b. Monografie di alcuni operai braccianti nel comune di Ravenna, pt. 2. *Giornale degli Economisti* 5: 411–427.

Perdisa, Luigi. 1935. *La distribuzione del lavoro manuale in poderi a mezzadria della Romagna.* Osservatorio di Economia Agraria per l'Emilia, no. 13. Faenza.

Pesciullesi, Antonella. 1978. *La popolazione e le famiglie del comune di Sesto Fiorentino nel primo decennio unitario (1861–1871).* Laurea thesis, University of Florence, under the direction of Antonio Santini.

Peyronnet, Jean-Claude. 1975. Famille élargie ou famille nucléaire? L'exemple du Limousin au début du XIXe siècle. *Revue d'Histoire Moderne et Contemporaine* 22: 568–582.

Pitkin, Donald S. 1959–1960. Land tenure and family organization in an Italian village. *Human Organization* 18: 169–173.

Plakans, Andrejs. 1977. Identifying kinfolk beyond the household. *Journal of Family History* 2: 3–27.

———. 1979. The study of social structure from listings of inhabitants. *Journal of Family History* 4: 87–94.

———. 1982. Ties of kinship and kinship roles in an historical Eastern European peasant community: A synchronic analysis. *Journal of Family History* 7: 52–75.

Poni, Carlo. 1969. *Gli aratri e l'economia agraria nel bolognese dal XVII al XIX Secolo.* Bologna: Zanichelli.

———. 1977. La famiglia e il podere. In *Cultura popolare nell'Emilia Romagna*, ed. Giuseppe Adani and Gastone Tamagnini, 99–119. Milan: Silvana Editoriale d'Arte.

———. 1978. Family and *podere* in Emilia Romagna. *Journal of Italian History* 1: 201–234.

———, and Silvio Fronzoni. 1979. L'economia di sussistenza della famiglia contadina. In *Cultura popolare nell'Emilia Romagna, vol. III. Mestieri della terra e delle acque.* Milan: Pizzi.

Poumarède, Jacques. 1979. Famille et tenure dans les Pyrenées du moyen-age au XIXe siècle. *Annales de démographie historique 1979*: 347–360. Paris: Mouton.

Poussou, Jean-Pierre. 1970 Les mouvements migratoires en France et a partir de la France de la fin du XVe siècle au début du XIXe siècle. *Annales de Démographie Historique*: 11–78. Paris: Mouton.

Preti, Luigi. 1955. *Le lotte agrarie nella valle padana.* Turin: Einaudi.

Priore, Gennaro Orazio. 1906. Una famiglia di mezzadri nella Media Valle del Tevere. *La Riforma Sociale* 16: 602–635.

Proietti, Rita Buffi. 1980. *La struttura demografica di Casalecchio di Reno nella seconda metà del XIX secolo.* Laurea thesis, Faculty of Economics and Commerce, University of Bologna, directed by Andrea Schiaffino.

Rabbeno, Aronne. 1895. Consuetudini rurali e divisioni dei contadini nella provincia di Bologna. *Annali* 35: 59–88.

———. 1899. I patti colonici nei rapportii colla odierna coltura. *Annali* 39: 41–58.

Ramponi, Agostino. 1892. La mezzadria e la coltura intensiva. *Annali* 32: 95–132.

Reddy, William. 1975. Family and factory: French linen weaving in the Belle Epoque. *Journal of Social History* 9: 102–112.

Riley, Matilda White. 1973. Aging and cohort succession: Interpretations and misinterpretations. *Public Opinion Quarterly* 37: 35–49.

———, Marilyn Johnson, and Anne Foner. 1972. *Aging and society, Volume III: A sociology of age stratification.* New York: Russell Sage Foundation.

Ring, Richard R. 1979. Early medieval peasant households in central Italy. *Journal of Family History* 4: 2–25.

Rozat, Maryse. 1977. Les échanges de population entre villages voisins: Le cas d'Antony et sa couronne. *Annales de démographie historique 1977*: 21–48. Paris: Mouton.

Santini, Antonio. 1977. The family life cycle as a context for the measurement

Bibliography

of nuptiality and fertility. In *International population conference*, vol. 1, 371–388. Liège: International Union for the Scientific Study of Population.

Saporiti, Angelo. 1978. Famiglia e studi di comunità in Italia: Appunti e osservazioni sulla letteratura di lingua inglese. *Sociologia* 12: 13–48.

Sardi, Deanna. 1973. *Economia e demografia di un comune del comprensorio bolognese: Granarolo dal 1881 al 1911*. Laurea thesis, University of Florence, under the direction of Giuliano Procacci.

Scarselli, Antonio. 1890. Delle condizioni morali delle nostre campagne. *Annali* 30: 27–39.

Schiaffino, Andrea. 1975. Una questione aperta: La "rappresentatività" delle famiglie ricostruite nelle ricerche storico-demografiche. *Statistica* 35: 165–181.

———. 1976. Ricerche nominative in demografia storica: Il caso della città. *Atti della XXVIII Riunione della Società Italiana di Statistica*. Padua: Società Italiana di Statistica.

———. 1977. *Per una ricostruzione nominativa dei menages*. Bologna: Istituto di Statistica.

———. 1981. Analysis of life strategies in the household context: Methodological perspectives. Paper presented to the general conference of the International Union for the Scientific Study of Population, Manila.

———, and David I. Kertzer. n.d. New perspectives on old households: Toward a processual view of coresidence. Unpublished manuscript.

Schiavi, Alessandro. 1904. *La disoccupazione nel basso emiliano. Inchiesta diretta nelle provincie di Ferrara, Bologna e Ravenna*. Publicazioni dell'Ufficio del Lavoro della Società Umanitaria, no. 4. Milan.

Schneider, Jane, and Peter Schneider. 1976. *Culture and political economy in western Sicily*. New York: Academic.

Schofield, Roger S. 1970. Age-specific mobility in an eighteenth century rural English parish. *Annales de Démographie Historique 1970*: 261–274.

Segalen, Martine. 1976. Evoluzione dei nuclei familiari di Saint Jean Trolimon, Sud-Finistère, a partire dal 1836. *Quaderni Storici* 33: 1122–1182.

———. 1977. The family cycle and household structure: Five generations in a French village. *Journal of Family History* 2: 223–236.

Sereni, Emilio. 1957. Note per una storia del paessaggio agrario emiliano. In *Le campagne emiliane nell'epoca moderna*, ed. Renato Zangheri, 27–54. Milan: Feltrinelli.

———. 1968. *Il capitalismo nelle campagne (1860–1900)*. Turin: Einaudi.

Seward, Ruby Ray. 1978. *The American family: A demographic history*. Beverly Hills: Sage.

Sezioni di Agricoltura ed Amministrativa, Società Agraria Provinciale di Bologna. 1889. Riferimento sulla memoria del Cav. Dott. Antonio Bernardi. *Annali* 29: 53–68.

Bibliography

Sharlin, Allan N. 1977. Historical demography as history and demography. *American Behavioral Scientist* 21: 245–262.

Shaw, Robert. 1975. *Migration theory and fact*. Philadelphia: Regional Science Research Institute.

Shorter, Edward. 1975. *The making of the modern family*. New York: Basic Books.

Silverman, Sydel F. 1968. Agricultural organization, social structure, and values in Italy: Amoral familism reconsidered. *American Anthropologist* 70: 1–20.

———. 1975. *Three bells of civilization: The life of an Italian hill town*. New York: Columbia University Press.

Smelser, Neil J. 1974 (1967). Sociological history: The Industrial Revolution and the British working-class family. In *Essays in social history*, ed. M. W. Flinn and T. C. Smout, 23–38. Oxford: Clarendon.

———, and Sydney Halpern. 1978. The historical triangulation of family, economy, and education. *American Journal of Sociology* 84: 288–315.

Smith, Richard M. 1981. Fertility, economy, and household formation in England over three centuries. *Population and Development Review* 7: 595–622.

Società Agraria Provinciale di Bologna. 1883. Questionario su la mezzadria. *Annali* 22: 69–86.

Sonnino, Eugenio. 1975. Sviluppi recenti della ricerca di demografia storica in Italia. In *Demografia storica*, ed. Ercole Sori, 99–104. Bologna: Il Mulino.

Stack, Carol. 1974. *All our kin*. New York: Harper and Row.

Stearns, Peter N. 1967. *European society in upheaval: Social history since 1800*. New York: Macmillan.

Stephenson, Charles. 1979. A gathering of strangers? Mobility, social structure, and political participation in the formation of nineteenth-century American workingclass culture. In *American Workingclass culture*, ed. Milton Cantor, 31–60. Westport, Conn.: Greenwood Press.

Stone, Lawrence. 1981. Family history in the 1980s: Past achievements and future trends. *Journal of Interdisciplinary History* 12: 51–87.

Tanari, Luigi. 1881. *Atti della giunta per la inchiesta agraria sulle condizioni della classe agricola*. Vol. 2. Rome.

Tentori, Tullio. 1976. Social classes and family in a southern Italian town: Matera. In *Mediterranean family structures*, ed. J. G. Peristiany, 273–285. Cambridge: Cambridge University Press.

Tilly, Charles. 1978. The historical study of vital processes. In *Historical studies of changing fertility*, ed. Charles Tilly, 3–55. Princeton: Princeton University Press.

———. 1979. Did the cake of custom break? In *Consciousness and class experience in nineteenth-century Europe*, ed. John M. Merriman, 17–44. New York:

Holmes and Meier.

———, and Richard Tilly. 1971. An agenda for European economic history in the 1970's. *Journal of Economic History* 31: 184–198.

Tilly, Louise A. 1979a. Individual lives and family stategies in the French proletariat. *Journal of Family History* 4: 137–152.

———. 1979b. The family wage economy of a French textile city: Roubaix, 1872–1906. *Journal of Family History* 4: 381–394.

———. 1979c. Occupational structure, women's work, and demographic change in two French industrial cities, Anzin and Roubaix, 1872–1906. In *Time, space and man*, ed. Jan Sundin and Erik Soderlund, 107–132. Atlantic Highlands, N.J.: Humanities.

Todd, Emmanuel. 1975. Mobilité géographique et cycle de vie en Artois et en Toscane au XVIIIe siècle. *Annales: Economies, Sociétés, Civilisations* 30: 726–744.

Toscanelli, Giuseppe. 1861 (1976). La famiglia colonica nella mezzeria toscana. In *Un'Italia sconosciuta*, ed. Massimo Giudetti and Paul H. Stahl, 257–269. Milan: Jaca Book.

Urtoller, G. 1898. I movimenti agrari in ordine al diritto e all'economia sociale. *Annali* 38: 199–229.

Van de Walle, Etienne. 1976. Household dynamics in a Belgian village, 1847–1866. *Journal of Family History* 1: 80–94.

———, and Olivier Blanc. 1975. Registres de population et démographie: La Hulpe, 1847–1880. *Population et Famille* 36: 114–128.

Verdon, Michel. 1979. The stem family: Toward a general theory. *Journal of Interdisciplinary History* 10: 87–105.

Vinovskis, Maris A. 1977. From household size to the life course: Some observations on recent trends in family history. *American Behavioral Scientist* 21: 263–287.

Wachter, Kenneth, Eugene A. Hammel, and Peter Laslett. 1978. *Statistical studies of historical social structure*. New York: Academic.

Wall, Richard. 1978. The age at leaving home. *Journal of Family History* 3: 181–202.

Watkins, Susan C. 1980. On measuring transitions and turning points. *Historical Methods* 12: 181–186.

———, and James McCarthy. 1980. The female life cycle in a Belgian commune: La Hulpe, 1847–1866. *Journal of Family History* 5: 167–179.

Weber, Adna Ferin. 1968. *The growth of cities in the nineteenth century*. Ithaca: Cornell University Press.

Wheaton, Robert. 1975. Family and kinship in Western Europe: The problem of the joint family household. *Journal of Interdisciplinary History* 5: 601–628.

Bibliography

Wilkening, E. A., Joao Bosco Pinto, and José Pastore. 1968. Role of the extended family in migration and adaptation in Brazil. *Journal of Marriage and the Family* 30: 689–695.

Wrigley, E. A. 1961. *Industrial growth and population change.* Cambridge: Cambridge University Press.

———. 1977. Reflections on the history of the family. *Dædalus* 106: 71–85.

Yanagisako, Sylvia Junko. 1979. Family and household: The analysis of domestic groups. *Annual Review of Anthropology* 8: 161–205.

Young, Michael, and Peter Willmott. 1962. *Family and kinship in East London.* Baltimore: Penguin.

Zangheri, Renato. 1957. I moti del macinato nel bolognese. In *Le campagne emiliane nell'epoca moderna*, ed. Renato Zangheri, 101–144. Milan: Feltrinelli.

———. 1969. The historical relationship between agriculture and economic development in Italy. In *Agrarian change and economic development*, ed. S. Jones and S. F. Woolf, 23–40. London: Methuen.

Index

Age: household composition in Bertalia and, 65–69; household type and, 94; kin link analysis and, 173, 175; kin links and migration and, 185–186; marriage and, 58; migration analysis and, 118–119, 123, 125–126, 127–128; mobility and, 134–136

Agriculture, 14, 90, 91, 101; Bertalia and, 12, 13; as economic base of Bologna region, 20–23; economic transition and crisis and, 50, 52–55; landownership and, 4, 25–26; peasant landownership and, 10; preindustrial, 10; sharecropping system as principle of, 17–20

Anderson, Michael, 2, 88, 111; kinship and, 162–163; nuclearization theory and, 107–108

Angeli, Aurora, 76

Anthropology, European family history and, 188–190

Apprenticeship, 5

Armstrong, W. A., 88

Artisans, 38; kin ties and, 179

Austria, 112

Aymard, Maurice, 11

Bachelors, 159–160

Balugani, Angela, 75

Bellettini, Athos, 76

Berkner, Lutz K., 131; complex family structure and, 83; simple family structure and, 137

Bertalia (parish in Bologna), 76, 132, 143; economic change and coresidence in, 91–100; household composition in, 61–73; household size in, 99; industrialization and urban expansion in, 90–91; kin tie studies in, 163–164, 173, 174, 175, 179, 187; migration analysis of, 115, 116–122; migration and coresidence in, 122–129; study conclusions and, 196–198; study of coresidential processes in, 12–14

Birth: life chances and order of, 5; migration and data on, 117–118

Birthrate, 58

Boarding (meals and lodging), 128–129

Boari. See Salaried farmers (*boari*)

Bologna, 12, 191, 198; agricultural crisis and, 50–55; *braccianti* and sharecropper households in, 77–78; as commercial center, 89–90; economy of, 20–26; industrialization in, 90; migration and preindustrial, 116, 117, 118, 130; mobility and, 132–133

Braccianti (agricultural wage laborers): agricultural crisis and, 53–55; analysis of, 40–42; case histories of, 42–45; composition of house-

241

Braccianti (continued)
holds of, 70, 71, 72, 77, 97, 102–103, 161, 196; diet of, 46–47; growth in population of, 23; household size and, 74–75, 84, 100; kin links and, 179, 181–182, 184; life course coresidence studies and, 150–152; living conditions of, 46; marriage and, 58–59, 159; morality question and, 49; occupational mobility and, 133, 134, 135, 136; percentage of Bertalia's population as, 13; proprietors and, 39; remarriage and, 161; rural areas and, 24-25; as servants, 39–40; sharecroppers and, 47–48; sharecroppers' contract and, 30; social unrest and, 55–56; types of, 38, 41
Brintazzoli family (sharecropper case history), 152–153
Broccoli, Armide, 35
Brothers: kin links and, 165, 167; relationship between married, 160

Cane family (*bracciante* case history), 151–152
Capital goods, 35; sharecropper contract and, 29
Capitalism, 50, 111
Casalecchio (commune), 77
Census (annual parish), 11, 61–62, 114
Chickens, 30, 46
Children: abandonment at orphanage of, 195; acquiring (through apprenticeship), 5; *braccianti* case history and, 44; coresidence experience of, 65; coresidence and parents and, 107–108; death of parents and, 194; family duties and, 33; geographic mobility and, 130; kin link analysis and, 173–174; poverty and *braccianti*, 47
Cholera, 60. *See also* Disease
Church, 31; replacement of papal authority and, 48
Climate, 23
Collomp, Alain, 81
Coltelli family (sharecropper case history), 153–154
Comizio Agrario of Bologna, 49
Commerce, 20
Communication, 90
Complex household structure. *See* Households, complex
Conenna, Lucia Bonelli, 37
Conjugal household structure. *See* Households, conjugal
Conscription, 48–49
Contract of sharecropper, 197; elements of, 26–32; inheritance of livestock and, 37; mobility and, 133
Coresidence: Bertalia parish and, 12–14; *braccianti* life course case histories and, 150–152; characteristics of preindustrial, 3–7; economic change and, 91–100; flux in patterns of, 159; followed through time, 15, 136–149; in France, 80–83; importance of son to sharecropper and, 160–161; Italy's pattern of, 8, 190–194; Italy and study of, 8–12; kin links and, 168–172; land tenure and, 10; life course methodology and, 131–133; migration and Bertalia's, 122–129; migration and changes in Bertalia's, 113–115; occupational mobility and, 133–136; patrilocal postmarital, 159; postmarital residence rules and, 189; sharecropper life course case his-

Index

tories and, 152–155; sharecropper residence case histories and, 155–159; urbanization and industrialization and, 108–110. *See also* Households

Corniglio (parish in province of Parma), 78

Crops: commercial, 52–53; diet and, 46; grown in Bologna region, 23; hemp, 23, 24, 49; sharecropper contract and, 29–30, 31; theft of, 49

Cultural norms: marriage and living standard and, 191; relationship to social practice, 189–190

Culture, family studies and, 192–193

Currency (1880 value of lire), 41

Darroch, A. Gordon, 129

Data, 61–62; background, 14; composition of households in Bertalia and, 65–66; cross-sectional and longitudinal, 131–133; demographic records, 3, 11; Italian wealth of coresidential, 10–11; kin ties and, 163; migration analysis and, 114, 115, 117–118; sources of, 2–3

Daughter-in-law, 167

Daughters: kin links and, 165–166, 170–172; moving into husband's household and, 34; in sharecropping households, 160–161

Davey, Ian E., 108

Day laborers (agricultural). *See Braccianti* (agricultural wage laborers)

Death. *See* Mortality

Debt, sharecropper and, 30–31

Delille, Gerard, 11

Diet, 46–47

Disease, 47, 60

Douglass, William A., 193

Dowry, 37, 59

Economic factors: agricultural crisis and, 50–55; augmenting family size and, 83; Bologna and, 20–26; coresidence in Bertalia and, 91–100; household composition and, 5–6; urban expansion in Bertalia and, 90–91

Eggs, 30, 46

Elderly: complex households and, 125–126, 127–128; composition of households in Bertalia and death of, 65; coresidence with children and, 108; coresidential norms and, 95–97; extended households and, 142; family duties and, 33–34; in preindustrial Europe, 6; urbanization and, 105

Emigration: *braccianti* and, 42; parish data and, 115

England, 8, 86, 88, 91, 112; kin tie studies and, 163; Preston study and, 107–108; study of households in, 6, 7

Europe: coresidence in preindustrial, 3–7; family life studies and, 191; migration in, 112–113. *See also names of specific European countries*

Evangelisti, Valerio, 54

Extended household structure. *See* Households, extended

Faenza (commune), 78

Family: analysis of sharecropper, 32–38; anthropology and study of, 188–190; augmenting size of (France), 83; patriarchal structure of, 32, 34, 49, 82; sharecropper contract and, 26–27, 29, 30; stem

Index

Family (*continued*)
  system of, 82, 84; women who married into, 34–35. *See also* Kin ties
Family life, concept of, 1–2
Farm produce, sharing of, 29–30. *See also* Crops
Farm size: family size and, 35–36; household size and, 75; sharecropping and, 25–26
Ferrara, 78
Fertility, 6; changes in childbearing patterns and, 4; kin ties linking households and, 175–177; sharecropper and *braccianti* and, 59–60
Fertilizer (chemical), 52
Fine-Souriac, Agnès, 82
Fiorini family (*bracciante* case history), 150
Firth, Raymond, 87
Flandrin, Jean-Louis, 83
Flour, tax on, 31. *See also* Taxes
Food. *See* Diet
Foremen, 41. *See also* Overseers
France, 80–83, 112, 113
Fronzoni, Silvio, 75

Garzoni. *See* Servants (agricultural, *garzoni*)
Geographic mobility. *See* Mobility (geographic)
Goode, William J., 9, 87
Goretti, Cesare, 34
Granarolo (commune), 77–78
Grassilli family (*bracciante* case history), 152
Gulandi family (*bracciante* case history), 151

Hamilton (Canada), 108
Hareven, Tamara K., 9
Harris, C. C., 8
Herlihy, David, 10–11, 79–80

Hospitals, 60
Household heads: coresidence and life course and, 69–70; household composition and occupation of, 97, 98; ideal sharecropper family and, 34; kinship ties and age of, 175; kinship ties and female, 166–167; kinship ties and male, 165–166, 169, 170, 171, 173–174; migration and, 123, 127; *reggitrice* (female), 33, 34–35, 49; *reggitore* (male), 26–27, 32–33, 34, 35, 49; sharecropper contract and, 26–27; urbanization and, 103, 104
Households. *See also* Coresidence
—categorization of, 63–64
—characteristics of, 6
—complex, 51; age groups in Bertalia and, 66–69; analysis of Italian, 193, 194; in Bertalia, 64, 71–73, 91–92, 94–95; in Bologna, 78; *braccianti* and, 97, 102–103, 196; in Britain, 91–92; coresidence through time and, 137–142; diminution of, 108–110; in France, 80, 81–82, 83; kin links and, 169; migration and, 15, 112, 113, 122, 124, 125–126, 127–128; minimizing significance of, 7; as norm, 75; in northern Europe, 81; occupation and, 97–98; in Preston (England), 107–108; in Ravenna, 78; in rural communities, 14; sharecroppers in Bertalia and, 70, 71, 103, 196; study conclusions and, 196; in Tuscany, 79
—composition of Bertalia's, 61–73
—composition of sharecropping area households (Italy) and, 75–80
—composition and size of, 73
—conjugal, 84, 87; joint family households and, 193; sharecropper

244

Index

households and, 76–77; as standard (Laslett), 6–7
—death of parents and, 37
—distance of migration and structure of, 114
—economic factors and structure of, 5–6
—extended: in Bertalia, 63; coresidence through time and, 142–148; defined, 64; elderly and, 97; kin links and, 170; migration and, 112, 126–127; as rarity, 6–7, 8; sharecropper households and, 79; sharecropper patrilaterally, 34; sharecroppers in Bertalia and, 70, 71; stability and, 149; urbanization and, 105
—kinship ties between, 165–168, 177
—methodology and study of, 199–210
—multiple, 75; analysis of Italian, 193; in Bertalia, 64; *braccianti* and, 77, 78; child care and, 60; coresidence through time and, 142–148; death of son and, 84; defined, 64; elderly and, 95, 97; in Emilia-Romagna region, 78; farm and family size and, 75; in France, 81, 83; kin links and, 169, 170, 171–172; migration and, 128, 130; in northern Europe, 81; occupation and, 97; pressures on sharecroppers and, 79–80; sharecroppers and, 76, 77, 78, 79, 97, 106, 191; sharecroppers in Bertalia and, 70, 71; sharecropping areas and, 57; stability and, 149; in Tuscany, 79; urbanization and, 105, 106
—nuclear: in Bertalia, 92–93; in England, 91–92; in France, 81; industrialization (debate) and, 86–90, 107; kin ties and, 198; migration and, 15, 111, 113, 123, 126; peasantry and, 8; urbanization and, 104–105; western Europe as characterized by, 9
—simple: age groups in Bertalia and, 66–67; analysis of Italian, 193; in Bertalia, 64; *braccianti* and, 77, 161; coresidence through time and, 137, 142–148; defined, 63; economic change and, 93–94; elderly and, 95; in France, 82, 83, 84; industrialization and, 86; kin links and, 169, 170, 171, 172; migration and, 113, 124–125; in northern Europe, 81; occupations and, 97; sharecroppers and, 76, 78, 79; sharecroppers in Bertalia and, 70, 71; stability and, 149; urban areas and, 105
—study objectives and, 14–16
—three-generation, 95; age groups and, 68; in Bertalia, 64, 71–73; idealized, 191–192; minority living in, 65; mortality rate and, 9; as rarity, 7
—as units of production, 5–6, 27, 35, 89, 101–102, 103, 104, 190
—urbanization and, 100–107
Household size: *braccianti* and, 74–75, 84; sharecroppers and, 73–75, 80, 84, 99–100, 192; urbanization and, 98–100
Housing, 45–46
Hunting and gathering societies, 111

Immigration. *See* Migration (rural-to-urban); Mobility (geographic)
India, 109
Industrialization, 2, 101; Bologna region and, 23–24; coresidence conclusions and, 197; impact of, 7, 108–110; migration and, 129–130;

245

Index

Industrialization (*continued*)
nuclear households and, 9; nuclearization debate and, 86–90, 107; urban expansion in Bertalia and, 90–91. *See also* Preindustrial era

Inheritance, 10; property division and, 37–38

Italy, 85; coresidence conclusions and, 190–194; family history and, 8–12; household composition and Laslett and, 83; sharecropper household composition in, 75–80; sharecropping system in, 17–20; unification of, 23–24, 34

Jacini, Stefano, 54

Katz, Michael B., 108

Kin ties: coresidence and, 168–172; coresidence and industrialization and, 108, 109–110; household to household, 165–168; indirect affinal, 167–168; industrialization and migration and, 87; informal relations and, 88; life course changes and, 172–177; little change in (1880–1910), 179–180; methodology and significance of, 162–164; migration and, 87, 112, 122, 128, 129; nuclear family and, 198; occupation and, 177–184; parish records and, 62; study objectives and, 16; urbanization and, 106. *See also* Family

Klapisch, Christine, 79–80

Labor exchange (*zerla*), 47

Landowners: labor power and, 102; sharecropper's family size and, 35, 36

Landownership: in Bertalia, 13; *braccianti* and, 24; crops and, 23; data on, 25–26; peasantry and, 9–10, 23, 84; work for wages and, 4

Land prices, 26

Land reclamation, 39, 41

Land tenure, 10, 79, 81

Laslett, Peter, 107, 111, 112, 131; categorization of households and, 63–64; complex family structure and, 81; extended family as rarity and, 8–9; influence of, 76; Italian family structure and, 83; kin ties and, 163; preindustrial European households and, 6–7; sharecroppers and, 192; simple family households and, 86, 88; Tuscan communities and, 79; urbanization and household size and, 98

Lemaitre, Nicole, 82

Levy, Marion, Jr., 7, 9

Life course perspective: approach to household composition studies and, 194–196; in Bertalia (1910), 94; *braccianti* coresidence case studies and, 150–152; complex households and, 105; composition of households in Bertalia and, 65; coresidence pattern flux and, 159; coresidence through time and, 136–149; cross-sectional data and methodology and, 131–133; household heads and, 69–70; importance of sharecropper sons and, 160–161; kin links and, 165, 172–177; occupational mobility and, 133–136; sharecropper coresidence case studies and, 152–155; sharecropper residence studies through time and, 155–159

Limoges, 83

Literacy, 28

Litwak, Eugene, 87

Index

Livestock, 46; inheritance and, 37; sharecropper contract and, 29
Livi, Livio, 87
Loans to sharecroppers, 30–31

Macfarlane, Alan, 112
Manufacturing, 50
Marriage, 6, 194; *braccianti* and 58–59, 159; coresidence and, 15; cultural norms and living standards and, 191; disincentives to, 159–160; dowry and, 37, 59; migration and, 128, 130; migration and sex differential and, 119; postmarital residence and, 159, 189, in preindustrial Europe, 5; remarriage and, 161; sharecropper contract and, 27; sharecroppers and, 159–160; sharecroppers becoming *braccianti* and, 54; sharecroppers and *braccianti* and, 58–59; simple household structure and, 143; son bringing bride home and, 15, 34, 65, 84, 159, 166
Mechanization (agricultural), 52, 54, 55
Men: *braccianti* and, 41–42; composition of households in Bertalia and, 65; division of labor and, 32–33; family structure and, 34, 35; as household heads (*reggitori*), 26–27, 32–33, 34, 35, 49; kinship household ties and, 165; migration and, 119–120; sharecropper and *braccianti* relations and, 48. *See also* Sex; Women
Mendel, Franklin F., 197
Merchants, 179
Merriman, John M., 10
Methodology, 63; categorizing households and, 203–210; coresidence in life course perspective and, 131–133; importance of, 199; individuals and, 83; kin links and longitudinal studies and, 172; life course approach to, 194–196; rural-urban migration and, 113–155; significance of extrahousehold kin ties and, 162–164; study of households and, 199–203
Mezzadria system. *See* Sharecropping system
Middleton, Russell, 111
Migration (foreign). *See* Emigration
Migration (rural-to-urban): in Bertalia, 116–122; *braccianti* and, 42; coresidence in Bertalia and, 122–129; coresidence and social stability and, 129–130; in Europe, 112–113; household relationships methodology and, 113–115; industrialization and, 87, 129–130; kin links and, 175, 181, 184–187; overview of European, 111–112; population of Bertalia and, 12; population growth and, 51; as social force, 15
Mobility (geographic): class differential, 87; as long-standing way of life, 129, 192; migration studies and, 114, 130; occupational changes and, 133–136; proprietor and sharecropper and, 36–37; social implications of, 112
Mobility (occupational), 133–136
Molinella (commune), 57
Montecastello (Silverman's study of town of), 79
Morality, 48–49
Mortality, 7; coresidence and, 15; death of parents, 37, 84, 194; household composition in Bertalia and, 65; kin ties linking households and, 175, 177; migration

Mortality (*continued*)
  codes and, 115; sharecroppers and *braccianti* and, 58, 60–61; simple households in France and, 82; tables on statistics concerning, 61, 62; three-generation households and, 9
Mother: child care and, 60; priorities of, 2. *See also* Parents
Multiple household structure. *See* Households, multiple

Nerozzi family (sharecropper case history), 154–155
Nimkoff, M. F., 111
Nuclear household structure. *See* Households, nuclear

Occupational mobility, 133–136
Occupations, 90; agricultural sector and, 103; in Bertalia, 12–13, 91; *braccianti* and, 41–42; changes in, 92; complex household structure and, 196; household composition and, 97–98; kin ties and, 177–184; migration and, 120; in rural areas, 40
Onoranze (tribute), 28
Oral history, 2
Overseers, 26. *See also* Foremen
Owens, Raymond, 109

Pagani, Aldo, 42
Parents: age at marriage and, 58–59; coresidence of married children and, 107–108; death of, 37, 84, 194; economic characteristics of, 5; inheritance and death of, 37; kin links and, 170–172, 173; leaving home of, 4, 6, 29, 88–89, 173–174; son bringing bride home to, 15, 34, 65, 84, 159, 166; three-generation households and, 7
Pasolini, Countess Maria, 42, 44, 47, 59
Peasants, 1, 50; feudal system and, 18–20; geographic mobility and, 112, 129; geographic stability question and, 111; industrialization and, 88; international market system and, 4; landownership and, 9–10, 23, 84; nuclear family and, 8; transformation to urban proletariat and, 3. *See also* Braccianti (agricultural wage laborer); Sharecroppers
Pesciullesi, Antonella, 79
Peyronnet, Jean-Claude, 83
Pichat, Carlo Berti, 75
Plakans, Andrejs, 10
Poletti, Luigi (*bracciante* case history), 43–44
Population: Bertalia's, 91, 143; growth, 51–52; migration and Bertalia's, 12
Population register (*anagrafe*), 11
Poumarède, Jacques, 82
Poverty, *braccianti* children and, 47
Preindustrial era, 9; characteristics of coresidence in, 3–7; migration and, 115; nuclear households and, 88; popular conception concerning, 2; sharecroppers in Italy and, 10. *See also* Industrialization
Preston (city in England), 107–108
Priests, 62
Priore, Gennaro Orazio, 191
Produce (farm), sharing of, 29–30. *See also* Crops
Property division. *See* Inheritance
Protests of rural proletarians, 50
Public works, *braccianti* and, 41, 42

Index

Ravenna, 78; *braccianti* case histories and, 42
Remarriage, 161. *See also* Marriage
Revolt, 55, 56
Rural areas, 50, 101; analysis of residents in, 38–40; children remaining in parental home and, 107–108; complex households in, 14; industrialization and, 89; kin ties and, 180; landownership of peasantry and, 10; morality and, 48–49; occupations in, 40; sharecropping families in, 24–25; wage labor and, 3

Salaried farmers (*boari*), 13, 38, 103; arrangements for, 39
San Giovanni (commune), 77
Saporiti, Angelo, 192
Schofield, Roger S., 111
Seasonality, 41–42
Servants (agricultural, *garzoni*), 43, 45, 196; leaving parental home and, 173–174; sharecropper and *braccianti* households and, 39–40
Servants (domestic), 112–113, 130
Sesto Fiorentino (commune), 79
Sex: family duties and, 32–33; life chances and sibling's, 5; migration analysis and, 119–120. *See also* Men; Women
Sharecropper labor exchange (*zerla*), 47
Sharecroppers, 16; agricultural crisis and, 53–55; cash and subsistence crops and, 23; composition of households and, 34, 57, 70, 71, 75–80, 103, 196; conscription and, 48–49; contract of, 26–32, 37, 133, 197; death of son and, 84–85; diet of, 46; family of, 32–38; in France, 81, 83; household composition research (Italy) and, 9–10; household size and, 73–75, 80, 84, 99–100, 192; importance of son and, 160–161; kin links and, 178–179, 183; life course coresidence studies and, 152–155; living conditions of, 45–46; marriage and, 58–59, 159–160; morality question and, 48–49; occupational mobility and, 133–134, 135, 136; percentage of Bertalia's population as, 13; pressures on, 84; residence case studies and, 155–159; rural neighbors of, 38–40; rural sector and, 24–25; servants and, 39; social relations with *braccianti* and, 47–48; social unrest and, 55–56; study objectives and, 14–15. *See also* Peasants
Sharecropping system, 18, 23, 102; change in, 85; essential elements of, 17–20; in France, 81; importance of sons in, 160–161
Shorter, Edward, 2
Siblings: kinship household links and, 165–166, 169–172, 174–175; life chances and sex of, 5
Silk, 24
Silverman, Sydel F.: idealized coresidence of sharecroppers and, 191–192; sharecropper system and, 18; Umbria study of, 79
Simple household structure. *See* Households, simple
Sisters, kin links and, 165
Smith, Richard, 190–191
Socialism, 55–56
Social practice, relationship to cultural norms and, 189–190
Società Agraria, 49

Index

Sociologists, 189
Solitaries, 63, 168
Somogyi, *braccianti* food expenditures and, 47
Sons: bringing bride home to parents' households and, 15, 34, 65, 84, 159, 166; conscription and, 48–49; importance of (in sharecropping system), 160–161; kin links and, 165–166, 170–172; sharecropper and death of, 84–85
Spinsters, 159–160
Stability (geographic), 111–112
State, 31–32, 48
Status animarum. See Census (annual parish)
Stephenson, Charles, 129
Stone, Lawrence, 9, 110
Strikes, 55, 56
Sugar, 53

Tassinari, Angiolo (*braccianti* case history), 44–45
Taverns, 55
Taxes: sharecropper contract and, 30; sharecropper hostility and, 31–32
Theft, 49
Three-generation households. *See* Households, three-generation
Tilly, Louise, 109
Topographical analysis of Bologna region, 20–23
Toscanelli, Giuseppe, 32–33
Transportation, 90
Tribute (*onoranze*), 28
Tuscany, 24, 37, 79

Urban areas, 101; children remaining in parents' home and, 107–108; expansion in Bertalia and, 90–91; kin ties and, 179; occupation and household composition and, 98; social unrest in, 56; wage labor and, 3
Urbanization, 2; coresidence conclusions and, 196–198; decline in household size and, 98–100; impact of, 7, 100–107, 108–110; industrialization in Bertalia and, 90–91; leaving home and, 89; migration and, 119, 120, 129–130; nuclearization and, 86; population growth and, 51; study objectives and, 15

Van de Walle, Etienne, 132
Vinovskis, Maris A., 9

Wage labor, 3
Wage laborers. *See Braccianti* (agricultural wage laborers)
Wages, *braccianti* arrangements and, 41
Women: *braccianti*, 42; division of labor and, 33; family structure and, 34–35; household head (*reggitrice*), 33, 34–35, 49; inheritance and, 37; kinship household ties and, 166–167; marrying into sharecropper family, 54; migration and, 119–120, 130; sharecropper and *braccianti* relations and, 48. *See also* Men; Sex
Wrigley, E. A., 88

Zirudelle (winter carnival custom), 47

LIBRARY OF DAVIDSON COLLEGE

Books on regular loan may be checked out for **two weeks**. Books must be presented at the Circulation Desk in order to be renewed.

A fine is charged after date due.

Special books are subject to special regulations at the discretion of the library staff.

NOV 24 1986			